D0375438

DEMOCRATIC TRANSITION IN
THE MUSLIM WORLD

RELIGION, CULTURE, AND PUBLIC LIFE

RELIGION, CULTURE, AND PUBLIC LIFE

Series Editor: Katherine Pratt Ewing

The resurgence of religion calls for careful analysis and constructive criticism of new forms of intolerance, as well as new approaches to tolerance, respect, mutual understanding, and accommodation. In order to promote serious scholarship and informed debate, the Institute for Religion, Culture, and Public Life and Columbia University Press are sponsoring a book series devoted to the investigation of the role of religion in society and culture today. This series includes works by scholars in religious studies, political science, history, cultural anthropology, economics, social psychology, and other allied fields whose work sustains multidisciplinary and comparative as well as transnational analyses of historical and contemporary issues. The series focuses on issues related to questions of difference, identity, and practice within local, national, and international contexts. Special attention is paid to the ways in which religious traditions encourage conflict, violence, and intolerance and also support human rights, ecumenical values, and mutual understanding. By mediating alternative methodologies and different religious, social, and cultural traditions, books published in this series will open channels of communication that facilitate critical analysis.

After Pluralism: Reimagining Religious Engagement, edited by
    Courtney Bender and Pamela E. Klassen
Religion and International Relations Theory, edited by Jack Snyder
Religion in America: A Political History, Denis Lacorne

Edited by

ALFRED STEPAN

DEMOCRATIC TRANSITION IN THE MUSLIM WORLD

A Global Perspective

Columbia University Press / New York

Columbia University Press
Publishers Since 1893
New York   Chichester, West Sussex
cup.columbia.edu

Copyright © 2018 Columbia University Press
All rights reserved

Library of Congress Cataloging-in-Publication Data
Names: Stepan, Alfred C., editor.
Title: Democratic Transition in the Muslim World: A Global Perspective /
edited by Alfred Stepan.
Other titles: Religion, culture, and public life.
Description: New York : Columbia University Press, 2018. | Series: Religion,
culture, and public life | Includes bibliographical references and index.
Identifiers: LCCN 2017037856| ISBN 9780231184311 (pbk. : alk. paper) |
ISBN 9780231184304 (cloth : alk. paper) | ISBN 9780231545419 (e-book)
Subjects: LCSH: Democratization—Islamic countries. | Democracy—Islamic
countries. | Islam and politics—Islamic countries. | Islamic countries—Politics
and government—21st century.
Classification: LCC JQ1852.A91 D447 2018 | DDC 320.917/67—dc23
LC record available at https://lccn.loc.gov/2017037856

Columbia University Press books are printed on permanent
and durable acid-free paper.

Printed in the United States of America

Cover Design: Martin Hinze

CONTENTS

2. THE CHALLENGES OF DEMOCRATIZATION IN THE ARAB WORLD:

Some Reflections on the Egyptian Case

Carrie Rosefsky Wickham

3. MUTUAL ACCOMMODATION:

Islamic and Secular Parties and Tunisia's Democratic Transition

Alfred Stepan

4. THE ROOTS OF EGYPT'S CONSTITUTIONAL CATASTROPHE:

The Necessity of Marrying an Analysis of Context, Process, and Text

Nathan J. Brown

5. PURISTS AND PLURALISTS:

Cross-Ideological Coalition Building in Tunisia's Democratic Transition

Monica Marks

6. PATTERNS OF CIVIL-MILITARY RELATIONS AND THEIR LEGACIES FOR DEMOCRATIZATION:

Egypt Versus Tunisia

Hicham Bou Nassif

7. THE FAILURE OF THE INTERNATIONAL COMMUNITY TO SUPPORT TUNISIA

Radwan Masmoudi

PART II
RETHINKING OTHER DEMOCRACIES WITH LARGE MUSLIM POPULATIONS:
What Policies Helped in Indonesia and India?

FOREWORD

MONICA MARKS

S THIS VOLUME was going to press in September 2017, its editor, Alfred C. Stepan, passed away at his home in New York City. He was a pathbreaking scholar and educator in federalism, comparative politics, democratization, democratic transitions, and patterns of relations between religion and state, particularly in Muslim-majority democracies.

His death represents an enormous loss for these fields and for his many friends, colleagues, and students, including the contributors to this volume. Al was an extraordinarily kind and inquisitive human being—a wonderful mentor and role model to generations of scholars who will follow the paths he forged.

During his distinguished career, Alfred Stepan (1936–2017) authored and edited over fifteen books, including *Problems of Democratic Transition and Consolidation* (with Juan Linz), *Arguing Comparative Politics*, and *Boundaries of Toleration* (with Charles Taylor). His works have been translated into dozens of languages. From 1983 to 1991, Stepan served as dean of Columbia University's School of International and Public Affairs (SIPA). In 1993, he became the first rector and president of Central European University (with campuses in Budapest, Prague, and Warsaw), and he was Gladstone Professor of Government at All Souls College, Oxford University, from 1996 to 1999. He returned to Columbia University's SIPA in 1999 as the Wallace S. Sayre Professor of Government.

This book is Professor Stepan's final edited volume. It grew from his deep fascination with and concern for Tunisia's democratic transition, a fascination that spurred him to make seven separate research trips to the country since its revolution in 2011. It was during one of those trips, in March 2013, that I met Professor Stepan. At the time, I was based in Tunisia conducting riveting interviews but completely unsure which direction to channel my doctoral research. Instead of sloughing off young scholars, Professor Stepan sought their expertise in the field. Despite his enormous knowledge and distinguished stature, he cultivated an electrically curious mind—constantly learning, seeking, and nurturing other scholars. This book is the product of his immense work on Tunisia and of a lifetime spent studying the comparative politics of democratic transitions.

Until his very last, Professor Stepan kept seeking and sharing knowledge. In January 2017, just months before this volume went to press, he was in Tunisia, conducting up to six interviews a day by my side. The tenacious energy with which he approached his sharply insightful, question-driven research and the genuine concern he had for Tunisia, its people, and the survival of its fragile young democracy were unparalleled.

To have known Professor Stepan was to have received a rare education and to have encountered an extraordinary role model in research and in life. We are all in his debt.

ACKNOWLEDGMENTS

T HANKS TO COLUMBIA University's Institute for Religion, Culture, and Public Life and the Center for the Study of Democracy, Toleration, and Religion for bringing this community of scholars together to examine Tunisia, democracy, and Islam in comparative perspective.

Monica Marks, a doctoral candidate at Oxford University and expert on Tunisia and Islamism in political transitions, provided critical feedback that helped this volume from conceptualization to publication.

Emad El-Din Shahin, a professor at the American University in Cairo and at Georgetown University, and Laryssa Chomiak, director of Centre d'Etudes Maghrébines à Tunis, made invaluable contributions to the discussions that influenced this volume. Nader Hashemi, the author of the widely acclaimed *Islam, Secularism, and Liberal Democracy*; Donald L. Horowitz, the major comparativist and constitutionalist; and Karen Barkey, an award-winning author on toleration, gave detailed and constructive comments to all the authors.

Finally, I would like to thank Melissa Van, for shepherding the book from draft to published volume, and the Henry R. Luce Foundation and their Initiative on Religion and International Affairs, which gave us invaluable support that helped us sponsor research on democracy in Muslim-majority countries and prepare this publication.

DEMOCRATIC TRANSITION IN
THE MUSLIM WORLD

INTRODUCTION

ALFRED STEPAN

THIS VOLUME EMERGED out of an engagement, from a comparative perspective, with the Tunisian democratic transition. Contributors to this book are particularly interested in expanding our understanding of what helps—or hurts—successful democratic-transition attempts in countries with large Muslim populations.

Tunisia allows us to do an analysis of this crucial question by comparing two "least similar" recent case outcomes, democratic success in Tunisia and democratic failure in Egypt. Tunisia also allows us to do an analysis of four "most similar" case outcomes by comparing the successful democratic transitions in Tunisia, Indonesia, Senegal, and the country with the second- or third-largest Muslim population in the world, India.[1] Did these countries face some common challenges concerning democratization that are undertheorized in the founding literature on democratic transitions?[2] Did all four of these successful cases in fact use some common policies that, while democratic, had not normally been used in transitions in countries without significant numbers of Muslims? If so, did these policies help the transitions in Tunisia, Indonesia, Senegal, and India? If they did, I believe we should incorporate them in some way into our comparative theories about successful democratic transitions.

Such incorporation is an exceptionally urgent political and intellectual task because *none* of the three most-cited and translated works on democratic transitions focus on successful democratic transitions in Muslim-majority countries. Islam is not discussed in the classic four-volume work edited by Guillermo O'Donnell, Philippe C. Schmitter, and Laurence Whitehead, *Transitions from Authoritarian Rule* (1986), nor in Juan J. Linz and Alfred Stepan's book *Problems of Democratic Transition and Consolidation: Southern Europe, South American, and Post-Communist Europe* (1996), because the successful democratic transitions in Muslim-majority Indonesia, Senegal, and Tunisia all occurred *after* the publication of these two books.[3] The third-most-cited book of course is Samuel P. Huntington's *The Clash of Civilizations and the Remaking of the Modern World* (1996), but his central focus is on how Islam impedes democratization. For example, he asserts flatly that "in Islam God is Caesar. . . . The underlying problem for the West is not Islamic Fundamentalism. It is Islam."[4]

In a moment of growing despair and religious conflict relating to ISIS, this volume is an effort to expand our knowledge and imagination about how and why new democracies, ones with strong Islamic influences, have actually emerged in the contemporary world.

"LEAST SIMILAR CASES": WHY SUCCESS IN TUNISIA AND FAILURE IN EGYPT?

In January and February 2011, Tunisia and Egypt both witnessed similar successful protests that ousted their long-standing dictators. Similar demands in both countries were made for new accountable governments to generate equitable economic growth and democracy. Unfortunately, the outcomes concerning democracy were "least similar."

In October 2011, Tunisia held free and fair elections for a National Constituent Assembly. For the next two years, from November 2011 to January 2014, Tunisia was ruled by a three-party coalition chaired by the Islam-inspired Ennahda (Renaissance) Party, with two secularly oriented political parties as partners. On January 27, 2014, a consensual constitution was approved by over 90 percent of the members in the National Constituent Assembly, and the Ennahda-led coalition peacefully stepped down so that a caretaker technocratic government could supervise parliamentary and presidential elections in late 2014. The secularly oriented leaders who won both elections were congratulated on their victories by the president of Ennahda, Rached Ghannouchi. Thus by December 2014, Tunisia had completed the first phase of a difficult but successful transition to democracy.[5]

In sharp contrast, the Egyptian military, with strong civilian backing from secularists and many of the one-time liberal Tahrir Square protestors, seized power in a coup d'état and suspended the constitution on July 3, 2013. Within a month of this event, the authorities had killed over 1,100 protestors. Within two years one judge alone had summarily sentenced 186 dissidents to death, and by 2015, Egypt had constructed the hardest authoritarian regime in the country's history. One of the military regime's announced goals is the complete "eradication" of the Muslim Brotherhood.[6] Correctly, Freedom House in 2016 gave Egypt its second-lowest-possible ranking for political rights, a 6, in contrast with Tunisia's highest-possible score of 1. Whereas Tunisia had completed all four of the necessary tasks a democratic transition requires by January 2015, as of this book going to press in late 2017, Egypt has completed none. Worse, a peaceful democratic transition is nowhere on the horizon in Egypt.

What accounts for these "least similar" outcomes in terms of democratic transition? Since in both Tunisia and Egypt the first elected government was headed by an Islamically inspired party, it seems we should begin our inquiry with an analysis of these two parties to see if they contributed to democratic success, or failure, in their country, and if so, how.

We are very fortunate that the founder and president of the Ennahda Party in Tunisia, Rached Ghannouchi, agreed to address the question (in his first article of this kind in English) of the political strategies his party chose to pursue a successful democratic transition. The founding literature on democratic transitions never included religion because it was not a major problem during the transitions of the 1970s and 1980s. Ghannouchi's words in the opening article of this volume highlight that religion was a relevant problem for Tunisia's transition. "There is an ongoing debate in our country," he says, "between secular currents, which may be described as extremist, and Islamist ones, which may be described in a like manner." To transcend this situation, Ghannouchi favored a proportional-representation electoral system that would be majority inhibiting and coalition inducing. "Two center-left secular parties responded to our call . . . and we formed a coalition that proved to be a great model of coexistence between secularists and Islamists, the two trends that had been in conflict for the proceeding half-century." This mutual accommodation was only possible because, as the articles in this volume by Ghannouchi, Stepan, and Marks make clear, for twenty years before the formation of this coalition Ghannouchi and Ennahda increasingly developed what I call a "democratically friendly Islamic political theology." In Ghannouchi's article, he also stresses (as I do in mine) that in any democratic transition, but particularly in one where trust needs to be built and maintained between secularists and Islamic activists, governing decisions should be based on "consensus building rather than majoritarian democracy."

The second article in the volume is a talk by America's leading scholar on Egypt's Muslim Brotherhood, Carrie Rosefsky Wickham. A close reading of her chapter leaves the reader with a clear sense of two major differences between the Muslim Brotherhood and Ennahda. First, the Muslim Brotherhood's conception of democracy was majoritarian, not consensual. For example, she writes that the Muslim Brotherhood interpreted their electoral victories as "granting them a popular mandate to govern the country as they saw fit." Second, Ghannouchi and Ennahda adapted theologically and politically to make a ruling coalition with secularists possible. In contrast, in Wickham's judgment, the Achilles' heel of the Muslim Brotherhood was their attitude toward the secular opposition, which the Brotherhood "from their perch at the apex of state power . . . felt free to condescend to or ignore." The Brotherhood paid a heavy cost for this: many secularists sought out military protection and eventually supported the authoritarian military coup that attempted to "eradicate" the Muslim Brotherhood.

My own contribution to this volume is an analytic narrative that complements Ghannouchi's article, in that I raise conceptual and empirical issues about conditions under which secular-Islamic coalitions are virtually impossible and conditions where they not only become possible but happen. Crafting prodemocratic coalitions among secularists and Islamists presents a special obstacle that must be addressed by theorists and practitioners. Such coalitions will not happen if potentially democratic secularists are part of what I call the authoritarian regime's "constituency of coercion," because they are afraid that free elections will be won by Islamists who threaten them even more than the existing secular authoritarian regime. In Indonesia, Senegal, and Tunisia, one of the most effective ways to erode or prevent such a constituency for coercion has been to create a democratically friendly Islamic political theology. Drawing on decades of interviews I conducted with Ghannouchi and seven field research trips to Tunisia, I examine how Ghannouchi and Ennahda first did this within the party; later through eight years of mutual accommodations, including joint statements with secularists; and finally in the Islamist-secular coalition government that was in power when the constitution was drafted.

We are beginning to assemble a reasonable literature that addresses the question of Islamic fundamentalist purists and how they might moderate and become pluralist.[7] However, we still have almost no literature on the possible moderation of secular fundamentalists who often support exclusionary authoritarian policies against Muslims in the name of hard-line secularism and modernity. Fortunately, Monica Marks, a Rhodes Scholar and doctoral candidate at Oxford who has conducted over 1,200 interviews in Tunisia since 2011, breaks new ground by comparatively exploring moderation hypotheses in regard to both secular and Islamic purists. In a convincing analysis, Marks shows how and why the party mechanisms of Ennahda that emphasize discussion, negotiation, and voting have helped move their Islamic fundamentalists toward a series of compromises and reduce to a minimum actions that Juan J. Linz would call those of "semi-loyal democrats."[8] In fact, as Ghannouchi has told both Marks and me, he accepts secularism as necessary for democracy, but he continues to dislike hard-line 1905 French-style laïcité secularism, which he believes inhibits pluralism and democracy.

In contrast to Ennahda, the secularly oriented party, Nidaa Tounes, while in opposition, included a hard "secular" wing—a term Marks deconstructs—whose members were at best semiloyal democrats. The problem did not go away when Nidaa Tounes became the ruling party in 2015, largely because, as Marks makes clear, they are such a loosely organized party that they seldom have discussions and votes on key policy issues and thus, unlike Ennahda, have great "difficulty transmitting . . . pluralism-expanding rationales down through party ranks." Indeed, Marks argues that many of Tunisia's secular purists are not modern democratic "post-secularists" in Habermasian terms, because they are still not "epistemically adjusted to the continued existence of religious communities."[9] To the extent that such secular fundamentalists do not accept a "twin tolerations" view of inclusive democracy for moderate Muslims, they may well complicate Tunisia's eventual achievement of democratic consolidation.

The leading scholar of comparative Middle Eastern constitutions is Nathan J. Brown. He opens his article on constitution making in Egypt and Tunisia with the comment that "rarely have success and failure been so closely twined as with Egypt and Tunisia." Brown advances the argument that modern constitutional analysis should begin with a close examination of the political context, go on to study the drafting process, and end with an analysis of the winners and losers as revealed in the constitutional text. The distance and hostility in Egypt between Islamists and liberal secularists we have just discussed partly explain why the political context was so conflictual in Egypt. Brown shows how three conflictual camps—Islamists, young secular activists, and deep-state officials, especially from the military and the judiciary—had their own goals and power bases, which complicated the political context and constitutional drafting process. In the end, whereas in Tunisia efficiency and speed were "sacrificed for the sake of inclusion, bargaining, and deliberation," so that only after three years were the "various forces . . . able to produce a consensus text," in Egypt, the sacrifice in the final text was democracy itself. "The primary winners in Egypt's constitution were the state institutions that had banded together to oust Morsi. The constitution enshrines autonomy for the military. . . . The judiciary, which strongly supported the military takeover from the Brotherhood, also won autonomy." Egypt's authoritarian "deep state" is thus constitutionally entrenched.

This brings us to another variable, the military, which played a major role in democratic failure in Egypt but not in Tunisia. Why? After the overthrow of the monarchy in Egypt, the country was under continuous military rule from 1952 until the fall of Mubarak in 2011. In sharp contrast, the military in Tunisia has never ruled, even for a day. Thus the task of controlling the military, even under the best of circumstances, would always have been more difficult in the Egyptian transition attempt than in the Tunisian transition attempt.

Also, the legacy of almost sixty years of continuous military rule left a powerful set of incentives for the Egyptian military to retain a major role in the state apparatus, incentives not found in Tunisia. We are very fortunate to have pioneering research on these incentives by Hicham Bou Nassif. Many scholars think detailed research on the Egyptian and even Tunisian militaries is difficult or even impossible. However, Bou Nassif discovered that the Egyptian and Tunisian states have always posted in the official gazette all major appointments, such as to governorships or major state agencies. Bou Nassif meticulously gathered and analyzed these publicly available documents. He demonstrates that from 1981 to 2011, 40 percent of all the governorships appointed in Egypt (and most of the crucially important political governorships) went to retired military officers, in contrast to less than 2 percent in Tunisia. Perhaps even more significantly, he shows that many of the well-paid and powerful positions in the state apparatus, such as the president of the Suez Canal Authority or the head of civil aviation, are assigned to retired Egyptian military officers, as are many posts in the economy, which are run by the military and thus unaccountable, since all military-run economic activities are secret parts of the national security state.

The Egyptian-Tunisian comparison concludes with a disturbing article by Radwan Masmoudi on the paucity of international aid that has been distributed to democratizing Tunisia versus to authoritarian, military-led Egypt. The United States, no matter how authoritarian the Egyptian military is, has always given at least 1.3 billion dollars a year in aid with no strings attached, owing to Egypt's geopolitical weight and its recognition of Israel since the Camp David Accords. No matter how democratic

Tunisia has been in the period 2011–2015, it has never received more than 70 million dollars a year in aid, funds, moreover, highly tied, as the U.S. ambassador stressed to me, to the purchase of U.S. goods and services.

INDONESIA AND INDIA

The volume concludes with articles on Indonesia and India. Why? For the last ten years, of the eleven members of the Association of Asian Nations (ASEAN), the country that has *always* been ranked as having the best democratic performance by Freedom House is not Roman Catholic Philippines, nor Confucian Singapore, nor Theravada Buddhist Thailand, but rather the world's most populous Muslim country, Indonesia.

The Indonesian democratic transition started with the successful democratic protests in 1998 that led to the fall of General Suharto, who had headed the military regime since 1965. One of the world's most prominent constitutional scholars, Donald L. Horowitz, recently published a book, *Constitutional Change and Democracy in Indonesia*, in which he asserted that Indonesia from 1999–2002 managed to craft a "meticulously consensual" constitution.[10]

Democracy in Indonesia shares much in common with its "most similar" cases of democratic success in Muslim-majority Tunisia and Senegal, in that sharia is not part of the constitution: key Muslim political leaders worked hard to create a democracy-friendly political theology and to develop good relations with democratic secular leaders. A disproportionate number of compulsory paid holidays are assigned to minority religions, and the state pays for pilgrimages for minority religions and for many minority-religion schools. But most importantly, *none* of these three countries (nor India, as we will see shortly) follow John Rawls's injunction to keep religion *off* the public agenda.

Jeremy Menchik spent the better part of three years doing field research on the three major Muslim political groups in Indonesia, which he presents in his chapter "Crafting Indonesian Democracy: Inclusion-Moderation and the Sacralizing of the Postcolonial State." Using a wonderful combination of ethnography, history, and political science, Menchik shows how Indonesia, without violating democracy, has been able to develop a high degree of state-religion cooperation in policy areas such as education. He suggests that for democratization to succeed in states like Tunisia and Indonesia, it is just as important that Islamic actors never fully "lose" as it is that they never fully "win." In comparative perspective, given the salience of religion in contemporary Europe, Menchik suggests that politics in peripheral states like India, Indonesia, and Tunisia where religious actors are central to the crafting of mutual accommodation may illuminate aspects of Europe's present, rather than its past.

India, of course, is unlike Tunisia, Indonesia, and Senegal in that it is not a Muslim-majority but a Hindu-majority country. I chose to retain India in this volume because if we are rethinking the question of the role of Muslims in successful democratic transitions, it seems to me useful to include some reflections on the Muslim impact on the quality of democracy in a country where Muslims constitute a very large minority. Before independence, India had the largest Muslim population of any country in the world, and Hinduism and Islam to some extent became *mutually constitutive*.[11] Even now, India, with a 2011 census estimate of 172 million Muslims, is the country after Indonesia, and possibly Pakistan, with the world's largest Muslim population. Thus Mahatma Gandhi, Jawaharlal Nehru, the great leader B. R. Ambedkar, and Mulana Azad, a Muslim who was president of the Congress Party in 1923 and 1940–1945 and the first minister of education in independent India, all had to think hard about how to create a democratic political culture and democratic political practices that incorporated their large Muslim minority. Though assertive Hindu nationalism under Prime Minister Narendra Modi and his Bharatiya Janata Party (BJP) threatens to destabilize its pluralist gains, India merits consideration for inclusion in the "success" category. Indeed, with the increasing interpenetration in Europe of secularism, democracy, and Islam, the Indian experience becomes more important than ever for comparativists and policy makers interested in new models of secularism and democracy for European countries with large Muslim minorities.[12]

In terms of attitudes toward democracy in India, Muslims are not non-democratic outliers. For my book with Juan J. Linz and the great Indian survey specialist Yogendra Yadav, *Crafting State Nations: India and Other Multinational Democracies*, we carried out a survey of 27,145 Indians, including large samples of Hindus, Muslims, and Sikhs, concerning their attitudes toward democracy.[13] The results were surprising. All three religions affirmed by 71 percent that "democracy was always preferable to an authoritarian regime" and only an identical 4 percent in all three religions said "sometimes authoritarianism is preferable to democracy."[14] When we discussed these results with scholars and activists, a number of them tended to dismiss our results concerning Muslims because they felt that we had not examined authoritarian attitudes among "intensely practicing Muslims," whom they assumed would be less supportive of democracy. To test their hypothesis, we divided Muslims (and Hindus and Sikhs) into low, medium, and high intensity of religious practice and measured their comparative support for democracy for all three categories. The results for Muslims, Hindus, and Sikhs were the same: "the greater the intensity of religious practice the greater the intensity of support for democracy."[15]

To examine some of the policies and practices that may have produced these results in India, and to explore whether such strategies might possibly be of use in other democracies with large Muslim minorities, this volume concludes with a theoretically and historically broad essay by Hilal Ahmed and Sudipta Kaviraj, "Indian Democracy and the World's Largest Muslim Minority."[16]

NOTES

1. For a discussion of research designs comparing "least similar" and "most similar" cases in terms of final outcomes of the dependent variable being studied, see Alexander L. George and Andrew Bennett, *Case Studies and Theory Development in the Social Sciences* (Cambridge, Mass.: MIT Press, 2005), esp. 49–54. Given that we do not have a large enough n for our comparisons, and given that most of our cases are so recent, our analysis of least- and most-similar cases is meant to be heuristic rather than rigorous and is focused appropriately on hypothesis generation rather than hypothesis verification.

2. Senegal does not have a separate chapter in this volume, but I incorporate it into my analytic framework in this introduction, in my chapter in this volume, and in my article

"Rituals of Respect: Sufis and Secularists in Senegal in Comparative Perspective," *Comparative Politics* (July 2012): 379–401. Senegal is the West African country with the longest ranking as a democracy. Democracy in Senegal was built with the help of the Sufi-inspired Muslim majority and features reciprocal and vertical "rituals of respect" between the Sufi religious majority and secular state officials and reciprocal and horizontal rituals of respect among all the Sufi orders and toward the Roman Catholic minority. The Institute of Religion, Culture, and Public Life at Columbia has published a very relevant volume on Senegal and democracy, Mamadou Diouf, ed., *Tolerance, Democracy, and Sufis in Senegal* (New York: Columbia University Press, 2013), and is also nearing publication of a related volume.

3. These books were both published by the Johns Hopkins University Press in Baltimore.

4. Samuel P. Huntington, *The Clash of Civilizations and the Remaking of the Modern World* (New York: Simon and Schuster, 1996), 70.

5. In my chapter, I discuss in detail the four requirements for a completed *democratic transition*. Of course, there are additional requirements for a *democratic consolidation* that Tunisia must still address, as I discuss in my chapter.

6. See Human Rights Watch's 188-page report "Egypt: Rab'a Killings Likely Crimes Against Humanity: No Justice Later for Series of Deadly Mass Attacks on Protesters," August 12, 2014. For systematic documentation of the "eradication" campaign against the Muslim Brotherhood, see Emad El-Din Shahin, "The State, Liberals, and the Muslim Brotherhood in Egypt: From Competition to Eradication," paper presented at an international conference on Tunisia's democratic transition in comparative perspective, March 25, 2015, Columbia University, and revised October 1, 2015.

7. For a discussion of this general literature, see Julian Schwedner, "Can Islamists Become Moderates? Rethinking the Inclusion/Moderation Hypothesis," *World Politics* 63, no. 2 (2011): 347–370. For a discussion of the moderation thesis concerning Ennahda in Tunisia, see Francesco Cavatorta and Fabio Merone, "Moderation Through Exclusion? The Journey of the Tunisian Ennahda from Fundamentalist to Conservative Party," *Democratization* 20, no. 5 (2013): 857–875.

8. For the importance of the categories of "semiloyalty" and "loyalty" for democratic breakdowns and transitions, see Juan J. Linz, *Breakdown of Democratic Regimes: Crisis, Breakdown, and Reequilibration* (Baltimore, Md.: Johns Hopkins University Press, 1978), 28–45.

9. Jürgen Habermas, "Religion in the Public Sphere," *European Journal of Philosophy* 14, no. 1 (2006).

10. Donald L. Horowitz, *Constitutional Change and Democracy in Indonesia* (Cambridge: Cambridge University Press, 2013), 293.

11. For example, Romila Thapar, arguably the leading historian of ancient and medieval India, argues that, due to intensive cultural exchanges such as shared pilgrimages, a cultural fusion between Sufi Islam and non-Brahmanical varieties of Hinduism such as Bhakti was the de facto religion of "the majority of Indians, for at least five centuries" before Britain arrived and introduced divisive classificatory and bureaucratic categories

privileging Brahmanism and rigidifying Hindu-Muslim distinctions. See Romila Thapar, "Is Secularism Alien to Indian Civilization?" in *The Future of Secularism*, ed. T. N. Srinivasan (New York: Oxford University Press, 2007), 100.

12. See, for example, the pioneering conceptual and empirical book by Nilüfer Göle, *Islam and Secularity: The Future of Europe's Public Sphere* (Durham, N.C.: Duke University Press, 2015).

13. Alfred Stepan, Juan J. Linz, and Yogendra Yadav, *Crafting State Nations: India and Other Multinational Democracies* (Baltimore, Md.: Johns Hopkins University Press, 2011), 62–72.

14. Ibid., 70. According to a Pearson's chi-square test, the findings for all religious communities are statistically significant (p-value < .001). The probability of this occurring by chance is less than 1 in 1,000.

15. Ibid., tables 2.7 and 2.8.

16. The same religion can of course have very different attitudes toward democracy for contextual reasons. For example, one of the most influential Muslim organizations today in both Pakistan and India is Jamaat-e-Islami, which was founded in 1941 by the same thinker, Syed Abul A'la Maududi. However, by 1970 the Indian branch had become explicitly supportive of democracy and secularism and remains so to this day, but the Pakistani branch has always retained an authoritarian political theology. For the engagement in India of Jamaat-e-Islami in electoral participation and democratic practices, see Irfan Ahmad, *Islamism and Democracy in India: The Transformation of Jamaat-e-Islami* (Princeton, N.J.: Princeton University Press, 2009). This is one more example of the "multivocality" of any religion.

PART I

WHY DIFFERENT DEMOCRATIZATION OUTCOMES IN TUNISIA AND EGYPT?

Cross-Ideological Accommodations, Constitutions, Militaries, and the Content of International Assistance

1

ENNAHDA'S DEMOCRATIC
COMMITMENTS AND CAPABILITIES

Major Evolutionary Moments and Choices

RACHED GHANNOUCHI

THE STORY OF TUNISIA remained largely untold until seven years ago. In December 2010, after decades of stifling repression and authoritarian rule, the country arose to ignite the flame of the Arab Awakening. Since then, Tunisia has witnessed three democratic and fair elections, a consensual transition, and the adoption of a democratic and progressive constitution that enjoys broad support. The path to becoming a democratic and fair society is yet to be completed, but it has been preserved by painstaking efforts to build political consensus and foster an inclusive system based on coexistence. It is in this sense that Tunisia can be hailed as a model for the Arab region.

This democratic transition is unprecedented for our country and indeed the region. Tunisia's transition from a repressive dictatorship to a newborn democracy brought about an evolution—and in some areas a revolution—on the political scene and in society as a whole. This chapter charts an overview of the evolution of the Ennahda (Renaissance) Party over the transitional period, from an opposition party persecuted and refused legal recognition to being the leading party in Tunisia's first democratically elected government. It seeks to delineate the principles guiding the Ennahda Party's approach to Tunisia's delicate transition and to, in particular, the elaboration of its historic constitution, the cornerstone of the new democratic republic.

GUIDING PRINCIPLES OF DEMOCRATIC TRANSITION

FIRST PRINCIPLE: CROSS-PARTY PARTNERSHIPS AND COALITION BUILDING

The extraordinary transitional phase presented an immense challenge to Tunisia as a whole and in particular to the political parties that had the delicate task of managing the difficult journey from dictatorship to a democratic state. The transitional phase has provided an opportunity to build on existing partnerships and to form new ones, to implement previously learned lessons and to learn new ones.

The first principle that has guided the Ennahda Party's approach is the willingness to form cross-party partnerships. The principle of pluralism is one that the party adopted at its inception. As early as 1981, when the party was founded, it explicitly recognized the right of any party, regardless of its ideological background, to govern if supported by the popular will. This was ahead of both Islamic and secular parties in Tunisia, who hesitated for a long time—some up to this moment—in recognizing genuine pluralism.

The Ennahda Party's understanding of pluralism goes beyond merely the idea of coexistence; it embraces partnership with parties of different intellectual and political backgrounds. This was demonstrated in the October 18 Committee of 2005, which brought together political activists, journalists, and human rights activists from various parties as well as independents. The initiative began as a joint hunger strike on the occasion of the UN-sponsored World Summit on the Information Society in Tunis in order to draw attention to the continuing deterioration of rights in Tunisia and to call for an end to human rights violations and the release of political prisoners.

The October 18 Committee developed into a forum to elaborate a shared vision for a post–Ben Ali democratic Tunisia. The committee produced joint papers on fundamental questions such as mechanisms for the peaceful alternation of power, equality between men and women, freedom of belief in a modern Muslim society, and the relationship between religion and the state in a future democratic system. Forging a partnership between secular and Islamist activists was intellectually and politically challenging because the Ben Ali regime fiercely opposed and actively sought to obstruct any such rapprochement. However, the committee was critical in laying the groundwork for future partnership by concretely elaborating the principles for building a pluralistic democracy and imagining a free democratic Tunisia beyond dictatorship.

The revolution opened up further spaces for cross-party cooperation. In the immediate aftermath of the revolution, the Ennahda Party joined the Higher Commission for the Achievement of the Goals of the Revolution and cooperated with all of the other parties in the commission. Even before the first post–Ben Ali elections, Ennahda openly declared its firm belief that whatever the result of the elections, Tunisia needed a coalition government built on broad representation and cooperation between parties.

We were convinced that building the foundations of a democratic Tunisia was an immense challenge that could only be achieved by preventing polarization and fostering cooperation between parties, in particular between the two principal intellectual trends in our society—moderate secularism and moderate Islamism. These two movements have always been the two wings of the national reform movement and are both critical to the democratic project.

After winning the free and fair elections for the National Constituent Assembly in October 2011, we reiterated our call for a national unity government. We could have formed a coalition based on ideological similarity, but we consciously sought to establish a new democratic tradition in Tunisia—that of cross-ideological cooperation and rejection of any monopolization of power by one party or trend. Two center-left secular parties responded to our call: the Ettakatol Party and the Congress for the Republic (CPR) Party—and we formed a coalition that proved to be a pioneering model of coexistence between secularists and Islamists, the two trends that had been in conflict in the region for the preceding half-century.

SECOND PRINCIPLE: CONSENSUS BUILDING

The coalition between Ennahda, Ettakatol, and CPR was the result of our conviction that Tunisia should be governed through consensus and that transitions cannot be managed by the logic of majority versus minority.

In fact, Tunisia's political leaders have elaborated a new form of transitional democracy based on participation and consensus building rather than on majoritarian democracy. This principle is at the root of the Tunisian model. Our adoption of consensus as a principle and as a *methodology* for governing was based on a conviction that transitional phases must not be governed by a majority of 51 percent. Rather, a broad consensus must be forged between the broadest possible trends in society in order to establish stability and shared political traditions. A democratic transition is the moment in which new foundational rules are established and new political conventions forged. It is critical that it be structured in a way that enables and incentivizes all political actors to contribute and commit to these new rules. The consolidation of that commitment, when there is no going back to the old rules, is what marks the end of the transition and the beginning of a stable democratic system.

The *practice* of consensus is an extremely delicate art, a complex response to a complex reality. In the absence of an established political culture between political elites, simple majoritarian democracy cannot provide an adequate framework. Thus, the model of consensus building between political trends provided the most appropriate tool for constructing shared conventions and a common political framework within which political competition could take place, leading to the success of the democratic transition and preventing chaos and conflict. Consensus building succeeded in saving Tunisia and its revolution from the many major crises it faced.

THIRD PRINCIPLE: CRISIS MANAGEMENT THROUGH DIALOGUE AND COMPROMISE

Despite the best of intentions, the Tunisian transition brought no shortage of challenges and crises. The Ennahda Party's approach was to deal with political crises using the logic of dialogue and compromise. Following the assassination of the martyr Chokri Belaid in February 2013, Ennahda accepted a proposal to hand key ministries to independent figures and technocrats. Following the assassination of the parliamentarian Mohamed Brahmi in July 2013, we took a similar approach. When a number of parliamentarians suspended their participation in constitutional debates in order to protest the assassination, Ennahda could have continued the debates and proceeded to the adoption of the constitution without their participation. However, we did not seek to rush through the adoption of the constitution nor impose a hurried transition. We understood that while finding a compromise might take time, it would be better than making the Tunisian constitution the constitution of a majority imposed on a minority.

Thus, following a national dialogue, we signed a road map according to which the Ennahda-led coalition government would resign and hand over power to an independent technocrat government, once agreement had been reached on a new prime minister, the adoption of the constitution, and the election of an election commission. The aim was not to remain in power but to ensure that the National Constituent Assembly, the supreme representative body, could complete its work of drafting a constitution to set the political foundations for a democratic Tunisia. This required broad agreement and a climate of national unity, not a logic of conflict and confrontation.

Ennahda's departure from government was a sign of the success of the national dialogue in resolving conflict. Prime Minister Ali Laarayedh's resignation was a rare example of peaceful transfer of power in our region and of Ennahda's commitment to democratic governance. As the largest party in the country, we believed Ennahda was required to give the greatest concessions to protect the revolution and the democratic transition process. These sacrifices helped preserve the country's unity and its democratic transition, crowned by the adoption of a new constitution by a striking 94 percent of the National Constituent Assembly and the holding of the country's second free and fair elections.

FOURTH PRINCIPLE: INCLUSION

In light of the dangers of polarization and division, whose consequences can be seen in the countries in crisis around the region, Ennahda chose to adopt the inclusive approach of consensus by incorporating the old system into the new. We rejected all the roads leading to exclusion or division between Tunisians and chose not to adopt a law of political exclusion such as the one introduced in Iraq and Libya. Anyone who enters under the political roof of democracy, as set out in the new constitution, is a Tunisian with full rights and without any discrimination. If they are proven to have wronged or violated anyone's rights, it is for the judicial system and the transitional justice commission to judge them according to the law. Barring that, everybody should enjoy their full rights of citizenship, including running for political positions. Opposing the proposed Law for the Protection of the Revolution and an article in the electoral law that sought to exclude supporters of the former ruling party from standing for election was a key decision that differentiated Tunisia from neighboring countries that fell into civil war after division and polarization.

GUIDING PRINCIPLES OF A DEMOCRATIC POLITICAL SYSTEM

FIRST PRINCIPLE: THE DEMOCRATIC CIVIL STATE

Ennahda's vision of the democratic civil state has been elaborated over a number of decades, starting with our Founding Declaration of 1981. The declaration embraced the principles of "the people's reclamation of their legitimate right to self-determination far from any internal or external tutelage . . . rejection of violence as a method of change . . . *consultation* as the means of deciding on matters of thought, culture, and politics. Rejection of authoritarianism and monopoly of power . . . and affirming the right of the people to exercise freedom of expression, assembly, and all legitimate rights, and to cooperate with all national forces to achieve this."

The cross-party October 18 Committee envisioned the state in a democratic system as a civil institution drawing its legitimacy from the people's free will and abiding both by the rule of law and by human rights. The committee recognized Islam as the religion of the majority of the Tunisian people and, alongside Arabic, as one of the main pillars of the country's civilizational identity, an identity in constant evolution in creative interaction with modernity. The state gives a special status to Islam, guarantees the teaching of Islamic education in educational institutions, maintains links of solidarity with Muslim nations, and defends the Arabic language as the language of administration, education, and culture, all within a framework of guaranteeing freedom of religion and belief, rejecting discrimination between citizens on the basis of religion or belief, and maintaining openness to world civilizations. Thus, the nature of the civil state was a matter of consensus among all major political trends prior to the revolution. The concept is outlined in the constitution, which stresses that Tunisia's political system is "a participatory, democratic, republican regime, under the framework of a civil state where sovereignty belongs to the people through peaceful rotation of power via free elections, and on the principle of the separation of powers and balance between them."

The role of sharia was debated following the desire of a section of the public, including some of Ennahda's supporters, to list sharia as one of the sources of legislation in the constitution. Whereas for some such a reference was simply a statement of fact—that a significant part of Tunisian legislation, including the Personal Status Code, is drawn from Islamic jurisprudence, in the minds of others, the term "sharia" was associated with negative connotations. After discussion at various levels of the party, its leadership reached the view that any term that can cause significant controversy had no place in the constitution and that the terms "Islam" and "Islamic teachings," which are included in the constitution's preamble and first article, encompass all aspects of the religion and are broader and more consensual than the term "sharia."

SECOND PRINCIPLE: FUNDAMENTAL RIGHTS

Tunisia's new constitution enshrines freedoms and rights newly enjoyed by Tunisians following the revolution, freedoms and rights of which they had been deprived for decades. The second chapter on "Rights and Liberties" includes twenty-nine articles that guarantee various rights and freedoms. Any limitations on these must be prescribed by the law, "necessary in a civil democratic state," and proportional, and such limitations must not compromise the essence of those freedoms and rights.

The constitution also mandates the state "to spread the values of moderation and tolerance" and promote "openness to foreign languages and human civilizations and spread the culture of human rights." As events around the world show, balancing the protection of fundamental freedoms with the need to challenge hate speech and incitement to violence is a key challenge of our time.

In addition to key civil and political rights, the constitution protects a number of economic and social rights, such as the right to free education at all levels, the right to preventative health care and treatment for every citizen, the right to culture and cultural innovation, the right to water, and the right to a sound environment. The extensive list of economic and social rights is innovative and more far-reaching than the constitutions of many other democratic states. The Ennahda Party is proud to have contributed to their constitutionalization as part of its vision of the role of the state in providing the basic conditions for a dignified life.

Two rights, freedom of belief and conscience, and gender equality, deserve specific mention, given their historical trajectory and symbolism in the Tunisian context.

Freedom of Belief and Conscience

The October 18 Committee debated the issue of freedom of belief and reached a common position: "Freedom of faith is a personal freedom far from any compulsion and part of freedom of opinion on which other freedoms depend. This freedom includes the right to embrace or leave a religion or belief, to express it, call to it, practice its rituals, and spread it through education and proselytizing." The committee pledged to "protect freedom of faith and conscience and to seek to abolish discrimination on the basis of religion or belief, as a condition of citizenship based on full equality of all members of society."

The constitution builds on this understanding by placing an obligation on the state to protect these rights: "The State shall protect religion, guarantee freedom of belief and conscience and religious practices." This raises the question of the nature of the relationship between state and religion. Throughout Islamic history, the state has always been influenced by Islam in its practices, and laws were made in light of Islamic values as understood at that particular time and place. Despite this, laws and procedures were not seen as being divinely revealed but were human endeavors open to challenge and criticism. Given the absence of an official "church" in Islam, there is room for broad freedom of thought and diversity of interpretation. When legislating, we are in need of a mechanism. In our view, the democratic mechanism is the best embodiment of the Islamic value of *shura* (consultation). In the absence of a church representing the sacred on earth, no particular scholar, party, or state represents divine will, and it is for each society to develop mechanisms for reaching consensus and making decisions.

There is an ongoing debate in our country between secular currents that may be described as extremist and Islamist ones that may be described in like manner. The latter would like to impose their understanding of religion from above using the state apparatus; the former aspires to strip the state and national culture of all religious influences. Both approaches endanger freedoms, rights, and social harmony. The approach we advocate is to find a balance that guarantees people's freedoms and rights because religion is here to do exactly that. There is no value in any religious observance that is coerced. People are created free, and while it is possible to have control over their external aspects, it is impossible to control their inner thoughts and convictions.

The primary ambit for religion is not the state's apparatus but rather personal conviction. The state's duty is to provide services such as health and education and to provide the framework for a dignified life—not to control people's hearts and minds. For this reason, and based on the Qur'anic verse that "there is no compulsion in religion," I have long opposed the imposition of religious practices in any form and have argued that the issue of *al-riddah* (apostasy) is not one for the state to regulate. It is a matter of individual freedom to adhere to or reject any religious creed.

The debate taking place today in Tunisia, and in many parts of the world, is often based on a misunderstanding of both secularism and Islam and their many forms. The Egyptian thinker Abd al-Wahhab al-Masiri distinguished between "partial" and "total" secularisms. In my view, secularism is not an atheist philosophy but a set of procedural arrangements designed to safeguard freedoms, particularly freedom of belief and thought. The new Tunisian constitution establishes a balance by mandating state neutrality and the neutrality of religious places of worship while protecting religious freedom and citizens' right to believe in whatever they desire within a framework of mutual respect and observance of the law.

Gender Equality

Equality between women and men is also a principle that has evolved throughout the democratic transition and now occupies a central place in the new constitution. After initial criticism of some articles of the Personal Status Code, the Ennahda Party officially embraced the code when it ratified the 1988 National Charter for democratic political competition, which it signed alongside other political parties. The October 18 Committee, as part of its joint work on elaborating a common vision for a democratic society, had produced joint papers on a number of topics, including on the equality of men and women.

Following the revolution, all parties, including Ennahda, had a chance to put these principles into practice. The Council for the Achievement of the Aims of the Revolution and the Democratic Transition in 2011 approved the principle of "gender parity" in the electoral system, introducing a quota system, according to which every electoral list had to include an equal number of men and women, to be alternated on the list. The Ennahda Party strongly supported the proposal for gender parity; over a quarter of the council's members voted against it. The result of the adoption of the gender parity rule was that fifty-nine women were elected to the National Constituent Assembly, forty-one of whom were from the Ennahda Party. Out of all parties, Ennahda had the highest percentage of women in its parliamentary group. Later, as some male members of the Assembly resigned and were subsequently replaced by the next candidate on the list, the number of women MPs rose to almost 31 percent—a percentage exceeding that of many European parliaments.

Ennahda's female members of parliament played a fundamental role in the Assembly's constitution-drafting, legislative, oversight, and outreach work. Ennahda put forward one of its female members of parliament for the position of Assembly vice president. Mehrezia Labidi thus became the highest-ranking elected woman politician in the Arab world. Of all Assembly committees (constituent, legislative, and special), the only committees headed by women were headed by Ennahda female members of parliament. Of the eight Ennahha heads of committees, four were women. The General Legislation Committee included seven Ennahda MPs out of twenty committee members. All seven were women, including the president of the committee, Kalthoum Badreddine. A similar pattern can be seen in the composition of the remaining committees in the Assembly.

The above figures demonstrate not only Ennahda's commitment to women in leadership but also the benefits Tunisia's transition brought to society, broadening women's participation at the political level. Their presence in the parliament was critical to ensuring that the constitution enshrines their rights—a number of articles emphasize the equality of all citizens, male and female, and the state's duty to eliminate discrimination and eradicate violence against women. The constitution also commits the state to developing women's rights further, ensuring equal opportunities in all fields, and removing all forms of discrimination. The constitution also includes an important and innovative article that requires all elected councils to respect the principle of gender parity in the election of representatives.

This is a pioneering step by Tunisia to constitutionalize gender equality in political representation, and it sets an example for countries around the world, including well-established democracies.

* * *

Tunisia has made significant strides toward democracy, despite living through tumultuous times in a tumultuous region. The horrific terrorist attacks that targeted the parliament and tourist sites in March and June 2015 sought to derail Tunisia's successful democratic transition. These despicable attacks are a grim reminder of the many challenges that lie ahead.

Terrorism is a multidimensional phenomenon that has been years in the making, and it requires a multidimensional and measured approach. Decades of the stifling of all aspirations and of political expression by despots in the region sowed the seeds of violent extremism. Political repression, social inequality, and economic deprivation have combined to create frustration, particularly among vulnerable youth, who are easily drawn to corrupted extreme ideologies that masquerade as religion.

Too many youth in our region have been suspended in a permanent state of hopelessness, unable to find dignified work, to access social and cultural opportunities for self-development, to build a family, or to see a future for themselves. Politicians must work hard to provide policies and structures within which young people have the opportunity to work for something and not to fight against something.

A unified political response is needed that respects the new framework of rights and freedoms that we have placed at the heart of our political system. When in government, the Ennahda Party worked to restore security after a tumultuous postrevolution period, reestablishing local police patrols and providing security forces with better equipment, with the assistance of international partners. The challenge was to reestablish order while creating new security solutions that respect the rule of law and human rights.

What is needed is a collective effort by political and social actors to set a comprehensive counterterrorism strategy. It is critical that the security challenges Tunisia is facing not be allowed to undermine the new democratic system. The solution to terrorism is not less freedom but more. The solution to terrorism is not to crack down on religion but to cultivate freedom of religion and moderate, balanced religious thought. Tunisia has a long heritage of moderate Islamic thought. I believe that this thought is the antidote to extremist ideologies that seek to create a false choice between tradition and progress, between modernity and authenticity, between secularism and religion. It is these false choices that continue to strangle development and progress in the Arab world—just as the false choice between stability and freedom justified despotism and created an ultimately unfree and unstable society. Through dialogue and consensus building, Tunisians can maintain their hard-won freedom both against the threat of terrorism and the lure of authoritarianism.

Despite the tragedy of these attacks, Tunisia remains on the right road. The principles of coalition building, consensus, and inclusion continue to guide the transition. The country continues to be battered by the high waves of political instability and chaos in the region. However, through maintaining these key principles and with international support, Tunisia can remain a beacon of hope and inspiration for the world, through the ideas and possibilities it represents.

2

THE CHALLENGES OF DEMOCRATIZATION IN THE ARAB WORLD

Some Reflections on the Egyptian Case

CARRIE ROSEFSKY WICKHAM

O N FEBRUARY 11, 2011, Egypt's President Hosni Mubarak resigned after just eighteen days of mass protest, and euphoric crowds poured into the streets to celebrate the dawn of a new era. Yet more than six years later, the uprising's goals of "Bread, Freedom, and Social Justice" have yet to be fulfilled. In fact, conditions in Egypt today are arguably worse than they were before the Arab Spring began. The free-wheeling public expression and assembly that blossomed in the wake of the uprising have been snuffed out in the name of order and security, and public officials of the "deep state"—headed by Abd al Fattah al-Sisi, the former military commander elected president in 2014—have achieved a near-total monopoly on power. Perhaps most remarkably, rather than mourn the loss of the uprising's democratic momentum, many Egyptians welcomed the resurgence of the very forces that the uprising had rallied against and have tolerated—if not openly supported—the al-Sisi regime's crackdown on any group or individual brave or foolhardy enough to call its actions into question.

This is the edited version of a lecture presented at a conference, "The Tunisian Democratic Transition in Comparative Perspective, with Reflections on Indonesia, India, and Egypt," at Columbia University, March 27, 2015.

So what went wrong? How do we explain the bitter disappointments of Egypt's transition and, in particular, the failure of the country's political elites to lay the foundations of a stable democratic order and hasten the arrival of a new era of freedom, development, and human rights?

The causes of democratic breakdown in Egypt remain hotly contested in scholarly and policy-making circles, and debate on the subject has become intensely polarized. On one end of the spectrum are those who lay primary—if not exclusive—blame for the disruptions of the transition era on what had been the largest and best-organized sector of the political opposition under Mubarak, the Muslim Brotherhood. Riding electoral victories to the heights of state power in the wake of the uprising, such observers contend, Brotherhood leaders exploited the authority of public office to advance a narrow partisan agenda over the objections of their critics. In so doing, they alienated potential allies in the secular opposition whom they could have enlisted as partners in the implementation of a sustained project of democratic reform. In addition, the administration of Muhammad Morsi, the veteran Brotherhood leader elected president in May 2012, was marked by epic levels of inexperience and incompetence, proving the Brotherhood ill-equipped to manage the affairs of a large, fractious, and resource-poor country on its own. Indeed, just one year into Morsi's tenure, massive protests broke out against him, fueled by the mounting frustrations of ordinary Egyptians awaiting relief from their daily hardships. The characterization of Morsi's brief tenure in power as nothing short of a spectacular failure is advanced by Michael Hanna in an article published in the journal *Foreign Policy* published five days after the president's ouster, titled "Blame Morsy: How to Wreck a Country in 369 Days."

Those on the other end of the spectrum, including, not surprisingly, prominent figures in the Brotherhood itself, vigorously contest this version of events. While acknowledging Morsi's lackluster performance as president, they take pains to point out that his room to maneuver was sharply limited from the outset, given the de facto veto power exercised by senior officials in the military, the judiciary, and the state administration carried over from the Mubarak era. Throughout his tenure, they claim, President Morsi attempted to meet the demands of the Egyptian people for economic relief, democratic restructuring, and justice for the families of the uprising's martyrs but was hampered in such efforts by the noncooperation—and at times, open hostility—of the very state administrators he depended upon to implement his directives. In addition, Morsi repeatedly invited prominent opposition figures to join his government in various capacities, and virtually all of these overtures were rebuffed. Hence it was the secular opposition's decision to boycott the Morsi government, rather than any impulse on the Brotherhood's part to monopolize power, that lent his administration a monotone Islamist coloration. Further, in the final days of Morsi's presidency, it was the country's secular politicians, including many of its self-professed liberal democrats, who "sold themselves to the tanks," that is, who supported military intervention as a quick and dirty fix to the problem of their own weakness rather than invest in the slow, hard work of building their own constituencies to compete with the Brotherhood through democratic channels. In sum, it was the refusal of the "deep state" and the secular opposition to accommodate themselves to the Brotherhood's authority as elected representatives of the Egyptian people that brought the democratic project crashing down, bringing the hard-won gains of the uprising along with it.

Though they reach polar-opposite conclusions, both of these narratives contain some grains of truth, yet they both are too partisan and self-serving to be convincing. A systematic analysis of the causes of democratic breakdown in Egypt exceeds the scope of this chapter, though this is a topic I take up in the afterword I wrote for the 2015 paperback edition of my book *The Muslim Brotherhood: Evolution of an Islamist Movement.* My objective here is more modest. Perhaps the greatest puzzle with respect to the Brotherhood's behavior during the transition era is why it abandoned the habits of pragmatic self-restraint that had enabled it to exploit previous openings without jeopardizing its own survival. I certainly do not claim to offer the final word on this matter; indeed, I'd go so far as to say that unless and until further information about the options, motives, and influence of key individuals and factions within the Brotherhood at critical junctures in the transition becomes available, the reasons it made the choices it did will remain unknowable. With that caveat in mind, let me offer a preliminary account of how and why the Brotherhood ended up on a collision course with other sectors of society and, in doing so, placed Egypt's democratic experiment—and its own gains—at risk.

The Muslim Brotherhood is the flagship organization of the Sunni movement of revivalist Islam and the "mother" institution from which various regional branches in other Arab states have sprung. Since its founding by Hasan al-Banna in 1928, the Brotherhood has sought to promote the comprehensive Islamic reform of society and state from the bottom up. Through the *da'wa*, its project of religious outreach, it has sought to win the hearts and minds of young Egyptians and enlist them in the noble task of restoring Islam to its rightful place as the foundation of society and state, arresting the spread of Western values which have alienated Muslims from their own identity and heritage, frayed communal bonds of social solidarity, and sown the seeds of moral decay. In addition to engaging in ideological outreach, the Brotherhood developed an impressive network of social service organizations that enabled it to forge robust ties with members of the mass public, endowing it with a mobilizing capacity far exceeding that of any secular group. During the Mubarak era, the Brotherhood drew on its supporters to win positions of elected office in parliament, student unions, and professional associations, where a new generation of dynamic, charismatic, and service-oriented Islamist actors displayed new forms of responsive leadership that stood in sharp contrast with the perceived avarice and corruption of the country's ruling elites.

Yet throughout its long history, the most senior posts in the Brotherhood's leadership structure have been occupied by veteran leaders known as the "old guard." Such figures have retained control over the recruitment and socialization of new recruits as well as the appointment of leaders and allocation of resources to the organization's branch offices. Further, they have remained encapsulated within Brotherhood movement networks, and whatever contact they had with other groups in Egyptian society was inflected by a confidence in the superiority of their cause, which, as they saw it, was consistent with the preferences of an overwhelming majority of the Egyptian public and consonant with divine instructions for humankind. During the Mubarak era, members of the old guard maintained a low profile, delegating the representation of the Brotherhood in broader domains of public life to other leaders better suited to the messy give and take of competitive politics and better equipped by disposition, ideological conviction, and life experience to frame the Brotherhood's agenda as consistent with global principles of democracy, pluralism, and human rights.

When Mubarak fell, it was the Brotherhood's old guard, together with loyal "organization men" from the Brotherhood's bloc in parliament, who took the lead in setting the group's agenda. The problem with the old guard and their allies in the conservative wing of the movement was not that they were ideologically committed to the application of an extreme, Taliban-like version of Islamic rule. There is no evidence that President Morsi and his advisors sought to impose a coercive version of Islamic law upon a reluctant citizenry; on the contrary, its brand of religious conservatism was not far off from the orientations of the median Egyptian voter. Rather, the problem was that the path chosen by the Brotherhood's top decision makers during the transition era was shaped by habits of thought and behavior forged during the Brotherhood's long years as an illegal, secretive, and highly insular organization that understood its mission as endorsed by God and supported overwhelmingly by the Egyptian people, however the votes in any given election tallied up. This outlook produced an exaggerated confidence in the Brotherhood's ability to manage the complex affairs of a modern state despite the limits of its actual governing experience. In addition, it made its leaders less attentive than they should have been to the risks of moving forward with the transition without the support of rival groups. It was this institutional legacy—as reflected in the mindset of the Brotherhood's top leaders—that placed the Brotherhood in direct conflict with other sectors of the revolutionary camp and, in so doing, set the stage for an authoritarian reversal.

Before proceeding further, however, let me strongly caution against blaming the disruptions of the transition era on the behavior of any one group or party alone. We must first bear in mind that several structural features of the environment in which Egypt's transition began hampered its progress from the outset. These include a stagnant economy, pervasive and unchecked corruption, chronic resource scarcity, and the conflicting interests and values of the country's major political forces, which encompassed a disparate mix of hard-line religious Salafis, mainstream Islamists, and secular leftists and liberals. A second element that functioned as a hard constraint on the transition process was the entrenched power of unelected officials in the military, the security establishment, and the judiciary. Such officials retained a de facto veto power over state policy, enabling them to block reforms that appeared to threaten their interests. In addition, they evinced a deep-seated suspicion and hostility toward the Brotherhood, which they had been trained to view as an existential threat to public order and security.

A third factor that paved the way to democratic breakdown was the tendency of nearly *all* of the country's major political actors, regardless of their ideological orientation, to spend more time and energy maneuvering for short-term partisan advantage than pursuing common goals. This tendency was just as pronounced among figures in the secular camp as it was in the Brotherhood. Both the Brotherhood and its secular rivals portrayed themselves as seeking to protect the democratic gains of the "revolution" (*thawra*) and justified their actions in this light. Yet as conflicts erupted over the timing, sequence, and rules of the transition process, as well as the meta-issue of who should decide them, positions taken in the name of principle came to function as proxies in a zero-sum competition for political gain. For the Brotherhood, the goal was to maximize the leverage deriving from its electoral victories; for secular groups, it was to challenge the Brotherhood and undermine its performance.

This analysis poses a direct challenge to the argument that responsibility for the failure of Egypt's democratic experiment lies with the Brotherhood alone. Yet there's no doubt that the Brotherhood's own actions undermined the democratic gains it claimed it sought to preserve. Both before and after Morsi's ouster, Brotherhood leaders have defended the group's actions as having been necessary to save the revolution from its enemies in the "deep state." Yet this characterization is not convincing. The path the Brotherhood took in the wake of Mubarak's resignation was just one of many it could have chosen. Throughout its long history, the Brotherhood's actions have been shaped by competing impulses toward pragmatic

self-restraint and bolder self-assertion. Historically, the Brotherhood vacil-
lated between such poles, but in the wake of the uprising, the pendulum
swung decisively toward the latter.

At the start of Egypt's transition, the Brotherhood's senior leaders kept
their ambitions in check, sensitive to the risks the group would incur by
asserting itself too forcefully and quickly. During the uprising and in its
immediate aftermath, the Brotherhood took pains to stress that it har-
bored no wish to dominate the new political order. In a mantra its leaders
would repeat ad nauseum in the heady days following Mubarak's departure, the Brotherhood insisted that it sought "participation, not domination." Yet in the months that followed, the Brotherhood made a series of
critical decisions indicating a progressive abandonment of this initial self-
restraint. These include its decision to run for a majority of the seats in
parliament and nominate its own candidate for president, in direct viola-
tion of earlier promises not to do so. Further, in the days leading up to the
presidential runoff, Morsi met with prominent opposition figures at the
Fairmont Hotel in Cairo. According to members of the Fairmont Group,
as such figures came to be known, Morsi promised to establish an inclusive
"national salvation government" if his bid for the country's highest office
was successful. When Morsi assumed the presidency, he did in fact reach
out to several presidential candidates and other prominent opposition figures to join the government in various capacities, and such overtures were
rebuffed. Yet he never showed any serious inclination to form a national
coalition government or initiate any other form of power-sharing arrange-
ment that included the Brotherhood's rivals as equal partners. As members of the Fairmont Group saw it, Morsi had turned his back on those
who endorsed his bid for the presidency. Indeed, Morsi never met with
them again after his victory at the polls.

As Egypt's new president, Morsi made several moves that further eroded
his rivals' good will and trust. He replaced senior editors in the state-run
media with Islamist allies and appointed controversial Islamist figures
to key posts in the state establishment. Further, the Brotherhood and its
Islamist allies dominated the commission involved in drafting a new constitution. When rumors surfaced that the commission might be dissolved

by court order, Morsi placed his actions above judicial review in order to allow the commission to complete its work, then moved ahead with a snap referendum on the text it produced, despite mounting protests. The Morsi administration's passage of a restrictive new law on nongovernmental associations; its crackdown on the opposition press; its sluggish response to numerous instances of intimidation and assaults on women, Coptic Christians, and Shi'ite Muslims; and several incidents in which anti-Morsi protesters were attacked by regime supporters were cited as further evidence of partisan bias.

Despite Morsi's repeated promises to serve as "the president of all Egyptians," various acts of commission and omission undertaken by the president and his supporters undercut this claim and alienated other civic and political forces who were initially inclined to give his administration a chance. What explains the failure of Morsi and the Brotherhood to govern in a more inclusive manner? The Brotherhood's behavior during the transition can be seen as an effort to seize the day, that is, to maximize its influence at a critical early phase in the transition and deal with the political fallout later. This strategy of self-assertion became even more pronounced after the Brotherhood's electoral victories, which its leaders interpreted as granting them a popular mandate to govern the country as they saw fit.

Yet the Brotherhood's decision to go for broke in the wake of the uprising has some deeper roots as well. The Brotherhood emerged from sixty years of authoritarian rule with its organization relatively intact, but its top leaders remained encapsulated within the movement's insular networks, convinced that they were uniquely qualified to manage society's affairs. Moreover, despite progressive changes in its public rhetoric, the Brotherhood remained a highly parochial organization marked by a high level of ideological discipline and conformity, an emphasis on uncritical loyalty and obedience to the group's elders, and a belief in the intrinsic superiority of the Brotherhood's mission as an embodiment of the higher purposes of Islam itself. Further, the Brotherhood entered the political fray in the wake of the uprising with habits forged during its long years at chronic risk of repression, including an emphasis on secrecy, a lack of transparency, and a stance of aloofness from—and suspicion of—outsiders, all of which were particularly ingrained among members of the organization's powerful old guard. In sum, in a clear demonstration of path dependence, key aspects of the Brotherhood's institutional culture left its leaders psychologically and practically ill-equipped to pursue a strategy of negotiation and compromise with other groups as equal partners in the work of democratic reform.

On the ideological front, critics of the Brotherhood have portrayed the group as anti democratic, but I believe that this label misses the mark. The problem was not that the Brotherhood knowingly and actively opposed democracy but something more nuanced.

First, the Brotherhood's conception of democracy was too thin. In particular, it understood and supported the procedural aspects of democracy as a system for the selection of leaders through free and fair elections. By contrast, it exhibited a much weaker commitment to other aspects of democracy, including its tolerant and inclusive ethos, its legal protection of dissent, and the predication of its effective functioning on a robust system of institutional checks and balances to prevent any branch of government from exercising absolute power. In addition, less sophisticated members of the Brotherhood simply equated democracy with majority rule and asserted their right to pursue an Islamist agenda regardless of its adverse effects on Egyptians' civil and political rights.

The second problem is what I would describe as a lack of *hikma*, the Arabic word for "wisdom," which, depending on the context, can also denote circumspection, judiciousness, prudence, or discretion. In forming a government with a pronounced Islamist coloration and moving ahead with the speedy passage of a new constitution, Morsi—and, by extension, the Brotherhood—were not, strictly speaking, acting undemocratically; on the contrary, one could say they were simply exercising the mandate they had gained via the ballot box. Yet at a time of institutional flux, when the authority of key actors remained vague and ill-defined and their relations distorted by mutual suspicion and distrust, the Brotherhood's behavior evinced a striking deficit of the *hikma*, or discretion, that the country's circumstances cried out for at the time.

If the Brotherhood had an Achilles' heel, it was not ideological extremism but hubris. One can see this in the attitude that Brotherhood leaders affected toward members of the secular opposition, who, from their perch at the apex of state power, they felt free to condescend to or ignore. Second, the Brotherhood's leadership was unwilling or unable to acknowledge the political inexperience and lack of technical expertise that limited their ability to govern the country on their own. Indeed, by monopolizing the privileges of executive authority, the Brotherhood ended up in sole possession of its burdens. There is no doubt that the magnitude of Egypt's problems would have tested the mettle of any new government. But the Brotherhood's insistence on retaining the upper hand placed it directly in the line of fire when its performance fell short of popular expectations, a trend that culminated in the spectacle of millions of Egyptians amassing in the streets on June 30, 2013, the first anniversary of Morsi's inauguration, calling on him to step down.

In the wake of Morsi's ouster, the Brotherhood has urged Egyptians to continue staging demonstrations until the "coup regime" is brought down and democracy restored. Indeed, the Brotherhood has pitched itself as democracy's greatest defenders and as those who have made the greatest sacrifices on its behalf. Further, Brotherhood leaders have yet to acknowledge publicly the grievances of Morsi's detractors or the alarming speed with which it squandered its reservoirs of public support. Meanwhile, supporters of the al-Sisi regime, including many of the country's leading secular politicians, have taken to describing the Brotherhood as a "terrorist" and "extremist" organization that, by its own actions, has forfeited its right to participate in the new political order. Hence in surveying the Egyptian political scene at the moment, one can't help but be struck by the yawning gap between how the Brotherhood views itself and the way it is seen by others.

The situation in Egypt today bears an eerie echo of a not-so-distant chapter in the history of the Southern Cone of Latin America, when military interventions against democratically elected leftist governments were welcomed by many upper- and middle-class citizens who saw the left as a pernicious threat that must be rooted out to save the nation from itself. The persistence of deep fault lines in society can make the transition to democracy a threatening proposition, particularly when those best equipped to succeed at the ballot box are seen as willing and able to exploit state power to advance a partisan agenda over the objections of their opponents. The Egyptian case is hence illustrative of a broader problem. When a country's major civic and political forces are divided against one another, it will be more difficult for them to confront the residual powers of the authoritarian state establishment head on. Indeed, those groups at an electoral disadvantage may choose to endorse an authoritarian system that excludes their opponents over one involving free competition for public office, out of fear that the victors at the polls will threaten their interests and those of the country at large. Such contingent—and ultimately reversible—support for democracy is arguably a common problem in faulted societies, particularly when the mobilizing capacities of rival groups are imbalanced. Under these circumstances, the need for thoughtful and intelligent attention to matters of transition sequencing and institutional design becomes magnified, as does the need for confidence-building measures to build goodwill and trust across partisan lines. This raises a broader question of general relevance for the analysis of democratic transitions. When and why are civic and political forces divided by interest or ideology inclined to join forces to advance democratic reform, rather than divert their time and energy into polarizing conflicts? This question, which lacks an easy answer, strikes at the heart of the challenges that must be addressed for Egypt to launch a successful transition to democracy in the future.

Taking a step back to compare Egypt with Tunisia, what broader trends can we discern that might help explain why Tunisian political elites managed to navigate the rocky terrain of the transition process more effectively than their Egyptian counterparts? I would suggest that key differences in the disposition of the countries' political elites, as well as in the power balance among them, help explain why their paths diverged, as do broader features of the societies in which they are embedded.

First, while elements of the Tunisian deep state survived Ben Ali's departure, their veto powers were less robust than those of their analogues in Egypt. Second, the members of Tunisia's revolutionary camp, though ideologically divided, were more disposed to consensus building through negotiation and compromise as well as more open to power sharing in the new political institutions forged in the wake of mass protests. Third, the Salafi current in Tunisia was smaller and less organized politically than its Egyptian counterpart, while Tunisia's secular parties and civil society groups were better endowed in terms of resources, organization, and public support to function as counterweights to the Islamic trend. Fourth, without dismissing the serious challenges posed by enduring poverty and socioeconomic inequality in Tunisia, it can nevertheless be argued that Tunisia's higher literacy rates and larger middle class compare favorably against lower levels of human development in Egypt, where an estimated 40 percent of the population struggles to survive on less than 2 dollars per day.

What is striking about each of these differences is that they are not matters of kind but of degree. Egypt, Tunisia, and many other states in the MENA region confront a similar set of challenges that will complicate any efforts at democratic reform. In many Arab states, the resources, organization, awareness, and habits of mind and behavior that enable citizens in well- established democracies to hold their leaders accountable for their actions have yet to coalesce. Such deficiencies are not intrinsic to the region's faith and culture; rather, I would argue, they stem from the region's twin institutional legacies of economic underdevelopment and authoritarian rule and the historic imbalance between state and societal power that have resulted from them and impeded the emergence of conditions in which civil and personal agency can flourish. If there is a broader point to be made here, it is that whatever democratic adjustments are made to the constitutions, laws, and electoral frameworks of Arab states, their effective functioning will hinge upon broader transformations in the distribution of power and resources and the purposes to which they are deployed. The processes by which "subjects" are transformed into "citizens"—which I refer to collectively as "deep democratization"—can be studied comparatively across different world regions and historical time periods, with particular attention to the junctures at which conscious and deliberate interventions by state and societal actors can exert a positive impact. A critically important issue is how the values and institutions of Arab Muslim societies can be enlisted in the development of effective, culturally resonant strategies of civic education and empowerment. In the meantime, we need to adopt a longer time horizon in assessing the prospects for democracy in the MENA region. The fits and starts of recent episodes of democratic experimentation, culminating, in the Egyptian case, in a full-blown authoritarian reversal, can best be understood as the first manifestations of a broader undercurrent of social and political change, with further instances of mobilization and countermobilization yet to come. As the members of Arab societies become more educated, aware, and technologically tuned in, they will become harder for authoritarian regimes to control. Future challenges to existing structures of authority are likely to unfold, but there is no guarantee that they will yield a democratic outcome. Whether future struggles will enhance or impede the fulfillment of citizens' aspirations for "Bread, Freedom, and Social Justice" will depend on the willingness and capacity of political actors to prioritize national reconciliation and consensus building over competition for partisan gain and on the capacity of reformers across the Islamist-secular divide to confront, co-opt, or find some other way to neutralize the power of veto holders in the "deep state" who seek to protect the perquisites, status, and opportunities for private enrichment that hinge on the continuation of authoritarian rule.

In conclusion, let me return once again to the case of Egypt. It goes without saying that the al-Sisi administration's exclusion of the Muslim Brotherhood, Egypt's largest civilian political organization, from any meaningful role in the country's political life is fundamentally at odds with the establishment of a democratic order. At the same time, the implications of the Brotherhood's reintegration, if and when it occurs, remain uncertain. Suffice it to say that whether the Muslim Brotherhood in its current form or some future incarnation can contribute to a future transition to democracy will depend on its ability to reform itself. In particular, it will need to separate its *da'wa* and political functions or revise its interpretation of Islam to align not just with the procedural aspects of democracy but also with its tolerant and inclusive ethos. Both of these adjustments are possible, but neither of them is inevitable. On the contrary, either of such developments would require a degree of soul searching, introspection, and self-criticism that are unlikely to achieve wider currency under present circumstances. Yet much the same can be said for Egypt's so-called liberals who welcomed the military's intervention in the summer of 2013, preferring to upend the democratic chessboard rather than work within its parameters to gain the support of the Egyptian public. Unless and until Egypt's leading civilian actors commit themselves to the establishment of an inclusive political framework, in which their rivals are afforded the same rights they demand for themselves, and convince the Egyptian people that such a system is worth fighting for, the former general al-Sisi, together with his cronies and henchmen, will continue to reign supreme, and the realization of a freer and more humane political order will be postponed to an indefinite time in the future.

3

MUTUAL ACCOMMODATION

Islamic and Secular Parties and Tunisia's Democratic Transition

ALFRED STEPAN

B Y THE END OF December 2014, Tunisia had finished its free and fair elections for a new parliament and presidency, agreed upon a constitution, had a peaceful alternation of power, and met the four standard conditions for a completed democratic transition.[1]

A crescendo of accolades followed. In December 2014, the *Economist* selected Tunisia as "the country of the year" for having its fairly elected National Constituent Assembly pass, with 92 percent of the votes, a progressive constitution, and because the Muslim-inspired Ennahda Party allowed a democratic alternation of power by peacefully leaving office when their coalition lost their parliamentary majority. Further recognition came in January 2015, when the world's most-cited democracy-ranking NGO, the U.S.-based Freedom House, for the first time in their seventy-four-year history awarded an Arab country, Tunisia, a "1" for political rights—the highest rank possible in their seven-point scale.[2] The crescendo reached its apex in October 2015, when four Tunisian civil society organizations were awarded the Nobel Peace Prize for having helped create a dialogue and eventually a national consensus about the necessity of peaceful compromises and democratic transition.

In a world where in the name of Islam organizations like ISIS are committing outrageous crimes against humanity and where many people increasingly believe there is an incompatibility between the fundamentals of democracy and the principles of Islam, it is particularly important to study the achievements of a country like Tunisia. Such an inquiry is especially relevant for democratization theory, given that neither of the two most-cited books on comparative democratization deal with any Muslim countries.[3]

My goal in this chapter is thus to put Tunisia's democratic transition, and the tasks it must accomplish if there is to be a democratic consolidation, in the comparative context of existing democratization theory.[4] How did Tunisia make such progress in political rights? What, if any, are the implications of this achievement for standard democratization theory? To address these questions, I will build upon my previous study on how democracy was actually constructed in Indonesia. For every year in the last decade, the highest-ranked democracy of the ten countries in the Association of South East Asian Nations (ASEAN) has not been Roman Catholic Philippines, Theravada Buddhist Thailand, or somewhat Confucian Singapore but the world's most populous Muslim-majority country, Indonesia.[5] Indonesia and Chile are also worth studying to see how religious parties that were once potential obstacles to democratic transitions ended up playing important cooperative roles.

Finally, democratization specialists who forget the fratricidal intolerance of the intra-Christian religious wars of the sixteenth century do so at their intellectual peril. Indeed, the great historian of the Reformation, Diarmaid MacCulloch, the Professor of the History of the Church at Oxford, states categorically: "Western Christianity before 1500 must rank as one of the most intolerant religions in world history."[6] What I call the "twin tolerations," by which I mean the mutual giving of the necessary space by religion to democracy for democracy to function and by the democratic state to religious citizens so they can exercise religious freedom and participate as full citizens in the public sphere, did not come easily in many democracies.[7]

Creating the twin tolerations is a contested issue in many Muslim-majority countries, especially those where an aggressive version of secularism meets an aggressive version of Islam. Rached Ghannouchi writes in this volume concerning Tunisia: "There is an ongoing debate in our country between secular currents that may be described as extremist and Islamist ones that may be described in a like manner. The latter would like to impose their understanding of Islam from above using the state apparatus; the former aspires to strip the state and national culture of all Islamic influences."[8]

It is possible that there are both secularist and Islamist citizens in some Muslim-majority countries who actually lean toward democracy as their preferred solution but cannot cooperate with one another against a dictatorship given the intensity of the secular/Islamist divide. If this is so, it is vitally important for the emergence of democracy that such citizens, via dialogue, doctrinal evolution, and mutual accommodation, come to the shared conclusion that they hate the dictatorship more than they hate and fear one another. Once they arrive at this conclusion, coordinated oppositional activities are enhanced and the prospects of postdictatorship cooperation, or even coalitions, are advanced. In what follows, I will attempt to show how and why constructive secular/Islamist accommodations were crucial to the successful democratic transition in Tunisia and how the absence of significant secular/Islamic accommodations contributed greatly to mutual fear and democratic failure in Egypt.

DEMOCRATIZATION THEORY: CREATING AN ANTIREGIME COALITION FROM ONETIME ENEMIES

A key general lesson in democratization theory is that successful democratic transitions often involve the formation of a coalition, within the opposition, of onetime enemies. Some might call this kind of transition a "pacted transition," except that a pacted transition is a four-player game involving a coalition of regime softliners and opposition softliners against regime hardliners and opposition hardliners.[9] What we are examining in this section is a three-player game, namely, how to get two opposition groups who do not trust each other somehow to work together against a hard-line authoritarian regime and, better still, craft some mutually supportive alliances, even a potential governing coalition, before any eventual effort at a democratic transition. I look briefly at how this task was accomplished in two important cases in which religion figured prominently: Chile and Indonesia.

In 1973, the Christian Democratic Party in Chile, with the tacit support of the U.S. government, in essence asked General Pinochet to overthrow the legally elected Socialist government of Salvador Allende. After this, from 1973 until the early 1980s, any possibility of joint cooperation against Pinochet by the Christian Democrats and Socialists was impossible. However, with the support of two German foundations, the Christian Democratic Konrad Adenauer Stiftung, and the Social Democratic Friedrich Ebert Stiftung, in the early 1980s the Chilean Christian Democrats and the Chilean Socialists began to discuss whether they hated each other less than they hated Pinochet. Eventually, by the mid-1980s, the two parties mobilized joint anti-Pinochet protest demonstrations. These shared activities slowly turned into shared political programs. They formed an electoral coalition with a joint platform in 1988 that defeated Pinochet in a plebiscite based on Pinochet's own 1980 constitution. In 1989, this coalition won the presidency and ruled together as a successful, reformist coalition from 1990 to 2010, with the presidency rotating from Christian Democratic Party presidents to Socialist Party presidents.[10]

In Indonesia, in the decade leading up to the fall of the thirty-six-year-long military dictatorship of General Suharto, Abdurrahman Wahid, the leader of the largest Muslim civil society group, created the Democratic Forum, in which all the potentially conflicting religious groups met regularly and increasingly released joint documents in favor of human rights, greater political freedoms, and democratic values.[11] These years of cooperation turned out to be very helpful in the surprisingly successful constitution-building process after the fall of Suharto in May 1998, a process that Donald L. Horowitz, a major comparative constitutional scholar, recently called "meticulously consensual."[12]

In Tunisia, one of the biggest obstacles to achieving democracy was the hostility between secularists and Islamists, which inhibited their joint cooperation against the nondemocratic regime of Ben Ali. One of the reasons for this was that, unlike in Indonesia, India, or even Senegal, by the time Tunisia became independent from France in 1956, the country formed a part of what I call the "iron triangle" of aggressive laïcité secularism. The three points in the triangle were made up of France, from 1905 to 1958 (before de Gaulle allowed the state to subsidize Catholic schools); Attatürk's Turkey; and Tunisia under Habib Bourguiba (1956–1967) and Zine El Abidine Ben Ali (1967–2011).[13]

Islam in Tunisia had been relatively progressive in the mid–nineteenth century. The country abolished slavery in 1846, two years before France. In 1861 Tunisia created the first constitution in the Arab world. This constitution, in Jean-Pierre Filu's judgment, "enshrined a political power distinct from religion" and built upon the previous Covenant of Social Peace emphasizing "freedom of religion."[14] The doyen of Arabists, Albert Hourani, highlights the progressive role of Zeitouna Mosque University during this period and the disruptive role of the French: "[This Tunisian] experiment in constitutional government . . . left its mark: it helped to form a new political consciousness in Tunis, and to bring to the front a group of reforming statesmen, officials, and writers . . . until they were scattered by the French occupation in 1881. This group had two origins: one of them was the Zaytuna Mosque [University]."[15]

After independence in 1956, Habib Bourguiba, in the name of modernism and laïcité, attempted to remove religion from the public square and from most programs of higher education and in essence closed the Zeitouna Mosque University (which had been founded in Tunis in 737, more than two centuries before Cairo's Al-Azhar University).[16]

From independence until 2011, Tunisia was ruled by only two presidents, Bourguiba and then Ben Ali. Across this entire period neither ever allowed one fully free and fair election. However, Bourguiba saw himself, and was seen by many, as a one-party-state modernizing leader. He passed the most progressive family code concerning women's rights in the Muslim world—and at the time, one of the most advanced in the world. Polygamy was banned and polygamists subject to imprisonment, men's right to divorce their wives unilaterally was abolished, and women's right to initiate divorce, receive alimony, and have greater child custody rights were put into law. Abortion was legalized under some conditions as early as 1965. Women's access to higher education soon matched men's.[17]

Bourguiba and Ben Ali skillfully used the progressive family code and women-friendly educational policies to help build what I call a "constituency for coercion." They crafted this constituency by regularly implying that if there were free elections, Muslim extremists would win and curtail freedoms, so it was better not to push too hard for elections. Parties with religious affiliations were forbidden, and many Muslim leaders were accused of being terrorists, then imprisoned and tortured. The autocratic state's discourse about Muslim terrorism strengthened the constituency of coercion and was intensified after events in Algeria in the 1990s: After an Islamist party won the first round of elections in December 1991, the second round was cancelled in January 1992 by the military. The outcome was a civil war between Islamists and the military that ravaged the country from 1992 to 1997, a war in which as many as one hundred thousand or more people died.[18]

In these circumstances, it was highly unlikely that potential democratic-secularist opponents of the regime in Tunisia would be trusted by Islamic activists, who viewed laïcité secularists as deeply antireligious and complicit in the repression of Islamic parties. Likewise, secularists who opposed the authoritarian regime of Ben Ali and wanted democracy did not see Islamists as desirable or even possible allies, given what they assumed were their antidemocratic ideologies and jihadist tendencies.

But from 2003 to 2011, something similar to Chile and Indonesia began to happen in Tunisia—an accommodation occurred among enemies. However, in the Tunisian case, this accommodation was helped greatly by the internal changes in a democratic direction that had developed within the major Islamic activist group, starting many years beforehand, in the early 1980s.

I focus here on the largest Islamist party and movement in Tunisia, Ennahda (Renaissance), and its most important thinker and political leader, Rached Ghannouchi, in order to analyze how and why Ennahda created, with two center-left secular parties, the ruling coalition in the National Constituent Assembly in 2011. In my judgment, the following

ideological and political processes that occurred in Tunisia are worth special attention.

GRADUAL IDEOLOGICAL AND POLITICAL
MODERATION: GHANNOUCHI AND ENNAHDA

One of Ghannouchi's key thoughts about democracy that eased Ennahda's
entry into electoral politics, first briefly in 1989 and then as the largest party
in the National Constituent Assembly from 2011 to 2014, was that, while
democracy has universal principles, each democratic country has some historic specificities that new political parties, such as Ennahda, should respect.
One such specificity for Ghannouchi was Tunisia's women-friendly educational and legal system. During a brief thaw during the transition from
Bourguiba to Ben Ali, Ennahda participated in the 1989 elections and articulated the reasons why good Muslims should treat men and women as equals.
Ennahda polled very well in the capital city, Tunis, before the party was
outlawed by Ben Ali on never-well-documented terrorism charges.

In the two decades of exile that followed for Ghannouchi in the United
Kingdom from 1991 to 2011, he wrote hundreds of articles in English, French,
and Arabic in which he increasingly advanced arguments against violence
and against the imposition of sharia on people (whether Muslims or not).[19]
He also insisted, along with the key Islamic democratic leaders in Indonesia and Senegal, that, as stated in one of the shortest and most explicit
injunctions in the Koran, "in matters of religion there can be no compulsion" (Sura 2:256). Ghannouchi further stressed that in the modern conditions of large cities with millions of people, the traditional Islamic virtue
of *shura* (consultation) is best achieved by consulting the citizens of a polity,
both Muslim and non-Muslim, in open competitive elections. Ghannouchi
often noted also that the Islamic juridical virtue of *ijma* (consensus), when
combined with the Koranic injunction against compulsion in matters of
religion, creates a space in Islam for a version of democracy that respects
individual rights and pluralism. To some extent, Ghannouchi, while often

sharply critical of the policies of specific democracies, by the mid-1990s had implicitly endorsed the view of Churchill that "Democracy is the worst form of government, except for all those other forms that have been tried from time to time."[20]

Notwithstanding the evidence that Ghannouchi and Ennahda were becoming increasingly supportive of democracy as a set of valuable procedures and norms, these changes in outlook would not have become politically important in Tunisian politics had Ennahda not been able to cooperate with some of the secularists, many of whom, as I have noted already, deeply distrusted any Islamist party. But, starting in 2003, a process of mutual accommodation between democratically friendly secularists and democratically friendly Islamists began, which weakened but did not entirely erode Ben Ali's "constituency of coercion."

GROWING EXCHANGES AND ACCOMMODATIONS BETWEEN ANTI–BEN ALI MODERATE SECULARISTS AND MODERATE ISLAMISTS, 2003–2010

In June 2003, representatives from approximately twenty opposition organizations met in France to see if they could overcome secular-Islamist differences and become more unified and powerful. Participants at the meeting included the Islamist Ennahda and two secular center-left parties, the CPR (Congress for the Republic) and Ettakatol. (Together, eventually, these three parties would constitute between October 2011 and January 2014 the ruling coalition in Tunisia's National Constituent Assembly. The largest party in the coalition would be Ennahda; the president of the National Constituent Assembly, Mustapha Ben Jaafar, would come from Ettakatol; and the president of Tunisia, Moncef Marzouki, would be from the CPR).

The first meeting in Aix-Marseille, France, in 2003 of the twenty political groups from Tunisia resulted in an only recently widely known or available document, "Call from Tunis."[21] This document in essence endorsed the two fundamental principles of the "twin tolerations." First, any future elected government would have to be "founded on the sovereignty of the people as the sole source of legitimacy." Second, the state, while showing "respect for the people's identity and its Arab-Muslim values," would provide "the guarantee of liberty of beliefs to all and the political neutralization of places of worship." Ennahda accepted both these fundamental agreements. The "Call from Tunis" also went on to demand "the full equality of women and men."[22]

The three main opposition political parties at the meeting, together with representatives of smaller parties and some civil society leaders, met nearly every year after 2003 to reaffirm, and even deepen, their commitment to the "Call from Tunis" principles. Their key 2005 manifesto, "Collectif du 18 Octobre pour les droits et les libertés," stated that after a "three-month dialogue among party leaders," they had reached consensus on a number of crucial issues. All the parties, including Ennahda, supported in great detail the existing liberal family code. Moreover, the manifesto added that any future democratic state would have to be a *civic state* . . . drawing its sole legitimacy from the will of the people," for "political practice is a human discipline [without] any form of sanctity." Finally, the manifesto reasserted that "there can be no compulsion in religion. This includes the right to adopt a religion or doctrine or not."[23]

Agreement on a "civic state" in which citizens were to be the *sole* source of legitimacy helped weaken any antidemocratic claim against elections along the lines that "only God, not men, makes laws." As we have discussed, Ennahda could easily accept that "there can be no compulsion in religion" because this is a Koranic verse that Ghannouchi in Tunisia, Abdurrahman Wahid in Indonesia, and Sufi leaders in Senegal such as Souleymane Bachir Diagne have constantly employed in their arguments against their own fundamentalists and to reassure classic secularists.

Ghannouchi could not participate directly in these meetings because he was forbidden from entering France. Unlike the British government, the French government insisted on designating Ghannouchi a terrorist. However, the extraordinary exchanges between some secular leaders and Ghannouchi were made possible by human agency and goodwill. One of the leading secular leaders of the democratic opposition, Moncef Marzouki, made over twenty trips from France to London to meet with Ghannouchi.[24] Trust and cooperation between the secular and Islamist democratic opposition were deepened by the fact that Marzouki had taken the risk of a major confrontation with Ben Ali by using the Tunisian League of Human Rights, an organization he had once headed, to defend the basic human and political rights of Ennahda. Democracy in Tunisia was beginning to be built with many secular and Islamic democrats working jointly.

However, while I consider these accommodations and agreements of great importance, it would be a mistake if I left the impression that all secularists and feminists were in agreement with these conversations. A militant core of secularists never joined these dialogues; indeed they denounced them in their own documents.[25] Nonetheless, in comparison to Egypt, the existence of secular-Islamic dialogues in Tunisia was of critical importance.

EGYPTIAN DEMOCRACY WITHOUT DEMOCRATS: BRUMAIRIANISM AND ERADICATIONISM

It is crucial in efforts at democratization to broaden agreement among most of the potential opposition groups to the authoritarian regime. Unlike in Tunisia, nothing like this occurred in Egypt, and this was a major cause of the failure of the democratic transition in that country.

Nothing comparable to Ennahda's internal reforms and external outreach to secularists was aimed for by the Muslim Brotherhood in Egypt. The leading U.S. scholar of the Muslim Brotherhood, Carrie Rosefsky Wickham, concludes her recent book with the flat statement that "leaders affiliated with the reformist trend have never gained more than a marginal presence in the Guidance Bureau, the group's highest decision-making body."[26]

Given this doctrinal opposition within the Muslim Brotherhood to internal reform, and given secularists' hostility to Islamists, intensive negotiations among leading secularists and leading Islamists to overcome mutual fears, of the sort we have documented for Tunisia, never really occurred in Egypt. This may account for why in Egypt, after the fall of Mubarak, the attitudes and behavior of many citizens were, at best, those of a "hybrid democracy." In December 2011, 68 percent of Egyptian respondents agreed that "democracy in which multiple parties compete for power through free elections is the best system for governing Egypt." However, in the same poll, six months *before* the Muslim Brotherhood's Morsi became president, 62 percent of respondents hedged their democratic bets by also agreeing that the military "should continue to intervene when *it* [the military] thinks necessary."[27] This explains why a columnist in a widely read Cairo publication, *Ahram Online*, asserted that "in general, liberal parties would like the constitution to be written before the elections take place, fearing that a post-election constitution-making process will be dominated by Islamists."[28]

Thus, in classic Eighteenth Brumaire fashion, many Egyptian citizens were willing to abdicate their right to rule by passing their power instead to a nondemocratic force such as the military, in return for protection from a potential and unwanted, but democratically elected, government.[29]

The responses to the assertion that "democracy is preferable to any other form of government" were slightly more positive in Egypt (68 percent) than in Tunisia (63 percent). But more significant politically is the fact that in 2013 (the year of the Tunisian crisis I examine shortly), Tunisia had a relatively low percentage of respondents who gave a Brumairian answer to the assertion that "in some circumstances an authoritarian government can be preferable to a democratic government." Approving answers to this non-democratic option in South Korea were 27 percent, Brazil 21 percent, Chile 18 percent, Tunisia 17 percent, Spain 9 percent, and Uruguay 8 percent.[30] Compare this with the 62 percent of Egyptians polled who were willing to abdicate power to the military to act "when *it* thinks necessary."

THE GROWTH OF POLITICAL AND CIVIL SOCIETY IN TUNISIA

At the beginning of the so-called Arab Spring, both Egypt and Tunisia had creative civil societies. If anything, Egypt's civil society was much deeper and more diverse.[31] However, while civil society can break a dictatorship, civil society by itself cannot construct a democracy, because this latter requires actions by political society, such as intensive and widely collaborative discussions about procedures for elections, the organization of political parties, and negotiations and bargaining until at least a working agreement is achieved on how the incipient polity will organize itself to rule democratically.

In the first four months after the fall of Ben Ali in Tunisia in 2011, 155 members of a diverse group were tasked with forming a commission, usually referred to as the Ben Achour Commission; its purpose was not to write the new constitution but to deliberate on what political choices had to be made before elections could even be held, that is, to create an even stronger political society.[32]

A key provision the Ben Achour Commission agreed on was that the first polity-wide election should be to elect a constituent assembly but not a president, because it was agreed that the decision as to whether the political system should be presidential, parliamentary, or semipresidential should be made by an elected constituent assembly and not an unelected working group such as the Ben Achour Commission.

The commission also agreed that there could not be an election without an electoral law and without agreed-on procedures on how to run the elections and that transparency should be enhanced by a large network of national and international election observers. They decided to use an electoral system of proportional representation (PR) rather than a "first-past-the-post" single-member-district system (as is used in the United Kingdom) because the general agreement, shared by Ennahda, was that the British system would produce an overwhelming Ennahda majority. In an interview in Tunis in early March 2011, Ghannouchi told me that should Ennahda win 90 percent of the seats under a first-past-the-post system, it could well produce an antidemocratic, Algerian-style backlash. Ghannouchi went on to estimate that with a PR system, Ennahda would not get more than 40 percent of the seats and would thus need to govern with one or two secular parties, an outcome he believed would help democracy get started in

Tunisia because it would preclude Islamic "majoritarianism."[33] There was also a decision, backed strongly by Ennahda, to have what is called a closed-list PR system, with every other name, on each electoral list, being that of a woman.

The final April 11, 2011, vote on all the proposals saw only two abstentions and two walkouts; all the other members of the commission voted yes. This exceptionally creative and consensual political society work helped contribute to the success of the October 2011 election for the National Constituent Assembly, an election that was widely considered by national and international observers alike to be free and fair. The results were roughly as predicted, with Ennahda receiving just under 40 percent of the vote and therefore forming a coalition government with the two secular parties. Once again, nothing remotely like this process of consensual political society building occurred in Egypt.

THE NATIONAL CONSTITUENT ASSEMBLY: INNOVATIVE CONSENSUS BUILDING IN THE MIDST OF CRISIS

Some commentators on the democratic transition literature argue that the word "transition" is teleological, in that it implies achievement of its goal. This is wrong. Linz and Stepan, on the first page of their preface, stated categorically:

As comparativists we are painfully aware that most political transformations away from a once stable non-democratic regime do not end in a completed democratic transition. . . . Precisely because we believe that completed democratic transitions are an empirical minority of all major political transformations . . . this book is explicitly devoted to the analysis of the conditions and practices that make such outcomes possible.[34]

Indeed, most transitions encounter numerous setbacks and crises that are overcome only by skilled political leadership, whether individual or collective. I have in mind the leadership in Spain from 1976 to 1982, which allowed it to survive the nearly successful February 23, 1981, military coup attempt; or in Brazil in 1994–1995, which overcame a democracy-threatening, annualized inflation rate of over 2,000 percent, largely thanks to the future president Fernando Henrique Cardoso's political and intellectually convincing leadership, which resulted in an enduring, union-based constituency against inflation. Indonesia provides another example: from 1999 to 2004, the country, through consensual constitution making, managed to reverse threatening ethnic and religious conflicts and remilitarization.[35]

In this regard, Tunisia is no exception to the norm of some setbacks within democratic transitions. Despite an auspicious beginning, with free and fair elections in 2011, for a six-month period starting in July 2013, Tunisia experienced an intense crisis that threatened the transition process. But by December of that year it had managed to re-equilibrate and consensually pass an inclusionary, if at times excessively unclear, constitution in January 2014. Here I will explore how innovative consensus building, in the midst of crisis, enabled this democratic re-equilibration in Tunisia.[36]

The roots of the crisis lay in the constitution-making process and in expectations about its speed. As I have noted, most of the decisions made by the Ben Achour Commission about Tunisia's future system of governance were democratically sound. However, one very unsound political commitment was made after the election to the National Constituent Assembly (NCA). The vast majority of the members of the NCA publicly committed themselves (some say "solemnly pledged") to completing the new constitution within one year of starting their deliberations. This was unnecessary and dangerous. In comparison, India's postindependence constituent assembly took three years (1947–1950) to publish its new constitution. The Spanish constitution-writing process took two years (from the Law for Political Reform in November 1976 to the acceptance of the final constitution in December 1978).

In Tunisia, the then-president of the country, Moncef Marzouki, actually (and wisely) refused to make a one-year commitment for constitution
writing, saying the process might take three years. Nonetheless, some of
the major actors in Tunisia, such as Tunisia's (and indeed North Africa's)
most politically prominent trade union, UGTT, and Beji Caid Essebsi,
who had been the interior minister under Bourguiba and had founded a
new opposition party, Nidaa Tounes, in the summer of 2012, began to
declare that the NCA in Tunisia would become illegitimate on the first-
year anniversary of its opening session (namely, on October 24, 2012).[37]
Essebsi suggested that some other groups (of unclear origin) should draft
a new constitution and then send it to the reactivated NCA for its ratifica-
tion. It is not clear to this day whether Essebsi was serious about closing
the NCA (and thereby getting the elected "Troika" interim government
made up of Ennahda, the CPR, and Ettakatol parties to resign almost
immediately), but what is clear is that his actions were at best what Juan
J. Linz would call "semiloyal" to democracy.

In the middle of this real but still rather vague crisis over the constitution-
writing process, there occurred the violent assassinations of two leading
leftist Ennahda critics, in February and July 2013. The assassinations, and
the fact that they were not solved, led to charges of Ennahda's incompetence or, worse, complicity. Events in Egypt colored the interpretations of
those in Tunisia. The massive petition movement Tamarrod (Rebellion),
directed against the Muslim Brotherhood's president, Mohamed Morsi,
facilitated the Egyptian military's coup against Morsi on July 3, 2013. This
in turn appeared to have strengthened the copycat Tamarrod movement in
Tunisia. Demands for the closure of the NCA, on the grounds that it had
not yet completed the new constitution, and for the resignation of the
Ennahda-led government intensified, with large demonstrations being
held outside the parliament.

In this highly charged context, on August 6, 2013, the president of the
National Constituent Assembly, Mustafa Ben Jaafar, temporarily suspended
the work of the NCA in order to gain time for the democratic groups
inside and outside of the NCA to create new ways to move past the crisis.[38]

Ben Jaafar achieved something virtually unprecedented in the history of democratic constitution making within an already elected constituent assembly. He managed to convince every party with seats in the NCA, no matter how large or small, to agree to have only one "voice" in the decisions about every contested article in what came to be called the Consensus Committee. This was a major sacrifice in terms of power for Ennahda because although having 41 percent of the seats in the NCA, their representation in the Consensus Committee would be no more than that of a number of parties with less than 5 percent of the seats. It was also agreed that there would be no formal votes in the Consensus Committee. Rather, an article would be considered consensually agreed upon when it was approved as the "sense of the meeting" by two-thirds of the participants. Progress in overcoming deadlocks in this fashion commenced rapidly once Ben Jaafar reopened the NCA.

Ben Jaafar used the period during which the NCA was suspended to reach as many key actors in civil society who were *outside* the constituent assembly as possible, to widen the dialogue and explore possible compromises. He told us: "I spent the whole month of August bringing people together, talking to all the political parties, and even with political leaders who had nothing to do with the NCA. The UGTT was also bringing people together. So when I had these signals—sparks of light that people are indeed coming together to discuss—then step by step we started to bring people back to the [National] Constituent Assembly."[39] Once it was apparent that the Consensus Committee could work well and that constructive dialogues were beginning with the opposition, Ben Jaafa slowly reopened the NCA in early September 2013. In this new atmosphere, the copycat Tamarrod campaign to close the NCA and sack the electorally based Troika government rapidly lost momentum.[40]

An external secular group initiated by the trade union UCTT was rapidly supported by the Tunisian League of Human Rights and the Tunisian Bar Association and was eventually joined by the leading employer's association, UTICA.[41] These four groups intensified a process increasingly referred to as the Dialogue. This external group was never a formal part of the Consensus Committee, but its leaders told us that, with the agreement of the Consensus Committee, they regularly sent two people to listen to key meetings of the Consensus Committee and to give the committee the Dialogue group's suggestions.

The Dialogue leaders eventually brought other weighty political and social actors into discussions about a roadmap to move past the crisis. This roadmap, which approximately twenty groups and parties supported, entailed dates for signing the constitution, the voluntary resignation of the Ennahda-led Troika coalition, the appointment of an interim technocratic prime minister and government, the final appointment of an electoral commission, and the holding of parliamentary and then presidential elections.

Ennahda agreed to everything in this roadmap, except they refused to resign until the day the final constitution was signed. In my judgment, they were correct to insist on this latter point. Once the constitution was approved on January 27, 2014, Ennahda duly stepped down, the interim government of technocrats took over, with the interim prime minister, Mehdi Jomaa, receiving a very high approval rating of 81 percent in a public opinion poll before the parliamentary elections in October 2014. The crisis had been consensually resolved. Now: what was in the final constitution?

AN INCLUSIONARY, CONSENSUAL, AND DEMOCRATIC CONSTITUTION

The Tunisian constitution, after four drafts, was voted on and approved on January 27, 2014. The final vote of the 216 deputies to the NCA was quite consensual: two hundred voted yes, twelve no, with four abstentions. Some of the articles in the final constitution are the most progressive ever passed in an Arab country—indeed in any Muslim country or even in many long-standing democracies. For example, a subcommittee draft on human rights had stirred the intense opposition of feminists and human rights activists because in the French and English translations it appeared to describe women as only being "complementary" to men.[42] However, in the final, approved constitution, this offending phrase was removed, and the preamble states flatly that the Tunisian polity is based upon "equality of rights and duties between all citizens, male and female." Article 46 also affirms that "the state works to attain parity between women and men in elected Assemblies."

In many Muslim countries, to accuse a person of being an "apostate" often puts that person at great risk, possibly even of death. In Article 6 of the Tunisian constitution, probably for the first time ever in the constitution of a Muslim-majority country, making such a charge has been criminalized.[43]

Other improvements are the establishment of a Constitutional Court, which is particularly necessary in Tunisia, given that the semipresidential executive type of system selected by the NCA often generates conflicts of jurisdiction over the correct prerogatives of the president and the prime minister. The NCA also passed a "limitations clause" that may help prevent legislators and presidents from eroding constitutionally embedded human rights provisions by introducing new intrusive laws or decrees.

Although many members of Ennahda's base might have wanted sharia law, Ghannouchi very early in the constitution-drafting process gave a major speech arguing against sharia being in the constitution. This was followed by the chief executive body of Ennahda, the Shura Council, voting against including *any* reference to sharia in the constitution. Like Indonesia but unlike Egypt, there is no reference to sharia in the 2014 Tunisian constitution.[44]

To be sure, the constitution has many "creative ambiguities" that enabled its overwhelming approval but may create problems later. For example, there is Article 1, which in its entirety stipulates that "Tunisia is a free, independent, sovereign state; its religion is Islam, its language Arabic, and its system is republican. This article may not be amended."

Some analysts maintain that Article 1 creates an Islamic state. Others, myself included, note that it is identical to the article inserted into the 1959 constitution by the first president of Tunisia, Habib Bourguiba, who, along with Kemal Atatürk of Turkey and the French 1905 law on laïcité, constituted the iron triangle of aggressive secularist forces in the Middle East.

They thus defend the language as "sociologically descriptive" rather than "legally prescriptive." At some point, however, the language of Article 1 could possibly be less creatively ambiguous and become a source of conflict.

An article even more laden with dangerous creative compromises is Article 6. On the one hand, it criminalizes calling someone an apostate, but on the other hand, it stipulates that the state commits itself "to the protection of the sacred and the prohibition of any offenses thereto." The head of Human Rights Watch for Tunisia, Amna Guellali, argues that this clause is too vague and allows for "the most repressive of interpretations in the name of offense against the sacred. Citing the constitution, lawyers, judges, and politicians could interpret Article 6 however they see fit. This ambivalence could hold grave consequences for the country."[45]

DEMOCRATIC ALTERNATION OF POWER IN 2015

In 2014, during the lead-up to the first free parliamentary and presidential elections in Tunisia's history, Ennahda mistakenly assumed they would win the first plurality in the parliament and thus again play a leading role in any government-ruling coalition. They were worried that if they ran a presidential candidate there was a danger that they would be seen as having too much power. They thus decided, after many internal discussions and debates in the Shura Council, not to run a candidate for the presidency. As the elections approached, there was some indication that a Nidaa Tounes coalition, led by Beji Caid Essebsi and comprising anti-Ennahda secularists and many former activists of Ben Ali's RCD party, was gaining strength, so they debated again whether they should nominate a presidential candidate before the deadline for getting on the ballot. Ghannouchi, supported by other key Ennahda leaders, played a major role in deciding not to; he argued that Ennahda did not want, as the Muslim Brotherhood had done in Egypt, to break promises made—first to claim they would not run a candidate and then do so—which might prove to many that as a party, the Islamists were not to be trusted.

As it turned out, in the parliamentary elections Essebsi's party, Nidaa Tounes, won the first plurality (and the right to nominate the prime minister); three weeks later, Essebsi won the presidency in a tight, second-round runoff election.

Many commentators have argued that once an Islamic party wins power in elections, they will never relinquish such power. I talked to Ghannouchi after Ennahda's parliamentary defeat. He was philosophical, and his main reflections concerned the future of democracy in Tunisia, to which he was convinced Ennahda had contributed:

> In a period of transition it was useful we did not push religion too hard. We are very keen to make a success of the transition. We have a very heavy responsibility for the success of democracy. Even if we lose in elections, democracy gains. The main goal is to make a success of democracy. Tunisia has got rid of despotism. There is chaos in Syria, Yemen, Egypt, and Iraq. We saved our country. We lose power but we saved Tunisia. We will try to oblige Nidaa Tounes to accept the game of democracy. Moving from government to opposition, and preserving the right to come back—this is the point of democracy.[46]

On the night of the presidential elections, Ghannouchi quickly phoned Essebsi to congratulate him on his victory and to accept the results of the free and fair election.[47]

President Essebsi's party, Nidaa Tounes, won a plurality in the parliamentary elections with eighty-six seats, but this was twenty-three seats short of the absolute majority needed to form a government by itself. After first attempting, and failing, to form a minority government with one minor party, Nidaa Tounes put together a more inclusive coalition of five parties, including Ennahda, a coalition that gave them a comfortable majority of seventy-four seats.[48] The formation of this coalition was very unpopular with those members of Nidaa Tounes's base and its allies who had fought an especially anti-Islamist campaign.[49] The idea of the coalition was also initially quite unpopular with many of Ennahda's base, who feared a return of anti-Islamic repression and did not want to share the inevitable costs of government with opponents. There thus was wide support within the Ennahda base for the Shura Council's opposition to the first government proposed by Nidaa Tounes.

So why did the coalition that included Ennahda come about, even though Nidaa Tounes and Essebsi could have put together a majority without Ennahda and though Ennahda, despite its sixty-nine seats in parliament, was only given one ministry while a party with only eight seats in parliament was given three?

No one knows for sure. But let me offer one tentative proposition. Even before the presidential election I heard talk of the possibility of a "two-sheikh" compromise. The two-sheikh metaphor refers to the founder presidents of their parties, Nidaa Tounes's Beije Caid Essebsi and Ennahda's Rached Ghannouchi.

For Essebsi and the majority of the realist members of his still fragile party, the coalition offered the promise of majority support for many of their difficult economic reforms. They know that if one drew a series of circles representing the economic policies of the biggest parties in parliament, the only two large parties with significant overlaps—despite great ideological differences on Islam—are Nidaa Tounes and Ennahda. Furthermore, Essebsi is eighty-eight years old and on dialysis. If he wants to leave a legacy of statesman-led growth and party building, Ennahda, rather than an alliance with the Marxist-secularist Popular Front, can help him and his new party more.

For their part, Ghannouchi and the leaders of Ennahda may calculate that they are in a better position to "oblige Nidaa Tounes to accept the game of democracy" from within, rather than from outside, the ruling coalition. The Shura Council thus voted, without great opposition from its base, to join the now more inclusive coalition. There is some party and historical logic to this experiment. As a member of the coalition, Ennahda can more effectively pressure Essebsi and his allies to accept Ennahda as a normal part of democratic participation in Tunisia. Also, within the logic of parliamentary ruling coalitions, Ennahda retains the capacity to cause the fall of the government if, for example, the government ever attempted a Ben Ali–style, undemocratic repression of their Islamist party. For Ghannouchi and many of Ennahda's leaders, the achievement of the "normalcy" of Ennahda within a successful democratic transition in Tunisia would be their greatest legacy.

For something like this two-sheikh policy to work, both sheikhs must value democracy for the present and the future of Tunisia.

TUNISIA: BEYOND DEMOCRATIC TRANSITION TO DEMOCRATIC CONSOLIDATION?

We have seen how and why Egypt was unable to make a successful democratic transition[50] but Tunisia was. A cautionary note is necessary, however. In most cases after a democratic transition has been completed, there are still many tasks that need to be accomplished, conditions that must be established, and attitudes and habits that must be cultivated before democracy can be considered consolidated. Tunisia has completed a "democratic transition," but a fully "consolidated democracy" normally requires more time, a supportive geopolitical neighborhood, and more tangible socioeconomic benefits from democracy than Tunisia has had so far.[51] Many countries complete a transition but never achieve consolidation: Argentina from the mid-1980s and the Philippines since the mid-1990s are prominent cases.

The magnitude of Tunisia's recent democratic achievements and future democratic tasks become clear when we situate Tunisia in a comparative geopolitical framework. When the Warsaw Pact disintegrated, nine Central European countries suddenly found themselves in a supportive neighborhood of peace and prosperity and were rapidly able to join the European Union. For example, the second president of postcommunist Poland, Aleksander Kwaśniewski, in a recent interview said that in the first six years of membership in the European Union "we received approximately €30 billion." He went on to say that "after the transition, our region was a fantastic example of dialogue, cooperation and stability."[52] Unfortunately, through no fault of its own, Tunisia is obviously in what international relations theorists call a "difficult neighborhood"; it has ISIS recruiting, training, and arming camps close to its porous desert borders with failed-state Libya. Tunisia also borders authoritarian and economically troubled Algeria and is one country away from Egypt, and it has no hope of joining the European Union. Two ISIS-inspired attacks launched from Libya killed sixty people in the spring of 2015 at two of Tunisia's most popular international tourist destinations: the Bardo National Museum in Tunis and the beach resort of Sousse. However, no ISIS-related group in Tunisia has been able to hold any territory or set up a ruling council to implement the ISIS version of Islamic law, and thus it is not one of the eleven ISIS-recognized provinces of the so-called ISIS caliphate spreading from Iraq to Nigeria.[53] Nonetheless, such ISIS-type attacks, while they may not destroy Tunisia's fledgling democracy, will make a full consolidation of democracy much more difficult.[54]

From the very beginning of the Arab Spring until now, the U.S. government has considered good relations with the Egyptian military a central strategic concern and Tunisia a relatively unimportant sideshow. Before I went to Egypt and Tunisia in March 2011, I visited the National Security Council at the White House and the Policy Planning Staff at the State Department to exchange ideas about the possibilities of democratization or renewed authoritarianism as a result of the Arab Spring. It was clear that maintaining good relations with the Egyptian military and helping sustain what some of the people I spoke to considered "the good relationship between Egypt and Israel" were the highest priorities. Compared to the Marshall Plan's ambition and generosity toward Germany, Japan, and Italy after World War II and the European Union's almost instant support of the economies and fledgling democracies of postcommunist Europe, the neglect of Tunisia is greatly to be regretted because it fails to respond to the historic occasion and to help consolidate the first-ever Muslim-majority democracy in the Arab world.

So, no matter how authoritarian, the Egyptian army alone always receives $1.8 billion a year, with no strings attached from the United States (the Egyptian government, run by the military, gets even more), but Tunisia, no matter how democratic, receives less than $200 million a year, virtually all of which from 2011 to 2014 had to be spent buying U.S.-made goods, until grants for security were added in 2015.[55]

Tunisia should be a central concern. If Tunisia, the Arab country that has by far the best chance of consolidating democracy, fails, democracy as a credible prospect to aspire to withers everywhere in the Arab world.

NOTES

1. A transition is not complete unless four conditions are met: (1) there is sufficient agreement on procedures to produce an elected government; (2) the government comes to power as a direct result of free elections; (3) the government is in de facto possession of the authority to generate new policies; and (4) the legislative power generated by the new democracy does not have to share power with other bodies de jure, such as military leaders. On these points, see Juan J. Linz and Alfred Stepan, *Problems of Democratic Transition and Consolidation: Southern Europe, South America, and Post-Communist Europe* (Baltimore, Md.: Johns Hopkins University Press, 1996), chap. 1. By December 2014, Tunisia met all four of these conditions (with the partial exception of a judicial system still influenced by the previous nondemocratic regime), and Egypt had met none.

2. See the article "Our Country of the Year: Hope Springs," *Economist*, December, 20, 2014. On Freedom House's seven-point scale for political rights, the worst score is a 7 (awarded to a country like Saudi Arabia) and the best score is a 1, awarded to countries such as Sweden and, in 2015, to Tunisia.

3. None of the most important transitions in the Muslim-majority countries of Indonesia, Senegal, and Tunisia had yet occurred, so Islam is not discussed in the classic, four-volume work on transitions edited by Guillermo O'Donnell, Philippe C. Schmitter, and Laurence Whitehead, *Transitions from Authoritarian Rule* (Baltimore, Md.: Johns Hopkins University Press, 1986); nor in Linz and Stepan's 1996 book *Problems of Democratic Transition and Consolidation.*

4. To be sure, Tunisia is still far from what Linz and I would classify as a "consolidated democracy." For example, Freedom House correctly gives Tunisia a 1 for "political right" but only a 3 for "civil liberties" because of continuing problems (many related to legacies of the previous authoritarian "deep state" of fifty-five years duration) with establishing rule of law, a reformed judiciary, and a rights-respecting police, but some problems, such as the spread of Salafi and ISIS violence emanating from stateless Libya, really only became serious during the post–Ben Ali period.

5. See the annual ranking of democracy for every country in the world between 2006 and 2015 in the *Economist*'s "Index of Democracy" and Freedom House's "Freedom in the World."

6. Diarmaid MacCulloch, *The Reformation* (London: Viking, 2003), 653.

7. I define and discuss the "twin tolerations" in much greater detail in my "The World's Religious Systems and Democracy: Crafting the 'Twin Tolerations'" in *Arguing Comparative Politics* (Oxford: Oxford University Press, 2001), 213–254; a much shorter version is available in "Religion, Democracy, and the 'Twin Tolerations,'" *Journal of Democracy* 11 (October 2000): 32–52.

8. See Rached Ghannouchi's chapter in this volume, "Ennahda's Democratic Commitments and Capabilities." Muslim extremists and secular extremists both need to be studied in transitions in Muslim-majority countries, but to date secular extremists have received less attention in the literature. For a useful corrective, see the discussion of "secular purists" in Monica Marks's chapter in this volume, "Purists Versus Pluralists."

9. For the "scope conditions" for a four-player game, see Linz and Stepan, *Problems of Democratic Transition and Consolidation*, 55–65.

10. See Eugenio Ortega Frei, *Historia de una alianza política* (Santiago: CED: CESOC, 1992).

11. See Mirjam Künkler, "How Pluralist Democracy Became the Consensual Discourse Among Secular and Nonsecular Muslims in Indonesia," in *Democracy and Islam in Indonesia*, ed. M. Künkler and A. Stepan (New York: Columbia University Press, 2013), 53–72.

12. Donald L. Horowitz, *Constitutional Change and Democracy in Indonesia* (New York: Cambridge University Press, 2013), 293.

13. For a discussion of "aggressive secularism" in France and Turkey, in contrast to a religious-friendly "passive secularism" in the United States, see Ahmet T. Kuru, *Secularism and State Policies Toward Religion: The United States, France, and Turkey* (New York: Cambridge University Press, 2009); and Ahmet T. Kuru, "Passive and Assertive Secularism: Historical Conditions, Ideological Struggles, and State Policies Toward Religion," *World Politics* 59 (2007): 568–594.

14. Jean-Pierre Filiu, *The Arab Revolution: Ten Lessons from the Democratic Uprising* (London: C. Hurst, 2011), 14. The entire chapter is excellent and recommended.

15. See Albert Hourani, *Arabic Thought in the Liberal Age: 1798–1939* (New York: Cambridge University Press, 1983), 65. The university is sometimes spelled Zaytuna, as in this quote from Hourani, but often it is now spelled (in English) Zeitouna.

16. See Alfred Stepan, "Tunisia's Transition and the Twin Tolerations," *Journal of Democracy* 23 (2012): esp. 99–102.

17. See M. M. Charrad, *States and Women's Rights in the Making of Postcolonial Tunisia, Algeria, and Morocco* (Berkeley: University of California Press, 2001).

18. See Gilles Kepel, *Jihad: The Trail of Political Islam* (Cambridge, Mass.: Harvard University Press, 2002), 254–275.

19. Yale University Press is now in the process of a major translation effort, for the long-awaited publication of many of Ghannouchi's most important theological and political articles.

20. Made during a speech in the House of Commons, November 11, 1947.

21. "Appel de Tunis," June 6, 2003, three-page document, one copy given to me with the name of the twenty-three signatories by a participant from Ettakatol and an identical copy with the same names given to me by a participant from Ennahda in May 2011.

22. Some of the other twenty-two signatories were civil society and political society leaders or organizations such as PDP (a political party), Le Bâtonnier (a barristers' organization), various human rights organizations, and some prominent journalists and intellectuals in their personal capacity.

23. I received a copy of this document on November 11, 2011, while visiting the Tunis headquarters of Ettakatol, the most secular party in the CNA ruling coalition. The person who gave it to me was one of the drafters, Zied Dooulotli. The Arabic-to-English translation is the work of Mostafa Hefny. For a discussion of this document eight years later, see Farah Sami, "Eight Years Ago Today, When Leftists and Islamists Got Along," http://www.tunisia-live.net/2013/10/18.

24. Interview with Marzouki in Tunis and a separate confirmatory interview with Ghannouchi in Tunis, both in May 2013.

25. For example, Monica Marks and I recently found an important February 2006 document "A propose d'une derive," which criticizes those secularists who signed the accords: "What can we say about the haste with which some political formations and associations . . . known for their commitment to secularism and democracy have signed this so called manifesto of alliance with the movement of Mr. Rached Ghannouchi? This approach . . . blurs the boundaries between the secular view of politics and fanaticism . . . between religion and theocracy; in a word between democracy and nondemocracy." The statement had 109 signatories, including some prominent feminists from ATFD, unionists, and human rights activists.

26. Carrie Rosefsky Wickham, *The Muslim Brotherhood: Evolution of an Islamist Organization* (Princeton, N.J.: Princeton University Press, 2013), 286.

27. Emphasis added. Data supplied to me by Professor Stephen Whitefield of Oxford University, based on a not yet published poll he and his colleagues gave in Egypt in December 2011 with 2,001 respondents. They repeated this question with 2,051 respondents in March 2014 after the July 3, 2013, coup against the Morsi government and an eradication campaign against the Muslim Brotherhood, and 78 percent of respondents affirmed that the military "should continue to intervene when it thinks necessary."

28. This was written by Samir el-Ayed on September 23, 2011. In a March 2011 seminar I had with one of the most progressive and important parts of youth-led civil society, the April 6 Movement, one of their leaders told me emphatically that one of their most important projects was to figure out how they could get the military to write the constitution *before* the elections. For more like this, see my "The Recurrent Temptation to

Abdicate to the Military in Egypt" on the Freedom House blog, *Freedom at Issue*, January 13, 2012, https://freedomhouse.org/blog/two-perspectives-egypt%E2%80%99s-transition.

29. This survey data is quite evocative of Karl Marx's *The Eighteenth Brumaire of Louis Bonaparte*, in which Marx lists as a characteristic of Bonapartist regimes the abdication of the right to rule in exchange for other kinds of protection by the ensuing strong state.

30. The Tunisia data are from the previously cited Whitefield survey. For data from surveys of democratizing polities in Spain (1992); in Uruguay, Chile, and Brazil (1996); India (2004); and South Korea (2004), see Alfred Stepan, Juan J. Linz, and Yogendra Yadav, *Crafting State Nations: India and Other Multinational Democracies* (Baltimore, Md.: Johns Hopkins University Press, 2011), table 2.5.

31. For example, "civil society association members comprised a strikingly larger share of Egyptian revolutionaries (43%) than Tunisian revolutionaries (19%) (Chi-square=19.705, significant at the .001 level)." Mark R. Beisinger, Amaney A. Jamal, and Kevin Mazur, "Explaining Divergent Revolutionary Coalitions: Regime Strategies and the Structuring of Participation in the Tunisian and Egyptian Revolutions," *Comparative Politics* 48 (October 2016): 9.

32. I discuss this commission in my article "Tunisia's Transition and the Twin Tolerations," esp. 91–94.

33. Interview with Rached Ghannouchi, March 28, 2011.

34. Linz and Stepan, *Problems of Democratic Transition and Consolidation*, xiii. Adam Przeworski and Philippe C. Schmitter, in their writings on democratic transition, also insist on, and document, the "indeterminacy" of outcomes and the frequency of failures.

35. For the individual leadership contributions in Spain of seven major figures, most importantly Adolfo Suárez, see Linz and Stepan, *Problems of Democratic Transition and Consolidation*, 87–115, esp. 92–99. For Cardoso's innovative leadership against inflation, see Alfred Stepan, "Fernando Henrique Cardoso: The Structural-Historical Scholar-President of Brazil," in *Cardoso and Approaches to Inequality*, ed. Dietrich Rueschemeyer and Richard Snyder (Boulder, Colo.: Lynne Reiner, forthcoming). For how many different groups and leaders in Indonesia's constituent assembly consensually came to numerous crisis-ameliorating (or -avoiding) decisions, see Horowitz, *Constitutional Change and Democracy in Indonesia*.

36. This fascinating period deserves a book and was clouded in secrecy and somewhat conflicting accounts. At this time, however, I will attempt to make tentative arguments based on nineteen interviews with most of the major participants and a few key analysts between October 28 and November 3, 2015. I did these interviews with Monica Marks, a doctoral candidate at St. Antony's College, Oxford, who is writing her PhD on the role of Ennahda in the Tunisian democratic transition and is a fluent Arabic speaker. See her chapter in this volume.

37. For more on these events, see the Carter Center's 2013 report, "The Carter Center Congratulates Tunisia's National Constituent Assembly on Final Draft of Constitution and Urges Safeguards for Human Rights," June 12, 2013.

38. What follows concerning the new style of internal work of the CNA is based largely but not exclusively on a long interview Monica Marks and I had with Mustapha Ben Jaaffa, on November 4, 2014, in his CNA presidential office in Tunis.

39. Ibid.

40. Whereas the Egyptian Tamarrod knew it was being listened to closely by the military, which Tamarrod activists felt would eventually overthrow Morsi, the Tunisian prime minister, Ali Laarayedh (who the Tunisian Tamarrod campaign was insisting leave office), told us that the Tunisian military appeared to him to have ignored completely the Tunisian Tamarrod and that he never felt threatened by the Tunisian military. Interview in Tunis, on November 4, 2014.

41. Monica Marks and I talked to the president of UTICA, Mouldi Jendoubi, at her UTICA headquarters in Tunis, November 4, 2014; the president of the Tunisian Bar Association, Mohamed Fadhel Mahfoudh, at his office in the Justice Palace on October 30, 2014; the president of the Tunisian League of Human Rights, Mokhtar Trifi, on October 30, 2014; and the vice president of UGTT and the editor of their newspaper, *Chebab*, on November 3, 2014, and October 30, 2014, respectively.

42. For a deeper analysis of the motivations for and mistranslations surrounding this language, see Monica Marks, "Complementary Status for Tunisian Women," *Foreign Policy*, August 20, 2012.

43. In Senegal, stoning someone to death on a charge of apostasy is deeply against Sufi values. Souleymane Bachir Diagne, an expert on Islamic philosophy and Senegal, told me in a series of interviews in October 2015 that there is no historical evidence of anyone being stoned to death in Senegal.

44. For Ennahda's votes in their *shura* against containing any reference to sharia in the constitution, see Monica Marks, "Convince, Coerce, or Compromise? Ennahda's Approach to Tunisia's Constitution," Brookings Institution, February 10, 2014. For the role of compromise in the constitution, see Nadia Marzouki, "Dancing by the Cliff: Constitution Writing in Post-Revolutionary Tunisia, 2011–2014," in *Constitution Writing, Religion, and Democracy*, ed. Asli Bali and Hanna Lerner (Cambridge: Cambridge University Press, 2017).

45. Amna Guellali, "The Problem with Tunisia's New Constitution," *Human Rights Watch*, February 24, 2015.

46. Interview with Rached Ghannouchi, October 29, 2014, Tunis.

47. For more of Ghannouchi's reflections, see his op-ed in the *Wall Street Journal*, January 15, 2014. I find it significant that he now normally identifies himself as the president of the Ennahda Party in Tunisia. Sometimes in the past he stressed Ennahda as a movement. It is still both, but like the history of the Christian Democrats in Germany, Ennahda is increasingly becoming a political party.

48. For a balanced and informative eight-page political analysis of this coalition, see Monica Marks, "Tunisia Opts for an Inclusive New Government," *Washington Post*, February 3, 2015, https://www.washingtonpost.com/news/monkey-cage/wp/2015/02/03/tunisia-opts-for-an-inclusive-new-government/.

49. For example, the secretary-general of Nidaa Tounes, Taieb Baccouche, who is a champion of the anti-Ennahda "erradicationist" wing of the party, publicly denounced the inclusion of Ennahda in the coalition. Ibid.

50. For more on Egypt's failure, see chapter 2 of this volume.

51. For a definition and a more extensive discussion of democratic consolidation, see Linz and Stepan, *Problems of Democratic Transition and Consolidation*, chap. 1, esp. 5–15.

52. See his interview in Sergio Bitar and Abraham Lowenthal, eds., *Democratic Transitions: Conversations with World Leaders* (Baltimore, Md.: Johns Hopkins University Press, 2015), 251–275, quotes from 269.

53. See "Islamic State: Spreading Its Tentacles" and "Tunisia's Economy: The Other Victim," both in the *Economist*, July 4, 2015.

54. Ibid.

55. See the chapter by Radwan Masmoudi in this volume.

4

THE ROOTS OF EGYPT'S CONSTITUTIONAL CATASTROPHE

The Necessity of Marrying an
Analysis of Context, Process, and Text

NATHAN J. BROWN

O N FEBRUARY 11, 2011, a national uprising that took its own leaders by surprise succeeded in achieving two primary goals: it forced the resignation of President Hosni Mubarak, and it compelled the departing president to take the regime's constitution with him. Divided by class, religious orientation, and ideology, Egyptians were briefly unified by a demand for a new political order—one that was democratic and held its leaders accountable. And writing a new constitution was a way to express the people's unified demands.

But that unity soon dissolved in the face of differences over how a new constitution would be written and what it would say. Three years after Mubarak's departure, Egyptians had lived through a series of documents, but the final proved to be the centerpiece of a thoroughly revamped and harsher authoritarianism, not a new era of openness and accountability.

In neighboring Tunisia, a very similar process unfolded, but with a very different result. The president was forced out of the country, and the constitutional document that had been written to support his regime was discarded. A tumultuous political process, however, resulted not in a return of authoritarian practices but instead a constitution that was recognizably democratic and whose mechanisms were used to bring to office a political party that had stood in opposition to the one that had led much of the constitutional drafting and oust the incumbent from the presidency.

EVOLVING CONSTITUTIONAL WISDOM

Comparative constitutional studies have often been written with a focus on iconic cases that are seen as models of successful processes and outcomes, for example, the United States, France, and South Africa. Occasionally spectacular failures, such as Germany's Weimar experiment, enter the constitutional canon. But rarely have success and failure been so closely twinned as with Egypt and Tunisia.

In comparative constitutional analysis, scholars have shown a clear progression in their focus over the past half-century, shifting from text to context and then from context to process. In other words, traditional constitutional analysis focused on the textual provisions themselves, comparing them and probing how they might operate. While comparative constitutional analysis largely fell out of favor in political science beginning in the 1960s, what attention was given tended to shift to the political context in which constitutions operated—either with a nod to the overall authoritarian environment, which was generally seen as rendering constitutional texts irrelevant, or to electoral and party systems, which were seen as making similar systems on paper operate quite differently in practice. Text was a product of the much devalued "formal legal" order; the real locus of politics was seen to lie in struggles and practices that could not be understood by a study of paper documents.

But beginning with the transitions of the 1990s—especially those in South Africa and the former Soviet bloc—international expertise (both scholarly and practitioner) very quickly switched to stressing process. A healthy constitution was seen as most likely to emerge from a healthy process, one that was open, participatory, and inclusive in nature. Realism about context gave partial way to hope that writing a constitution the right way could give birth to the right kind of politics.

Yet the new stress on process, while apparently combining a strong dose of political realism with a strong emphasis on pluralism (lessons quickly were drawn that the best constitutions rely less on the fine print than on the consensus of the society; attempts to pick and choose who should be involved in the process of writing a constitution should give way to an attempt to include all), can actually betray strong naiveté: specialists quickly rushed to explore what the best process might be without considering who was supposed to implement it, why critical actors might balk at some of the processes proposed, and why attempts to be overly inclusive and public might lead not to a consensual outcome but to no outcome at all.

The Egyptian and Tunisian experiences might appear deceptively simple in their lessons: the Egyptians selected a bad process, and the Tunisians selected a good one. Indeed, there is much truth to that statement, but it obscures as much as it reveals. It passes over the critical political questions of who did the selecting and why any particular selections were made. Egypt illustrates nothing else so much as the necessity of marrying analysis of context, process, and text. In our understanding of the Egyptian catastrophe—and a popular revolution against an autocracy that resulted in a more robustly authoritarian order written up in constitutional form surely qualifies as a catastrophe—we will see (especially when we keep the Tunisian contrast in view) not only how text, context, and process are important but how they relate.

CONTEXT

When those interested in constitutional documents have focused on the context in which documents are written and operate, they have tended to look at long-term and large-scale issues, such as a country's historical constitutional development, the nature of its political system, and its political culture. But in Egypt what seemed to matter above all was the immediate political context.

Of course, a longer-range view does help to some extent. The country's more distant history provided some tools to the actors (most countries writing constitutions draw heavily from past texts and processes, if only to know what to avoid) but no firm answers to the questions facing them. It also helped shape the cast of characters and their goals and expectations. But there was one major distinctive feature of the environment in 2011 that made it more difficult to draw on the past: for the first time, Egyptians were writing a constitution when there was nobody clearly in charge. All of Egypt's previous constitutions were written by existing regimes that were seeking to establish sovereignty, rearrange themselves institutionally, or communicate new ideological messages.[1] Committees representing various bodies of expertise and perspectives drafted the documents, but always under the watchful eyes of existing rulers; those rulers called for amendments when the constitutions began to work in annoying ways or simply suspended or rewrote them when they felt the need.

In Egypt in 2011—as in nearby Tunisia—it was not quite clear what the regime was. In Tunisia, an interim structure was stitched together; in Egypt, the Supreme Council of the Armed Forces (SCAF) stepped into a vacuum at the top, claiming to represent the entire nation. But in neither country was there real experience in writing a constitution under conditions of such uncertainty. The problems inherent in Egypt's response should have been clear from the beginning—and indeed, they were noted early on by those familiar with regime transitions elsewhere or those who were paying attention to nearby Tunisia.[2] By seizing control of the Egyptian state and claiming the authority to set the rules of politics, the military high command robbed civilian political forces of the necessity to deal with one another; in Tunisia, by contrast, the process was guided by the Ben Achour Commission, a body more modest in its pretensions and often creaky and cantankerous in its operations but still one in which most actors were given a venue to negotiate rules. In Egypt, most major actors deferred to the military for the short term, hoping that the constitutional process would be one where the necessary long-term deals would be struck. Some members of the revolutionary coalition, to be sure, turned against the military's rule, but by the time they did so, their potential partners—especially

Islamists—saw that move (with some justification) as an attempt to disrupt a coincidence of interests between a military wishing for a quick transition and Islamists hoping for quick elections.

Thus the constitution writing took center stage. The decision was not an obvious one—the past experiences with constitutions might have led to popular repudiation of the very idea of a written document as a tool of political reconstruction. Constitutions had been issued in the name of the people, but political manipulation had in the past produced a ventriloquist effect in which the people always loyally expressed the ruler's will. Yet rather than insist that constitutions were bunk, revolutionary political forces called for a new one written by a plurality of political forces through an open and participatory process. There was a superficial agreement that the received international wisdom about inclusiveness and participation was helpful. This time, political questions were to be resolved through the political process using the constitution as a tool.

They did not ignore history; indeed, they were informed by it—but their goal was to correct the past, not repeat it. This was true in a procedural way, of course—they were going to write constitutions that emanated from political society. But it was true in a substantive sense as well—the constitutional issues drawing the most attention were those that grew out of bitter experiences with the constitutional flaws of the past. The topics discussed in 2011 focused on the domination of the political system by the presidency, the use of military trials and other tools to ensure the legal system served rulers rather than the rule of law, and the restrictions on civil and political liberties.

Of course, within three short years, Egyptian voters approved a constitution that provided for a strong presidency, allowed an expanded role for military trials, proved unable to block a judicial role imposing the new order, and clamped down on political and civil rights more than the Mubarak regime had done.

Countries go into constitution writing with the political societies they have, not the ones that might have evolved under better conditions. And in Egypt that society proved far more problematic than the revolutionary enthusiasts of 2011—who felt a new era was at hand—had reckoned for.

And that was where political context turned out to be determinative: Who were the political forces? What were their perceptions of their own strengths? And what did they expect of one another?

In Egypt, the map of political forces in 2011 consisted of three main camps. First was the state apparatus, its unity shattered by the uprising, still seemingly poised to coalesce around a vision of restored order if any part of it could take the lead; the military seemed to be the most likely candidate in 2011, and it was later joined by the security services as they began to reestablish themselves in the following two years. Second was a group of revolutionary actors, youth movements, and amorphous and ephemeral groupings of revolutionary enthusiasts able to call followers into the streets in support of a variety of visions of a freer and more just society. And third was the Islamist camp, dominated by the Muslim Brotherhood, a social movement that was rooted in parts of Egyptian society despite being deprived of legal status, but also joined by a less centrally organized Salafi movement and a host of charitable, self-help, and grassroots organizations unaffiliated with any political actor. That rich combination made the Islamist camp the most densely organized part of Egyptian society.

There were two problems that should have been apparent from the beginning but that were obscured by the wave of revolutionary enthusiasm. First, all three camps saw themselves not as part of a pluralist apparatus but as legitimately speaking for the entire nation, defending it against those who would hijack it for particularistic agendas. Second, the three camps were playing on different fields, and each felt it had the upper hand. For the state apparatus, it was laws, institutions, and procedures that mattered; those existed not to reflect the people's will but to give shape and protection to the people. For the revolutionaries, it was control of the streets and public spaces (real, such as Tahrir Square, and virtual, including mass media and social media) that mattered: they had brought down Hosni Mubarak by seizing control of such spaces and were convinced they could do so again if faced with another implacable foe. Finally, Islamists looked to the ballot box, persuaded that they not only represented the silent majority of Egyptians but also, through their proven ability to turn their organizational networks into electoral machines, the voting majority as well.

In 2011, it was the revolutionaries' field that seemed to have the upper hand, but the year closed with parliamentary elections that began a stream of electoral victories, apparently giving the Islamists an edge, one they used to begin work on a constitution that reflected their authorship. But in 2012, parts of the state apparatus began to balk: Egypt's administrative courts dissolved the first constituent assembly, the Supreme Constitutional Court dissolved the elected parliament that had chosen that assembly, and the military robbed the presidency of much of its authority before handing it over to newly elected Muhammad Morsi from the Muslim Brotherhood.

The political context in Egypt thus was not merely conflictual; it was also one in which the various actors despaired of (or perhaps neither had the skills nor felt the need for) reaching out to rivals. Tunisia was different. The state apparatus was much less of a player, with the military far less powerful and the security forces far more cowed. The other actors were similar to those operating in Egypt, but they were far more resigned to dealing with one another. This was not because the ideological gap was narrower: in Tunisia, Islamists and non-Islamists viewed each other with fear and disdain. But neither group had a dominant field on which it felt it could win, though hotter heads in both camps sometimes acted otherwise. The Islamists' comparatively poorer electoral showing, while still impressive, forced them to reach outside their camp, and the weakness of the state apparatus meant that there were fewer alternatives to the ballot box. To be sure, Islamists and non-Islamists had entered into prerevolutionary dialogue in Tunisia, as elsewhere.[3] For a variety of reasons, such efforts seemed to leave a stronger imprint in Tunisia than in Egypt. The Ennahda party of Rached Ghannouchi had shown an ability to voice positions less unfriendly to non-Islamists. But those positions, while they proved friendly to concerns of non-Islamists, still left considerable ambiguity,[4] and Ghannouchi himself was quite capable of angrily dismissing the "Francophones" in terms more reminiscent of Sarah Palin's contempt for the "lamestream media" than Rodney King's "can we all get along?" Those familiar with opposition dialogues in preuprising Tunisia stress how well they laid the groundwork for postuprising understandings. In Egypt, such dialogues also took place; they may have had less impact because of the Brotherhood's ambivalence about them and the comparative weakness of the non-Islamist opposition. Ghannouchi's personal commitment to a pluralist environment—seeing it as necessary to the long-term goals of his movement—was paralleled by the Egyptian Brotherhood's "participation, not domination" slogan. The former guided al-Nahda's post-2011 behavior, while the Brotherhood gradually pushed (or, in the eyes of its leaders, was forced) to move in a more assertive direction.

Islamists in both Egypt and Tunisia shared a belief that they represented the true values of the population against an arrogant, cosmopolitan, and self-appointed cosmopolitan elite. But ultimately softer parts of the al-Nahda vision were fostered in the immediate pre- and postuprising periods; in Egypt, by contrast, similar voices in the Brotherhood (such as that of 'Abd al-Min'am Abu al-Futuh) were marginalized.

Thus the problems in Egypt were less centuries and decades and more years in the making: the political forces active in the wake of the uprising were poised in a manner that made designing a functioning democratic constitutional order far more difficult.

PROCESS

There may be no surer way to provoke horror in any country undergoing dramatic political change than to call in a foreign expert who proclaims, "I am from Egypt, and I am here to help you design a democratic transition." Other canonical successes stories—South Africa, in particular—have, by contrast, spawned professional careers of those who can claim to assist in helping societies design transitions. Tunisians may soon join that body of international experts.

Tunisians suspended their constitution and allowed an interim oversight body to form—one that defined its task narrowly as paving the way for the election of a constituent assembly. That body, when elected, had an Islamist plurality but not a majority. It proceeded extremely slowly and for extended periods seemed paralyzed by the inability to eke out a text all could agree on; some clearly came to hope the body would fail and be replaced. But after three years, the various forces represented managed to produce a consensus text; efficiency and speed were sacrificed for the sake of inclusion, bargaining, and deliberation.

While there is much knowledge that has been gained about how to design constitutional processes, far less attention has been paid to understanding why societies make the choices they do. There is no doubt that Tunisia followed international best practice at critical junctures, following a process that was rocky and contentious but also slow and inclusive. Egypt, by contrast, rushed through a series of processes, each one of which seemed worse than the last in excluding or marginalizing critical political actors. Why were the Egyptians such bad students and the Tunisians such good ones?

In fact, constitutional processes are designed not by students, angels, or philosopher-kings but by real political actors. The rules of politics contained in constitutions are made not at a time when politics is suspended for long-ranged and disinterested contemplation but when bitter political struggles are at their most intense. And the rules about making those rules—that is, the processes for writing a constitution—are themselves outcomes of intense political struggles. The relationship between process and outcome is not lost on political actors; in an environment in which the stakes seem particularly high, each actor seeks to ensure that it will be included; international wisdom about inclusiveness is embraced most heartily by those who fear being excluded and forgotten (or politely ignored) by those who feel that sharper elbows are more likely to secure specific gains.

The process in Egypt—or the set of processes—was therefore a product of Egyptian politics and not ignorance of international wisdom. The context described above—one in which three actors reached for the tools they could use, convinced they were doing so in the national interest—produced a series of lurches in which suspicions and polarization grew, in which momentary coincidences of interest (between Islamists and the military, for instance) were viewed by those excluded as orchestrated plots, and where individuals or groups that sought to bridge differences found themselves suspect, pulled into one of the rival camps, or utterly marginalized.

In a first step, a military interested in a speedy restoration of order called for a limited number of constitutional amendments and appointed a committee to rush the drafting of some suggested ones. That committee designed a process that allowed for a restoration of the 1971 constitution but also a process for writing a new one at a more leisurely pace, with an elected parliament to select a drafting committee. Those amendments were then submitted to voters a mere five weeks after the suspension of the 1971 constitution and forced departure of Mubarak; Islamists (sensing that the rapid sequence of parliamentary elections, presidential election, and referendum on a new constitution would serve them well) called out their supporters; opponents (wishing to write a new constitution first and seeking to continue revolutionary activity through regular demonstrations) opposed the changes.

The Islamists won the referendum, but the SCAF demonstrated that it had the upper hand by issuing an entirely new interim constitution incorporating the approved amendments but also removing key parliamentary powers; it issued a series of supplementary constitutional declarations, the final one of which transferred authority from the presidency to the military on the eve of the presidential elections of June 2012.

With the military in interim control, attention shifted to the electoral process—or at least that is where the Islamists' attention shifted, persuaded that if political contests could be moved into the voting booths they would do well. Revolutionary groups, less sanguine about their electoral prospects or even the fairness of electoral competition in the midst of an inchoate but still authoritarian environment, continued to contest the military's role and maintained their public protests, culminating in a series of bitter clashes between security forces and demonstrators. The brutality of Egyptian security services and the continued use of military courts for some of those arrested led Islamist and revolutionary groups to escalate the charges against each other for betraying civilian unity. Islamists insisted that the best response was an electoral one because proceeding with voting would put in place a civilian leadership with the authority to exercise oversight and allow the constitutional process to move forward; revolutionaries charged that Islamists were pursuing short-term partisan interests by seeking to sacrifice revolutionary demands and tolerate official brutality only so that they could win a seat at the table.

Thus, when parliamentary elections were held—and Islamists won a resounding victory—suspicions had already grown quite deep. Islamists found that the parliament could not legislate or oversee the cabinet, because it had been deprived of its constitutional standing; revolutionaries felt that Islamists would use their parliamentary majority to stack the constitutional assembly (to be chosen by the parliament); and the SCAF and parts of the state apparatus appeared to fear that their ability to use the tools at their disposal would be devalued over time as Islamists completed their conquest of the presidency and wrote a constitution to their liking.

The constitutional process proceeded according to everyone's worst fears. Islamists did indeed stack the drafting body. Revolutionaries and other non-Islamist forces boycotted on the plausible grounds that Islamists had given them a small share, and Islamists retorted on the equally plausible grounds that their opponents could not accept the reality of the electoral outcome. The state apparatus heard noises about judicial reform, security-sector reform, and civilian command of the military, all of which suggested that the constitution might be a bit too innovative for their liking. And Islamists found their path blocked not merely on a interim basis—that is, by the SCAF trying to hold power in its hands by transferring authority away from the presidency in advance of presidential elections—but perhaps more ominously on an ongoing basis. In April 2012, an administrative court dissolved the constituent assembly, populated with a firm Islamist majority, and in June 2012, the Supreme Constitutional Court (SCC) dissolved the Islamist-dominated parliament on the eve of the Brotherhood's capture of the presidency. The parliament had been able to elect a second constituent assembly with an Islamist majority shortly before the SCC disbanded the body, so constitution writing proceeded under Islamist leadership. But from the summer of 2012 forward, the enmity between important judicial actors and the Islamists only increased, with the threat of politically portentous rulings always poised above the Islamists' heads and plans proceeding among the Islamists for a judicial "reform" that could purge senior judicial personnel.

The period from the overthrow of Mubarak to the presidential election seemed to persuade the state apparatus that the Islamists were the true challenge; the revolutionaries and other political forces could be ignored, reduced to scattered demonstrations and escalating rhetoric. And for their part, the Islamists seemed to calculate that they could not take on the entire state apparatus at once. They therefore shelved security-sector reform and seemed to reach a modus vivendi with the SCAF, asserting executive-branch control over most civil matters but treating the military as a sovereign body.

Yet the judiciary proved a source of great concern, and the newly elected Islamist president, Muhammad Morsi, thus sought to insulate the constitutional process from judicial involvement by issuing his own constitutional declaration exempting the assembly's work from court review. The resulting firestorm from the opposition—now suddenly seeing the judicial part of the state apparatus as an ally—led to bloody clashes and a determination by the Islamists to shove through their constitution, which they did as 2012 drew to a close.

Egypt's constitutional process, therefore, had been one that involved little bargaining among disparate forces; instead it reflected the will of dominant actors—and when the opposition to that constitution proved implacable in 2013 and the state apparatus continued both passive and active resistance to the Islamists (with parts of the bureaucracy simply failing to respond to presidential directives, the military positioning itself as above the presidency and the entire political process, and the judiciary operating as an opposition camp within the state itself), Egypt seemed completely adrift. With unsurprisingly poor policy performance and escalating tensions, the Islamists seemed to depend on their constitutional legitimacy, the prospect of parliamentary elections, and their perceived popular strength to outwait or intimidate opponents. The opposite occurred, with the opposition mobilizing against the Islamists and the state apparatus, including quite dramatically the military itself, forcing the Islamists out of office in July 2013 and underground when they refused to accept the outcome of the coup.

Egypt's constitutional process seemed to go from bad to worse—and soon went to worst of all with the violent overthrow of the Brotherhood in July 2013. After suspending the 2012 constitution, the military decreed a new "road map" that was sketched out in more detail by the man designated as interim president in the wake of the coup, SCC Chief Justice Adli Mansur. The new plan was to have jurists offer a series of amendments to the constitution; those would then be submitted to an appointed committee of fifty who would rush the suggestions to a referendum, followed by parliamentary and then presidential elections. The jurists convened, going over the 2012 document clause by clause; the committee of fifty then convened and pushed that work aside, doing its own comprehensive review. While non-Islamists composed almost all of the committee, what was remarkable was that most of the members drew a state salary; the process was not one of various social and political forces coming together either to write a new constitution or amend the old one. Instead it can best be described as a process in which the Egyptian state reconstituted itself.[5]

TEXT

If one were to read the various constitutions governing Egypt—those promulgated in 1971, 2012, and 2014—without knowing all the political background, one might be astounded to discover the bitterness of the political struggles surrounding them. The documents resemble nothing so much as one another.

There were, to be sure, important differences in the fine print. Those differences were very much a product of the context and process described in this chapter. Peculiarities of the final constitution can be understood as a reaction to the power struggles that took place not only during the year of Morsi's presidency but also during the nearly three years since the removal of Mubarak.[6] The military, judiciary, police, and other groups sought to protect themselves from the very sort of challenge they encountered from elected Muslim Brotherhood officials and non-Islamist revolutionaries. The leaders of institutions of the pre-2011 state saw in the post-coup anti-Brotherhood, promilitary popular climate an opportunity to retake—and even broaden—the powers they enjoyed under Mubarak. The primary winners in Egypt's 2014 constitution were the state institutions that had banded together to oust Morsi.

The constitution enshrines autonomy for the military, which had already been granted a considerable measure of autonomy by the now-suspended 2012 constitution. In effect, it is no longer treated as part of the executive branch of government but rather a branch unto itself. The most significant change is the requirement that the military approve the defense minister for the next two presidential terms (Article 234). Also notable was the continued broad jurisdiction of military courts over civilians. In the 1971 constitution (in force until 2011), this matter was left to legislation; the 2012 constitution took a similar approach. The 2013 document does the same, though it works to restrict this jurisdiction to specific kinds of cases (Article 204). The language is so broad, however, that the military courts are likely to have jurisdiction whenever they wish, such as in any area military officials declare a "military zone."

Mubarak used the military courts to try political cases in which he wanted to be assured of a quick guilty verdict. That abuse may be less of a problem now since that right depended on the declaration of a state of emergency that has come under greater restrictions in the post-2011 period. The real issue will instead become the military's own actions in dealing with protesters and critics, not the president's. The thousands of cases in military courts since 2011 have come from military prosecutors and courts acting on their own.

The judiciary, which strongly supported the military takeover from the Brotherhood, also won autonomy in the 2013 document. Judicial bodies receive their budgets in a lump sum, the judicial council selects the prosecutor general, and each judicial body is granted autonomy. Various judicial actors jockeyed to obtain specific mention in the draft constitution as well as independence from other actors; most got what they wished for, though some judicial bodies will inevitably feel slighted.

A third state institution to emerge victorious was al-Azhar, Egypt's premier religious institution, though a superficial reading of the text may suggest otherwise. The 2012 constitution included a controversial article requiring that al-Azhar be consulted in matters related to Islamic sharia; that has been eliminated. But such a constitutional responsibility would have exposed the institution politically as attempting to assert a Sunni version of Iran's clerically supervised system, and al-Azhar never sought such a role. Its authority was already established in law. Al-Azhar's current leadership seeks supreme moral authority and autonomy, and that is what the current text offers.

Finally, the police as well as the wider security and intelligence apparatus won little-noticed victories. The police are loyal directly to the people (Articles 206 and 207), the same definition of mission that the military used to intervene in politics in 2011 and 2013. They are supposed to honor human rights, but a reference to international human rights instruments was dropped from the final draft. According to the new document, a Supreme Police Council—likely dominated by senior officers—must be consulted on any law affecting the police, effectively ensuring that much-needed security reform will run through existing police institutions. General intelligence officers are subject to the military courts, not to civilian justice (Article 204), effectively giving them immunity from civilian oversight or prosecution. And Article 237 requires that the state fight "terrorism," a term deployed in an idiosyncratically broad manner by Egypt's current rulers.

Yet if context and process explain the constitutional variation, what is more remarkable is how much that same context survived the constitution, working through its provisions even when it did not change them. In other words, tremendous political upheaval in Egypt could occur while leaving the basic constitutional structures little changed on paper. The 2012 constitution (shoved through by Islamists) and the 2013 constitution (dictated by the state itself) are different not so much because of the fine print but because the 2012 constitution was operating in the context of an Islamist president, an excluded opposition that rejected the legitimacy of the document, and a state apparatus, important parts of which regarded the Islamists as a hostile alien force to be bypassed or ousted. The 2013 constitution enabled the election of a president who had spent his entire adult life in the military, and it was implemented in the midst of greatly weakened political forces and the most extensive and brutal political crackdown in two generations.

CONTEXT MATTERS

Constitutional texts can affect the way that politics operates. And different constitutional processes produce different constitutional texts. But there is a clear lesson from the Egyptian experience, especially when compared with the Tunisian one: Context matters considerably and helps shape both the process by which a constitution is written and the text. In that sense, process and text can be seen as outcomes—even though much prevailing analysis is based on seeing them as causes.

But the context that seemed to matter the most is short term and conjunctural. The Arab world's experience with written constitutions is now 150 years old, and the countries within that region have constitutional texts that have evolved over time but often incrementally—as in other places, the best way to predict what will be placed in one draft is what was in the preceding one. In that way, history matters.

But when it comes to the most fateful constitutional questions, what seems to matter more than distant history is who the actors are, what they can do, and what expectations they have of one another. Marx was right that men make their own history but not as they please, but he should have been a bit more myopic: it is their very recent past that needs to be weighed most heavily.

NOTES

1. See my article "Regimes Reinventing Themselves: Constitutional Development in the Arab World," *International Sociology* 18, no. 1 (March 2003): 33–52.

2. See, for instance, Alfred Stepan, "Tunisia's Transition and the Twin Tolerations," *Journal of Democracy* 23, no. 2 (April 2012): 89–103.

3. On such dialogues, and on their limited achievements prior to 2011, see Michaelle L. Browers, *Political Ideology in the Arab World: Accommodation and Transformation* (Cambridge: Cambridge University Press, 2009).

4. See Nathan J. Brown, Amr Hamzawy, and Marina Ottaway, "Islamist Movements and the Democratic Process in the Arab World: Exploring the Gray Zones," Carnegie Endowment for International Peace, 2006.

5. See my "Egypt's Constitutional Cul-de-Sac," Chr. Michelsen Institute Insight, March 2014.

6. I explored this with Michele Dunne in "Egypt's Draft Constitution Rewards the Military and Judiciary," Carnegie Endowment for International Peace, December 2013, on which this section is based.

5

PURISTS AND PLURALISTS

Cross-Ideological Coalition Building in
Tunisia's Democratic Transition

MONICA MARKS

O N FEBRUARY 2, 2015, Tunisia's prime minister Habib Essid announced the formation of a coalition government whose members included representatives of three secularly oriented parties and a sprinkling of posts for Ennahda, the center-right Islamist party that had placed second in Tunisia's October 2014 parliamentary election.[1] Ennahda's inclusion in the secular-led government, though largely symbolic—with just one ministerial seat and three secretarial posts—was historically significant.[2] For the second time since its January 2011 revolution, Tunisia had freely and fairly elected a government that opted for a cross-ideological coalition.[3] English-language media characterized the coalition as part of a distinctively Tunisian pattern of compromise. With dialogue and consensus as defining trademarks, Tunisia was again applauded as the "only success story of the 2011 Arab uprisings."[4]

Why have Tunisians managed to bridge certain secular leftist–versus-Islamist divides at key junctures in their transition from authoritarianism while attempts at cross-ideological coalition building elsewhere in the region have largely failed to materialize? Explanations have centered on Tunisia's structural advantages—its military had long been sidelined, and voters had elected secular and Islamist parties in relatively balanced proportion in the postrevolutionary elections of 2011 and 2014, thereby preventing either side from winning straightforward parliamentary majorities.[5] Tunisia's Islamists, too, adopted a more farsighted, self-restrained approach to power than Egypt's Muslim Brotherhood.[6] Outside analysts have frequently credited Ennahda's president Rached Ghannouchi, in particular, with helping steer the party toward inclusive pragmatism and away from the demands of more intransigent maximalists, including the well-known former Ennahda MPs Sadok Chorou and Habib Ellouze.[7]

While each of these factors holds important explanatory value, another important angle—namely, Tunisian secularists' willingness to engage in cross-ideological coalition building with Islamists—has remained under-recognized. Scholars, like journalists and policy makers, have almost exclusively scrutinized Tunisia's Islamists when locating ideological obstacles to political pluralism. This tendency to focus principally on whether and how Islamists compromise is borne out by the flourishing of studies on Islamist moderation versus the relative absence of studies asking whether, how, and why secular and leftist groups in the MENA region moderate, and the extent to which these groups should even be considered "secular" according to the most widely accepted definitions of the term.

While this chapter employs the word "secular" for convenience, it does so with a crucially important caveat—namely, that many actors in Tunisia whom Western journalists and academics label "secular" would be more accurately described as anti-Islamists, as self-identified modernists, and/or as proponents of state-led paternalistic authoritarianism. Traditionally, so-called secular autocrats in Tunisia and other countries across the Middle East and North Africa have not identified as secularists in Arabic—the word 'almani has a negative and politically unpopular connotation. Nor have they necessarily championed the separation of religion and state. Instead, they have often supported the state's top-down monopolization of religious authority. For instance, in Tunisia and in Turkey, all imams have traditionally been employees of the Ministry of Religious Affairs and the Diyanet, respectively. Being a preacher in either country requires one to be a state employee, a condition that has often seen religious leaders co-opted as handmaidens to illiberal regimes.[8] Similarly, the word "Islamist," which has been applied to actors as diverse as Al-Qaeda, the Egyptian Muslim Brotherhood, and Tunisia's Ennahda Party—often confuses more than it clarifies. Ennahda, for example, never explicitly championed classic "Islamist goals" like implementing sharia as a discrete set of rules or clearly endorsing the foundation of an Islamic state. Instead, from their beginnings in the 1970s, Ennahda has supported a vague program of Arab-Islamic cultural revival, sometimes adopting more "liberal" positions on homosexuality, women's rights, and other matters than secular-leftist counterparts.[9] Ennahda officially renounced the Islamist label at its Tenth Party Congress in May 2016, further complicating application of the "Islamist" label.

The terms "secular" and "Islamist" also foster subconscious feelings of solidarity or opposition among Western observers. Secularists, it is assumed, identify more "with us" and make naturally more effective champions of pluralism and liberal democracy than Islamists, who are not like us and whose values, it is assumed, more strongly oppose the adoption of liberal democracy. Finely grained case studies can upset these assumptions. In Tunisia, for instance, procoalition actors on both the "Islamist" and "secular-leftist" sides of the political spectrum struggled against purists within their respective camps to forge cross-ideological compromises, both before and after the revolution. Their efforts have proven crucial to the relative success of Tunisia's democratic transition.

This chapter highlights key moments in that struggle for pluralism and inclusive dialogue. In so doing, it demonstrates that the traditional framing of Tunisia's ideological landscape, that is, as a battlefield between ideologically intransigent Islamists and presumably pluralist secularists, elides important work secularists have done both to facilitate and impede the formation of inclusive institutions. Indeed, while broad segments of Tunisia's Islamist and secular camps now believe some measure of cross-ideological accommodation and even alliance building is necessary, the best-organized opposition to these coalitions frequently sprang from exclusionary segments of Tunisia's secular left, whose members—perceiving Ennahda as a reactionary party that seeks to impose an Islamic state ideal—have felt they stand to lose the most from Islamists' inclusion in electorally representative political structures.[10]

OPPOSITION TALKS IN THE 2000s: SETTING THE STAGE FOR CROSS-IDEOLOGICAL COOPERATION

Organized cross-ideological opposition to the authoritarian rule of Zine el-Abidine Ben Ali (1987–2011) emerged visibly in the early 2000s. In 2003, shortly after Ben Ali rammed through a constitutional amendment allowing him to stand for a fourth presidential term, three secularly oriented political parties—Congress for the Republic (CPR), led by the human rights activist Moncef Marzouki; the Democratic Forum for Labor and Liberties (FTDL), known as Ettakatol, led by the opposition politician Mustapha Ben Jaafar; and the Progressive Democratic Party (PDP), led by the lawyer and prominent opposition politician Ahmed Najib Chebbi—met formally in Aix-Marseille, France, with the Islamist party Ennahda and ten independent Tunisian civil society organizations dedicated to protecting human rights and prisoners' rights.[11]

Their meeting culminated in the publication of a document, the "Nida'a Tunis" (Call of Tunis; more commonly referred to by its French title, the "Appel de Tunis"), signed by all parties to the talks. The "Appel de Tunis" attempted to develop "a political contract establishing a democratic society," laying out "new norms" for the construction of a "pluralistic, tolerant society" that could guarantee freedom of belief as well as equality (*musaawa*) between men and women.[12] The document, signed by three top leaders in Ennahda—Amr Laarayedh, president of Ennahda's political bureau at the time; Mohamed Ben Salem; and Rafiq Abdessalem—identified popular sovereignty (*sayadat al-shaab*) as the sole source of legitimacy (*ka-masdar wahid lil-sulta*) and made no mention of Islamic law.[13]

Mokhtar Yayaoui, a prominent antiregime judge and independent secularly oriented human rights activist, released a letter in conjunction with the talks that described the Aix-Marseille meeting as a "qualitative leap" (*naqla nida'iya*) in the history of the Tunisian opposition. According to Yahyaoui, Tunisia's opposition was, for the first time, coming together to reject its regime-assigned role, which he described as "polishing the image of false democracy" that Ben Ali had promoted internationally.[14] In a second letter published in July 2003, Yahyaoui decried Ben Ali's "robbery" of Tunisia's democratic opposition, describing how the dictator had deliberately fomented divisions among opposition actors, creating "a confrontation that is still alive today."[15]

Yahyaoui and other leaders present at Aix-Marseille saw the 2003 talks as an important cross-ideological rejection of Ben Ali's divide-and-rule policies, which had stymied any formation of a united oppositional movement. Throughout the 1990s, Ben Ali had framed Ennahda as a fundamentally illiberal actor opposed to Tunisian moderate Islam. A steady stream of heavily censored, regime-compliant reporting delegitimized Ennahda as an essentially anti-Tunisian, violent, and Gulf-inspired actor—one that especially threatened Tunisians' standard of living and comparatively liberal lifestyles.[16] As Beatrice Hibou's excellent book *The Force of Obedience* explains, Ben Ali marketed a "security pact" in which citizens traded democratic freedoms for assurances that the regime would safeguard their lifestyle and living standards. This pact began to crumble in the late 2000s as Ben Ali's promises of economic development failed to materialize, but it still enjoyed significant, if often tacit, support from individuals, particularly many secularly inclined Tunisians who feared an Algeria-style scenario of unrest, illiberalism, and possibly even civil war if Islamists were brought into a democratic polity.[17]

On October 18, 2005, Tunisia's nascent cross-ideological opposition undertook a high-profile protest. Prominent opposition figures, ranging from secular and leftist figures like the PDP's Ahmed Najib Chebbi and the Tunisian communist party's leader Hama el-Hammami to the Ennahda activist and prisoners' rights campaigner Samir Dilou, staged a month-long hunger strike to coincide with a UN-sponsored international summit in Tunis regarding digital communications.[18] Through subsequent meetings organized in Tunisia, France, and Italy, the hunger strikers formalized their protest into a longer-term oppositional movement dubbed the

"October 18 Collective for Rights and Freedoms." The October 18 Collective sought to unify opposition to Ben Ali's regime, bringing together a wide spectrum of independent civil society activists, human rights groups, and political parties including CPR, FDTL, PDP, and Ennahda as well as leftist and Arabist parties including el-Hammami's Tunisian Communist Workers' Party (POCT) and the United Nasserist party.

A press statement and founding document released on December 4, 2005, stated that the October 18 Collective was a movement that aspired to "achieve a common vision of a minimum democratic standard" and to provide a forum in which different political and intellectual currents could collaborate to achieve three shared demands: (1) freedom of speech and of the press, (2) freedom of organization and association, and (3) release of political prisoners and enactment of a general amnesty law.[19] Two months later the collective published in Arabic a document titled "Defending the Rights of Society: Grounds for Common Political Work," in which fifty-seven signatories from the aforementioned groups signed on to three core principles governing the collective's work: (1) equality, that is, no discrimination based on social, sexual, or cultural origin; (2) national sovereignty; and (3) the rejection of violence both as a means to resolve political or ideological differences and as state violence to resolve political and social conflicts. Cross-ideological opposition to Ben Ali's rule was becoming more organized and outspoken than ever before.

FEBRUARY 2006: "A PROPOS D'UNE DÉRIVE"

As the October 18 Collective was releasing its foundational documents between December 2005 and February 2006, a separate group of Tunisian secularists and leftists met to issue their own manifesto. In February 2006, they released a statement with 109 signatories called "A propos d'une dérive" (Concerning a drift), which laid out their opposition to the October 18 Collective based on the movement's inclusion of Ennahda. Its signatories asserted that they repudiated Ben Ali's dictatorship but that including Ennahda in an oppositional coalition was unacceptable. "The signatories of this document would like to comment on the commotion that is rippling through the left and all who make claims to democracy and laïcité [secularism] in Tunisia," they said. "Democratic debate is one thing; alliance at all costs is another. We are not convinced that the choice of the October 18 Collective for Rights and Freedoms [to enter into dialogue with Ennahda] is timely or relevant. . . . For this movement [Ennahda] to have a place in the democratic family, it would have to renounce its Islamic state project."

The document's 109 signatories included representatives of major civil society groups and public intellectuals. Thirteen prominent members of Tunisia's best-known and most internationally supported women's rights group, the Tunisian Association of Democratic Women (ATFD), signed, along with at least three members of the Tunisian League for Human Rights (LTDH) and some of Tunisia's best-known public intellectuals, including the academics Hamadi Redissi, Dalenda Larguèche, and Souhair Belhassen. Political scientists, unionists, teachers, lawyers, students, feminists, and human rights activists—many of whom believed Ennahda's supposedly democratic commitments were insincere—signed on. The signatories asserted that though they, too, opposed Ben Ali's regime, forming a cross-ideological alliance with Islamists was dangerously unwise.

> What can we say . . . about the haste with which some political formations and associations . . . known for their commitment to secularism and democracy . . . have signed this so-called manifesto of alliance with the movement of Mr. Rached Ghannouchi? The approach is symptomatic of our left . . . blurring the boundaries between the secular view of politics and fanaticism . . . between religion and theocracy; in a word, between democracy and nondemocracy.

The statement goes on to call for debate rather than dialogue with Islamists and accuses the October 18 Collective of postulating "consensus before finalizing the discussion," in effect yoking democratic actors to an essentially antidemocratic Islamist Trojan horse. "As we know," its authors say, "the first defeat begins with words."[20]

The following month, Ahmed Najib Chebbi, the leader of the Progressive Democratic Party (PDP), spoke for secularly oriented members of the October 18 Collective in a rebuttal titled "Amorce d'un débat" (Start of a debate). In his letter, Chebbi defends the collective, saying it has been meeting with European partners, "none of whom raised reservations about the participation of the Islamist movement." Instead, he says, "all have praised" the movement for bringing an end to "the fragmentation of the Tunisian opposition" and its chaotic infighting. Chebbi asserts that under a dictatorship such as Ben Ali's all victims of oppression "have a clear interest to work together to enable the liberalization of public life." Referencing Ennahda members and their families, who bore the brunt of politically motivated repression, torture, and other police abuses under Ben Ali's rule, Chebbi says that Islamists "are more interested than others in establishing such alliances" because "they suffer the most pressure at present."[21]

"A propos d'une dérive" and the trove of documents related to opposition talks held in the 2000s shine a fascinating light on the nuts and bolts of cross-ideological coalition formation in Tunisia, with profound implications for scholars' understanding of alliances made and unmade in the years immediately following Tunisia's revolution.[22] Yet no English-language academic study has drawn significantly on these documents or discussed in any detail the vibrant intrasecularist debate surrounding Ennahda's inclusion in the October 18 Collective.[23] This likely reflects a tendency among scholars of the MENA region to investigate the ideological openness, coalitionability, and moderation of Islamist parties at the expense of looking simultaneously at tensions between antidialogue purists and procoalition pluralists within secularly oriented movements. Nevertheless, the documents cited above tell us much about why some secular and leftist actors remained skeptical of Ennahda well after the revolution—even to the extent of sometimes allying, either tacitly or explicitly, against Ennahda and with members of Ben Ali's disbanded party, the Constitutional Democratic Rally party (RCD).

AFTER THE REVOLUTION: FEARS OF ISLAMIST TAKEOVER AND THE RISE OF NIDAA TOUNES

After the revolution, many secularly oriented Tunisians continued to suspect strongly that Ennahda constituted an Islamofascist wolf in sheep's clothing. Commentators both within and outside the MENA region similarly worried that the Arab Spring uprisings would sweep illiberally majoritarian yet electorally legitimate Islamist parties into power. Many Tunisian secularists who had resented the heavy-handedness of Ben Ali's dictatorship—among them academics, feminists, and civil society activists—nonetheless feared that full democratic enfranchisement might bring Ennahda to power, dangerously disrupting Ben Ali's security pact, which, though repressive, had promised protection from Islamist assaults on secularists' lifestyles.

Numerous interviews I conducted and encounters I had with secular Tunisians in the summer of 2011 brought such fears into focus. On my way toward the then-unmarked Ennahda party headquarters in early July 2011, I asked Ibrahim Letaief, a secular radio personality who worked at the nearby Radio Mosaique headquarters, for directions. "Just watch out that you don't be their *idiot utile*," he warned. "These people [in Ennahda] are taking Tunisia back to the dark ages! They'd take you too if you lived here." In an interview at her home in Monastir, a feminist activist and supporter of the Democratic Modernist Pole, a now-defunct secular party, predicted a "*raz-de-marée Islamiste*" (Islamist tidal wave) would sweep the October 2011 elections and chided me for speaking with Ennahda women as part of my master's thesis research: "You can come and talk to *Nahdawi* [Ennahda member] women and believe what they tell you, but you're going back to Britain, and you won't have to live in an Islamist republic. I have to live here, even if this place becomes Iran."[24]

Many secularly oriented Tunisians with whom I spoke in 2011 made little or no distinction between Ennahda and Salafi actors, be they quietists or jihadi.[25] Some, drawing on decades of regime-mediated coverage, described Ennahda as a violently intolerant group, loyal to Wahabbi militancy and supportive of terroristic Al Qaeda–style practices. Though Tunisia is a small country, where families generally include Islamist and secularly oriented individuals, fear of Ennahda—and more general frustration with newly visible "others" in society—surged in the revolution's wake. Secular incomprehension of some Salafi women's decision to wear the *niqab*, a face-covering black garment banned under Ben Ali, for example, mirrored conservative frustration with the showing of secularly oriented films like Nadia al-Fani's *No God, No Master* and Marjane Satrapi's *Persepolis*. In a country where authoritarian regimes had purposefully conflated unity with uniformity, both sides seemed to be wondering, "Is this who Tunisians really are?"[26] Given the strict criminalization of Ennahda members, their families, and even many of their associates under Ben Ali, fear of the party and its intentions ran especially high.

Rather than ushering in an Islamist tidal wave, however, Tunisia's October 23, 2011, elections produced relatively comparable percentages of votes for Ennahda and secular parties.[27] CPR and Ettakatol, the centrist secular parties of the famed human rights fighter Moncef Marzouki and the long-time social democrat Mustapha Ben Jaafar, won second and fourth place, respectively, and joined Ennahda in a three-party coalition government commonly referred to as the "Troika." Interestingly, Ennahda's president, Rached Ghannouchi, had expressed support for such a coalition well before the October 2011 election. In a March 2011 interview with Alfred Stepan, Ghannouchi correctly predicted that deploying a Westminster-style first-past-the-post (FPTP) system in Tunisia would produce a landslide victory for Ennahda, inhibiting prospects for coalition building and fueling fears of an Islamist takeover. Instead, Ghannouchi lent his support, and Ennahda's backing, to a proportional representation (PR) Hare quota system, which is estimated to have reduced Ennahda's share of the final vote by a staggering 50 percent.[28]

Despite the formation of a cross-ideological coalition, fears of Ennahda dominating the government continued to worry many secular and leftist Tunisians. Some, including influential signatories of "A propos d'une dérive"—the February 2006 statement that had opposed the October 18 Collective's inclusion of Islamists—strongly opposed CPR and Ettakatol's decision to enter into the coalition. Immediately after the Troika coalition was announced, many members of the secular left, including a significant number of individuals in Ettakatol itself, denounced the decision, arguing that such a coalition would necessitate eventual betrayals of democratic-modernist values and contribute to legitimizing Ennahda's presence at the democratic table.[29]

For the segment of Tunisian secularists who had most vehemently opposed a cross-ideological coalition with Islamists, such as the signatories of "A propos d'une dérive," the 2011 elections came as a stunning defeat. Most had supported left-wing laïcist (French style-secularist) parties such as the Democratic Modernist Pole (PDM), which presented itself as a modernist alternative to Ennahda. These parties lost badly, along with PDP, a more centrist-oriented secular party, whose leader, Chebbi, had dialogued with Islamists in opposition talks throughout the 2000s.[30] "The day after the elections, we [on the secular side] were really asking ourselves what to do. There was a push to come together in a single, secular party organized against the Islamists," said Zeineb Turki, a former member of PDP, which is now known as Joumhouri.[31]

Beji Caid Essebsi—a charismatic eighty-seven-year-old veteran of the Bourguiba and Ben Ali regimes—emerged as the figure best poised to lead that large anti-Islamist front. In April 2012, Essebsi, who had won plaudits as the head of Tunisia's transitional government from February to December 2011, created the Nidaa Tounes (Call for Tunisia) party—a diverse coalition of anti-Islamist actors including leftists, secularists, trade unionists, Destourians, and ex-RCD members.[32] The creation of Nidaa Tounes stirred considerable excitement among secularists still stinging from Ennahda's electoral victory. Yet rumors that the party was built on a reactivation of ex-RCD money and manpower soon circulated. Outside the capital, particularly in Tunisia's interior and south, community residents were quick to describe Nidaa Tounes as "old *boukha* [Tunisia's traditional alcoholic brew] in new bottles," often claiming that leaders of local

Nidaa offices had been active members of the local RCD office, too.[33] Inside Tunis, the party was counting prominent ex-RCDists—including Mohamed Ghariani, the former secretary general of the RCD, and Faouzi Elloumi, a prominent MP in the former RCD—among its top leaders and financiers. Citing the prevalence of ex-RCD members and corruption within the party, some individuals who had defected from center-left secular parties to join Nidaa Tounes began to leave Nidaa as well.[34]

Despite recognizing such problems, many Nidaa Tounes members with secular-leftist political backgrounds defended the party as the sole vehicle capable of derailing Ennahda's electoral advance. In interviews with members of Nidaa's executive committee in the spring and summer of 2013, I routinely encountered self-described leftists who suggested that an implicit alliance with the ex-RCD was necessary and justifiable on the grounds that it would help combat the rise of Ennahda—which they described as a stubbornly "antimodernist" party, often using language reminiscent of the substance and style of "A propos d'une dérive." Mahmoud Ben Rhomdhane, a leftist who became one of Nidaa's chief economic advisors, said he opposed the RCD but felt realism was needed in the struggle against Ennahda: "Nidaa Tounes isn't the cleanest train . . . but it's the last train. It's the only train. If you want to reach the terminus of democracy, you've got to get on board. . . . Otherwise it will be Ennahda in power for the next two generations."[35]

Many staunch secularists and leftist-oriented leaders of Nidaa vowed that a purist secular party—one that would resolutely oppose entering into any coalition government with Ennahda—was needed. They described Ettakatol and CPR as pseudosecular sellouts who, by agreeing to participate in a coalition government with Ennahda, had betrayed their modernist principles. "Ettakatol claimed to be modernist, but then it went into coalition with Ennahda," said Mohsen Marzouk, a leftist-oriented former leader in Nidaa who headed the party's electoral campaign in the fall of 2014. "A lot of its supporters left. That's because they want a real modernist alternative. We are now that alternative."[36] Nidaa's opposition to cross-ideological coalition helped it achieve double victory in the fall 2014 parliamentary and presidential elections, as disillusioned voters hoped a sharp alternative might reverse the disappointments of the Ennahda-led Troika, which many perceived as having failed to provide security or economic stability to Tunisians.

OPPOSITION TO THE 2015 CROSS-IDEOLOGICAL COALITION

Despite its pre-electoral promises, Nidaa Tounes—which fell twenty-nine seats short of achieving a majority in Tunisia's 217-member parliament—ended up forging a fragile four-party coalition that included Ennahda, largely at the behest of ex-RCD pragmatists within the party who managed to override the voices of more ideologically purist secular leftists.[37] On February 2, 2015, following its first proposal of a noninclusive government composed of just two parties (Nidaa Tounes and the populist Free Patriotic Union party), the Nidaa-selected prime minister, Habib Essid, announced a revamped, more inclusive government that included a handful of posts for Ennahda members. Though Ennahda was granted just one of twenty-four ministries in the new cabinet, a vocal faction within Nidaa Tounes accused the party of betraying Tunisian democracy by accepting any Islamists at all.

Hamadi Redissi, a signatory of "A propos d'une dérive," was a well-known leftist and political scientist who enthusiastically supported Nidaa in a series of op-eds and interviews in 2013 and 2014. Five days after the Islamist-inclusive coalition government was announced, Redissi published a response in the well-known Tunisian political magazine *Leaders*. His op-ed, titled "Ennahda Enters the Government, Politicians Have Betrayed the People," excoriated what he perceived as Nidaa's hypocrisy and the fundamental untrustworthiness of Ennahda.

For months, the head of Nidaa Tounes [Beji Caid Essebsi] stressed that Nidaa and Ennahda were "two parallel lines," one eager to "return Tunisia to the twenty-first century," the other turning back "to the eighth century." . . . [Now] they sleep together in one bed. . . . This is blackmail. . . . Either the Islamists have converted to the identity of the nation and the rules of the civil state . . . or they threaten terror. . . . We cannot praise their civility and at the same time be wary of the Arab in them, always perfidious.[38]

Certain prominent feminist activists also wrote against the coalition government, arguing that the replacement of Khadija Cherif—an ATFD member and signatory of "A propos d'une dérive" who had been named minister of women in the first, noninclusive iteration of the Essid government— with a secular Afek Tounes member named Latifa Lakhdar represented a capitulation to conservatives.[39]

Vocal opposition to Ennahda's inclusion in the government also came from members of the Popular Front, a coalition of leftist and Arabist parties led by Hamma el-Hammami, two of whose MPs—Chokri Belaid, himself a signatory of "A propos d'une dérive" and a tenacious critic of Ennahda, and Mohamed Brahmi—had been assassinated by Tunisian jihadists in February and July 2013, respectively. El-Hammami, the only participant in the October 18 Collective to oppose Ennahda's inclusion in the government, grounded his party's position in accusations that Ennahda had supported, either directly or indirectly, the assassinations of Belaid and Brahmi.

For the most stalwartly anti-Islamist segment of Nidaa Tounes supporters, however, opposition to Ennahda's inclusion in the 2015 coalition had its origins in decades-old ideological prejudices and suspicions, some of which were echoed in "A propos d'une d'érive." Taieb Baccouche, a leftist and one of three vice presidents of Nidaa Tounes at the time, expressed sympathy with the frustrations of such stalwartly anti-Islamist Nidaa supporters. Immediately following the announcement of Ennahda's inclusion on February 2, 2015, Baccouche joined anticoalition protesters gathered in front of Nidaa Tounes's national headquarters in the Lac 1 neighborhood of Tunis, assuring them that he, too, wished the party had not gone into coalition with Islamists. "Excluding the Islamists was what we promised our voters," he later recounted. "They are backwards and can only pull us backwards . . . of course many people in Nidaa are extremely disappointed."[40]

NAHDAOUI PURISTS: CRAFTING CROSS-IDEOLOGICAL COMPROMISE AMONG ISLAMISTS

As Ahmed Nejib Chebbi correctly surmised in his 2006 rebuttal "Amorce d'un débat," Ennahda—the political actor most persecuted under Ben Ali—also stood to gain the most from cross-ideological coalition building before the revolution. Such coalition building helped destabilize the Ben Ali regime, laying groundwork for Ennahda's eventual political participation. But what about after the revolution, when a freshly empowered Ennahda could have sidelined its foes?[41] Predictions that Ennahda would adopt the Egyptian Muslim Brotherhood's more majoritarian approach were mistaken. Instead, key leaders in Ennahda, among them Rached Ghannouchi, the brothers Amr and Ali Laarayedh, Hamadi Jebali, and Rafiq Abdessalem, backed a long-term approach that prioritized pragmatism and self-constraining minimalism, even at the cost of angering its own supporters.[42]

As the sole Islamist party in a National Constituent Assembly composed mainly of centrists, secularists, and populists, Ennahda's margin of legislative maneuver was admittedly limited versus the Egyptian Brotherhood. The Brotherhood-backed Freedom and Justice Party handily won a plurality of votes in Egypt's 2011 parliamentary elections, producing a nearly two-thirds Islamist-controlled parliament when combined with seats won by the ultraconservative Salafi party Hizb al-Nour, which took second place. Ennahda's more minimalist approach to power, however, wasn't merely a response to weaker electoral gains. Ennahda helped set the stage for its electoral marginalization by supporting proportional representation (PR). Furthermore, core party leaders—especially Ghannouchi and his inner circle—seemed convinced even before the October 2011 elections that pursuing a coalition-friendly approach would help Ennahda, and Tunisia's transition, survive the democracy-reversing recoils that had followed Islamist electoral victories in Algeria in 1990 and 1991 and elsewhere in the region—including in Tunisia, after Ennahda-supported candidates' strong performance in the 1989 elections.[43]

Ennahda leaders' openness to entering into a cross-ideological coalition government was not a point of contention within the party during 2011, partially because electoral law at that time prevented parties formed by ex-RCD members from contesting elections. Nahdaouis I interviewed in the summer of 2011 generally felt that cooperation with existing parties would help Tunisia overcome its fearful aversion to Islamists and reduce the likelihood that old-regime policies, like the criminalization of Ennahda, could return. Unlike the purist wing of Tunisia's secular left, which opposed inclusion of Islamists on principle, Nahdaouis, who adopted more purist positions, did not voice opposition to dialoguing with secular leftists, signing on to coalitional documents alongside them, or even joining them in postrevolutionary coalitional governments. For Ennahda, including even the most conservative voices within its ranks, cross-ideological coalition building represented a self-preservational safeguard that could help prevent Tunisia from backsliding into another Ben Ali–era dictatorship, which persecuted Islamists by the thousands in the name of preserving Tunisian stability.[44]

However, opponents of compromise-driven politics certainly did and do exist within Ennahda. Many purist-oriented Nahdaouis in the party's base chafed against repeated compromises pushed through by their leaders on matters of both revolutionary and religious principle.[45] Their support for revolutionary principle—that is, rejection of the ex-RCD's return to political power—often led them to resent party leaders' rapprochement with elements of the old regime, including Beji Caid Essebsi. After months of agonizing and fierce internal debate, Ennahda opted to oppose a dangerous lustration law that would have excluded former RCD members, including President Essebsi himself, from running in the 2014 elections. Had it passed, the law would have sidelined many ex-RCDists and their supporters, possibly incentivizing them to form a disgruntled pro-coup coalition—something that would have toppled Tunisia's entire transition. Ultimately the lustration law dramatically failed to pass in the National

Constituent Assembly by just one vote: that of an Ennahda MP who had switched his vote of support to an abstention at the last minute. This proved a bitter pill for many Nahdaouis to swallow, especially Nahdaouis who strongly believed that ex-RCD members were inherently antidemocratic old-regime perpetrators who could never credibly moderate or uphold values of pluralism and human rights.[46]

Similarly, and despite mixed signals throughout much of 2012, Ennahda's leaders eventually coaxed the party's base to give up a constitutional article that would have criminalized blasphemy in clear, liberty-restricting terms. Ennahda leaders reverted to positions of more minimalist compromise on other religiously oriented issues, too, giving up over the course of constitutional drafting a preamble that would have directly referenced sharia and language that would have defined men and women's roles as "complementary" to one another within the family.[47]

Conceding to secular pressure did not always come easily to Ennahda, many of whose members felt the party deserved to advocate for what it believed to be the Tunisian people's true, long-suppressed Islamizing desires following decades of antidemocratic exclusion at the hands of so-called secular authoritarian regimes. During these years, tens of thousands of Ennahda members and their families were wrongfully arrested or imprisoned. Women who chose to wear the headscarf were frequently banned from attending school or university as well as from working at or receiving admittance into public institutions. Many frequently experienced degradation and harassment from police forces. Ennahda members experienced other sinister forms of abuse from the state: many were tortured, raped, forced to divorce their spouses, and/or blacklisted from employment or university attendance. Religious freedoms were also heavily circumscribed by the state. Under Ben Ali, police officers were stationed at mosques, Friday sermons often followed a regime-dictated script, and young men seen praying the dawn prayer at a mosque or sporting beards—actions identified with more conservative religiosity—were frequently arrested and harassed by police. After the revolution, many members of Ennahda felt the party had a special responsibility actively to recenter long-marginalized citizens and ideas. For many, this meant standing up more forcefully for principles of religious conservatism and political opposition to old-regime actors than Ennahda's leaders were prepared to do.

Drumming up support within Ennahda for compromise positions therefore often involved long periods of internal disagreement and prolonged dialogue, both among Ennahda's leaders and between leaders and the party's base. Early promises from key Nahdaoui leaders, including Ghannouchi himself, that the party would not seek to introduce sharia law, for example, rang hollow for many secularly inclined Tunisians, who saw some conservative figures within Ennahda, like the party's MPs Sadok Chorou and Habib Ellouze, reopen the sharia debate and push more maximalist positions.

In early 2012, Chorou and Ellouze encouraged Ennahda's primary decision-making body, the 150-member Shura Council, to consider inserting language into the new constitution recognizing sharia as a source of law. Chorou, Ellouze, and other members of Ennahda's Shura Council also sought to Islamize the purposefully vague language used in Article 1 of Tunisia's 1959 constitution and retained in subsequent iterations of the constitution, which described Tunisia as a free and sovereign state whose language is Arabic and religion is Islam. This language struck a delicate balance between conservative and liberal demands, since it could be interpreted as saying not that Tunisia is an Islamic state but rather that the religion of the majority of its citizens happens to be Islam—a sociological description rather than a legislative prescription. Though Ennahda's Shura Council rejected both propositions, the fact that prominent figures within the party succeeded in stirring up such debates—and therefore raised the possibility of referencing Sharia, which was something that Ghannouchi had promised the party would not do—reinforced the fears of many secularly oriented Tunisians. For many, such actions served as reminders that Ennahda was, at its core, a regressively conservative party whose promises to "convince, not coerce" Tunisians into adopting more religiously conservative lifestyles would at some point devolve into bald-faced legislative repression.[48]

More ideologically purist voices within Ennahda found it especially difficult to give up language inserted in the first draft of Tunisia's constitution (released on August 8, 2012) that would have criminalized "attacks on the sacred" (*tajrim muqadisaat*). Secular pushback within the National Constituent Assembly subcommittee that drafted the article, as well as sustained pressure from international human rights and constitutional advisory groups, ultimately convinced Nahdaouis that the constitution was not the appropriate place for such restrictive and rights-abusing language.[49] Fortunately the proposal to criminalize blasphemy—like ambiguous language that would have defined men and women's roles as "complementing one another within the family"—was dropped by the third draft of the constitution, released on April 23, 2013. Yet Ennahda, with the support of some other factions within the National Constituent Assembly, succeeded in keeping vague language that defines the Tunisian state as the guarantor of freedom of religion and protector of sacred things (*muqadisaat*). This signaled that, despite having made many compromises during and after the Troika period, Ennahda did not give its secularist critics all they had desired. Instead, Ennahda sometimes stubbornly pursued what its critics termed back-door channels, lobbying for the inclusion of less visible or more vaguely worded clauses that it might later use to justify the introduction of more conservatively oriented policies in the future.[50]

Ennahda's secular and leftist critics sometimes claimed its so-called compromises throughout the constitutional drafting process were insincere, part of a broader and highly manipulative "double discourse" that duped many Western researchers and journalists into viewing the party as genuinely committed to democracy. This duping effect was particularly pronounced among Anglophone researchers, they argued, because they championed a model of secularism that offered more freedom for religious expression than French laïcité. More purist Tunisian secularist-leftists, who embrace the French model of secularism, tended to view the Anglo-American model of secularism, which allows greater space for wearing religious symbols, for example, as dangerously naive.

Ennahda's critics were correct that its leaders sometimes pursued compromise positions because they viewed such compromises as strategically smart and better for the party's long-term survival and integration into Tunisia's political fabric and not out of ideological commitment to the positions themselves. Yet accusations that Ennahda's concessions were merely stage-managed posturings designed to dupe outside observers ignore important realities within the party. In fact, Ennahda's national and regional leaderships worked vigorously at all levels of the party—sometimes over the course of years—to convince party purists within its various leadership structures and its base that they should accept critical compromises. These compromises spanned a range of controversial matters that touched on both revolutionary and religious principles. To foster support for these compromises within the party, Ennahda's leaders marshaled a combination of arguments. Some rested on the logics of political pragmatism and strategic self-interest; others were grounded in Islamic principle and religious sources.[51]

Over the course of four years I spent based in Tunisia researching Ennahda's internal politics for my doctorate (2012–2016), I came to recognize a fascinating pattern play out again and again within the party. First, Ennahda's top leadership—represented principally by its Executive Committee and Shura Council—would consider adopting a position that was more pluralist than purist. Discussions on the matter would be held sometimes before, concurrently, or afterward within regional and local Ennahda offices. The purpose of these discussions was to solicit grassroots views and transmit those views upward, so that party leaders understood where the majority of base opinion stood. On especially controversial issues formal or additional Shura Council meetings would be held, in which all 150 Shura members would discuss, debate, and then vote on what position the party should adopt on an issue.

Shura discussions and votes took place, for example, on the matter of whether to include any references to sharia in the constitution, whether to criminalize blasphemy, whether Ennahda should support the lustration law, and whether it should enter 2015's cross-ideological coalition government. After the vote, representatives of the Shura Council—which is intended to function as a kind of representative parliamentary body within Ennahda—would then return to meet with their "constituents," as well as with regional party heads and representatives, who in turn met with the party's local office leaders to present and defend the rationales undergirding these compromises. This was an iterative, hugely time-consuming process. It often involved long question-and-answer sessions at local and regional offices, Ennahda youth gatherings, and other venues in which leaders fielded critical questions from disgruntled—and sometimes outright hostile—members of the base. Often but not always, grassroots supporters who initially opposed the leadership's compromises came to support the leadership's rationales.

For instance, some individuals I interviewed in Tataouine, a conservative southern region where Ennahda is very strong, in 2011 and early 2012 initially felt that sharia should be directly referenced in the constitution. However, by June 2013, these individuals had begun to internalize and repeat certain Islamically grounded arguments espoused by Ennahda's leadership that were transmitted down the ranks from the Shura Council, for instance, the argument that sharia is *shumuli*, or comprehensive enough, to encompass a constitution that adheres to principles of social justice without explicitly using the word "sharia" or including any *hudud* punishments. Another argument local leaders and base activists gradually adopted referenced the Caliph Omar, who, when exhorted to cut off the hand of a guilty thief, asked himself instead how he had failed in governance so that this man would resort to stealing in order to survive. The lesson of this illustration—employed frequently by Ennahda's national and regional leaders—was that government's primary responsibility should be providing socially and economically just conditions—in other words, broadly prioritizing Islam-inspired principles of good governance over specific, restrictive *hudud* punishments.

Faced with a parallel need to justify its own compromises—such as the February 2015 alliance with Ennahda—to its base, the anti-Islamist Nidaa Tounes party has experienced more difficulty. Transmitting rationales for cross-ideological compromise and coalition building among party leaders and between leaders and the base has proved more difficult for Nidaa Tounes in part because the party lacks strong representative structures capable of carrying out such top-to-bottom (and bottom-to-top) communication work. Frustrated and isolated, many secular and left-leaning purists within Nidaa have abandoned the party. Yet while such ideologically motivated defections have happened in Ennahda, they have been less common, especially at the regional and national leadership levels. This is true despite Ennahda members' deep dissatisfaction with many of their leaders' political and ideological concessions, especially the electoral inclusion of and outright coalition with ex-RCD members after 2014 and Ennahda's leaders' ongoing support for a proposed economic reconciliation law that would effectively amnesty old-regime officials. Other factors—including Ennahda's sense of tight-knit, even family-like solidarity, which developed over years of criminalization and pariah-like status in Tunisian society—have bound its supporters together even as their leaders pursue a path of compromise-oriented radical pragmatism that sometimes threatens the party's cohesion.[52]

Since Tunisia's 2011 revolution, Ennahda leaders have increasingly sought to paint the party as a center-right Tunisian version of the German Christian Democrats, a moderate party caught between two militantly ideological poles, "religious Salafis and secular Salafis," both of whom reject Ennahda's supposed centrism.[53] This is a self-serving portrayal that conveniently glosses over the existence of Ennahda's own ideological purists, some of whom would have likely sought a Brotherhood-style maximalist approach if Tunisia's Islamist factions had been as electorally successful as Egypt's. Yet Ennahda leaders do have a point when they remind observers that intransigently purist ideological currents exist on both sides of Tunisia's political aisle. Radically uncompromising Salafi currents, manifested in vocal and sometimes violent jihadi groups (ranging from Ansar al-Sharia and Hizb al-Tahrir to Oqba ibn Nafaa and other proto-ISIS groupings) gained traction in Tunisia following the revolution. These currents, along with some extreme slivers of Tunisia's quietist Salafi trend, represent the only conservative Islamists in Tunisia that wholeheartedly oppose dialogue and coalition building with secularists. Ennahda's casting of itself as friendly peacemaker pigeonholed between extremes is politically handy and can seem callously dismissive of the critical role that pluralist secularists—many of whom courageously confronted purist secularists to initiate and sustain a dialogue with them—played in crafting cross-ideological opposition to Ben Ali's regime, moving Tunisia's postrevolutionary transition forward, and helping Ennahda integrate itself as a normalized actor in Tunisian politics. It is, however, interesting to note that in the Tunisian context, individuals who completely reject cross-ideological coalition building between Islamists and secularists have tended to sit at the hard-Salafi and hard-secular extremes.

This brief examination of recent attempts at cross-ideological coalition building in Tunisia suggests it may be worthwhile to ask not just whether Ennahda has moved into what the scholar Asef Bayat termed a "post-Islamist" identity but also whether secularists in Tunisia have moved into what the philosopher Jürgen Habermas termed a "postsecularist" identity. In his 2006 reflection "Religion in the Public Sphere," Habermas defines a postsecular society as one "epistemically adjusted to the continued existence of religious communities." The postsecular society, he says, requires self-critical transcendence of rigidly secularist understandings of modernity—a change he describes as "no less cognitively exacting than the adaptation of religious awareness to the challenges of an ever more secularized environment."[54]

Indeed, the unspoken crux of Ennahda's argument with those it has termed "secular Salafis" revolves around the possibility of pluralizing Tunisian understandings of secularism to create, if not a Habermasian postsecular reality, then at least a post-laïque or poststate monopolization reality. In other words, a reality in which religion-restricting elements of French laïcité (which seeks to protect the state's freedom from religion) are replaced with a model of secularism that seeks to protect religion's freedom from the state (as is found in the United States) and in which Tunisia's history of top-down state manipulation and monopolization of religious authority is replaced with a model that gives more space for ground-up religious expression.[55] Multiple Ennahda leaders, including Rached Ghannouchi, have emphasized to me in interviews over the past four years that Ennahda "doesn't oppose secularism—it opposes laïcité."[56] Ennahda has attempted to introduce softer understandings of secularism closer to the Anglo-American model, thus pluralizing traditionally closed conversations in Tunisia over how to practice democracy and *modernité*, the mantle of which Nidaa Tounes has claimed while drawing on restrictive readings of French laïcité and on decades of paternalistic authoritarianism in Tunisia's recent history that saw so-called secular autocrats illiberally impose top-down policies to modernzie or "enlighten" the country.

Ultimately, cross-ideological dialogue in Tunisia has required proponents of pragmatic and pluralist ideals on both sides of the political spectrum to transcend the suspicions of more exclusionary purists within their ranks. More research is needed, though, on how and why some secularly oriented groups and leaders came to embrace pluralistic, antidictatorial coalition building and why others have, in Alfred Stepan's terms, acted as "constituencies for coercion" who sometimes lent indirect support to the preservation of authoritarian regimes by obstructing cross-ideological dialogue. More research is also needed on the varying and vibrant debates and interpretations of laïcité/secularism and its less controversial byword "modernity" in the MENA region and other Muslim-majority countries, on how and why secularism has sometimes been interpreted in more pluralism-expanding versus pluralism-contracting formulations, and on why the preponderance of Western scholarship regarding moderation theory in Muslim-majority contexts has centered on Islamist, rather than on secularly oriented or "modernist" actors.[57]

The story of Tunisia's thus far comparatively successful transition is not just a story of structural advantages or better-behaved Islamists; it is a story, too, of pluralist secularists willing to craft coalitions and talk across the table with Islamists. Concluding they might have more in common with ideologically opposed rivals than with the sitting dictatorial regime, these path-breaking liberal secularists helped initiate a series of trust-building, brainstorming dialogues that unified and empowered Tunisia's nascent opposition while also laying crucial intellectual and personal groundwork for cross-ideological coalitions formed after Tunisia's revolution. Their efforts helped destabilize Ben Ali's dictatorship and laid foundational planks for what John Rawls has termed an "overlapping consensus" for democracy, an effort that the October 18 Collective talks were explicitly supporting during the mid-to-late 2000s.[58]

NOTES

The author thanks the European Research Council's WAFAW program, which has supported her research through a doctoral fellowship.

1. Ennahda won sixty-nine of 217 total parliamentary seats, with 27.79 percent of the vote; its secular rival Nidaa Tounes won eighty seats, with 37.56 percent of the vote. On January 5, 2015, the newly elected president of Tunisia and founder of Nidaa Tounes Beji Caid Essebsi appointed Habib Essid, who held governmental posts under Zine el-Abidine Ben Ali as well as Caid Essebsi's 2011 transitional government and the Troika, head of government and asked him to form a cabinet.

2. Tunisia's government is composed of twenty-four ministerial seats and fifteen secretarial posts.

3. For more on the factors leading to the formation of this government, see Monica Marks, "Tunisia Opts for an Inclusive New Government," *Washington Post*, February 3, 2015, https://www.washingtonpost.com/news/monkey-cage/wp/2015/02/03/tunisia-opts-for -an-inclusive-new-government/.

4. Heba Saleh, "Tunisia Forms Coalition in Advance from Autocracy," *Financial Times*, February 2, 2015.

5. See Sharan Grewal, "Why Tunisia Didn't Follow Egypt's Path," *Washington Post*, February 4, 2015, https://www.washingtonpost.com/news/monkey-cage/wp/2015/02/04 /why-egypt-didnt-follow-tunisias-path/. Harvard University's Dr. Tarek Masoud stressed the importance of electoral outcomes in his remarks at Sciences-Po's "Whither the Arab World? Revisiting Democratic Transition Theory" conference in Paris, November 7, 2015.

6. See Shadi Hamid, *Temptations of Power: Islamists and Illiberal Democracy in a New Middle East* (Oxford: Oxford University Press, 2014); Anouar Boukhars, *The Reckoning: Tunisia's Perilous Path to Democratic Stability* (Carnegie Endowment, April 2015); Monica Marks, "How Egypt's Coup Really Affected Tunisia's Islamists," *Washington Post*, March 16, 2015, https://www.washingtonpost.com/news/monkey-cage/wp/2015/03/16 /how-egypts-coup-really-affected-tunisias-islamists/.

7. Chorou and Ellouze were both MPs in Tunisia's National Constituent Assembly but, in part because of pressure from Ennahda's leadership, did not run again as MPs for Ennahda in the 2014 parliamentary elections. Regarding Ghannouchi, see Larry Diamond, "Tunisia Is Still a Success," *Atlantic*, March 23, 2015. In Diamond's words, Ghannouchi "has, at every crucial turn on the sometimes troubled path from dictatorship, embraced flexibility and moderation." See also Noah Feldman, "A Peace Prize for Tunisia's Exceptionalism," *Bloomberg*, October 9, 2015.

8. For an excellent exploration of this topic, see Nathan Brown, "Official Islam in the Arab World: The Contest for Religious Authority," Carnegie Endowment, May 11, 2017.

9. For instance, when Tunisian prostitutes went on strike in the summer of 2012, the only member of parliament who met with them was Meherzia Labidi, a female Ennahda

MP. Similarly, in 2015 and 2016 Beji Caid Essebsi, the president of Tunisia and founding leader of Nidaa Tunis, a so-called secular party, strongly refused to decriminalize homosexuality, while Rached Ghannouchi, the cofounder and leader of Ennahda, publicly supported a softer "don't ask don't tell"–style position, saying the state does not have the right to intrude on people's privacy. Likewise, Ennahda supported legislation that required equal representation for women on party electoral lists, while some secularly oriented parties balked at the legislation, possibly because Ennahda, as a very large party, was more confident than smaller parties that they had enough female candidates to fill their lists. These are just a few of many examples.

10. Here I am discussing coalitions not merely in the parliamentary sense but in the broader sense of alliances and partnerships, such as the sort formed by the October 18 Collective discussed later in this chapter. It is important, too, to point out that during the years of Zine el-Abidine Ben Ali's rule, the best-organized opposition to cross-ideological coalition formation sprang from Ben Ali himself, who feared a united opposition might jeopardize his regime's survival.

11. Tunisia held a constitutional referendum in May 2002 abolishing the existing three-term limit for incumbent presidents and raising the age limit for incumbent presidents from seventy to seventy-five.

12. The "Appel de Tunis" laid out twelve democratic objectives for Tunisian society, the seventh of which was "the realization of equality [*tahqiq al-musaawa*] between citizens and especially between men and women."

13. Because of a French ban that restricted him from traveling to the country at the time, Rached Ghannouchi was not in attendance at these Aix-Marseille talks.

14. Mokhtar Yahyaoui, "Nida'a Tunis, Nida'a al-mustaqbal," part 1, May 2003.

15. Mokhtar Yahyaoui, "Nida'a Tunis, Nida'a al-mustaqbal" part 2, July 2003.

16. See Joshua S. Rogers, "There Is No Room for a Religious Party: Negotiating the Islamist Challenge to State Legitimacy in Tunisia, 1987–1991," master's thesis, Oxford University, 2007. See also Francesco Cavatorta and Fabio Merone, "Moderation Through Exclusion? The Journey of the Tunisian Ennahda from Fundamentalist to Conservative Party," *Democratization* 2, no. 5 (2013).

17. Beatrice Hibou, *The Force of Obedience: The Political Economy of Repression in Tunisia* (Polity, 2011).

18. The summit, titled the World Summit on the Information Society (WSIS), aimed to expand Internet access in the developing world but was marred by oppression of local human rights activists and international journalists covering the event.

19. See Collectif du 18 Octobre pour les Droits et les Libertés, "Communiqué de Presse," December 4, 2005.

20. "A propos d'une dérive," February, 2006.

21. Ahmed Najib Chebbi, "Amorce d'un débat," March 2006.

22. For instance, CPR and Ettakatol were arguably more willing to join the Islamist-led Troika coalition in 2011 because of a sense of familiarity and understanding had built up between these groups and Ennahda over the course of long talks during the 2000s.

23. French scholars, including Éric Gobe and Vincent Geisser, have tended to give more attention to the October 18 movement and related opposition talks. See Vincent Geisser and Eric Gobe, "Un si long règne . . . Le régime de Ben Ali vingt ans après," in *L'Année du Maghreb* (CNRS Éditions, 2008); Eric Gobe, "Les avocats tunisiens dans la Tunisie de Ben Ali: économie politique d'une profession juridique," *Droit et Société* 79 (2011).

24. Author interview, August 18, 2011.

25. Author interviews, 2011. For more on the distinctions between Salafis, see the work of Fabio Merone and Francesco Cavatorta. For instance, Fabio Merone and Francesco Cavatorta, "Salafist Mouvance and Sheikh-ism in the Tunisian Democratic Transition," Working Papers in International Studies, Dublin City University, 2012; Fabio Merone and Francesco Cavatorta, "The Emergence of Salafism in Tunisia," *Jadaliyya*, August 17, 2012.

26. See Monica Marks, "Who Are Tunisia's Salafis?" *Foreign Policy*, September 28, 2012.

27. The top five parties in Tunisia's 2011 National Constituent Assembly were Ennahda, with 89 seats; CPR, with 29 seats; Aridha Chaabia, with 26 seats; Ettakatol, with 20 seats; and PDP, with 16 seats.

28. See Alfred Stepan, "Tunisia's Transition and the Twin Tolerations," *Journal of Democracy*, April 2012; John M. Carey, "Why Tunisia Remains the Arab Spring's Best Bet," conference presentation for Dartmouth and IISS, September 9–11, 2013. For a discussion of the motivations behind Ennahda's support for proportional representation, see Marks, "How Egypt's Coup Really Affected Tunisia's Islamists."

29. Author interviews with members of Ettakatol, the Tajdid Movement, the Democratic Modernist Pole, the Tunisian Communist Workers' Party (POCT), and feminist associations including ATFD, December 2011 to August 2012.

30. PDM won five seats with 2.8% of the vote; PDP won 16 seats with 3.9% of the vote.

31. Author interview with Zeineb Turki, December 29, 2013.

32. Destourians identified with the presidency and modernist principles of Habib Bourguiba, the president of Tunisia from 1956 to 1987. For more on Tunisia's secularist parties, see Anne Wolf, "Can Secular Parties Lead the New Tunisia?" Carnegie Endowment, April 2014.

33. Author interviews in Beja, Gafsa, Jendouba, and Sidi Bouzid governorates, November 2012 to February 2013.

34. Author conversations with former MPs in Ettakatol and PDP, 2012–2013. Slim Ben Abdessalem, an Ettakatol MP who joined then left Nidaa, discussed his reasons for leaving the party in an interview with the BBC's Owen Bennet Jones in November 2014. See "Tunisia After the Revolution," *BBC*, November 17, 2014.

35. Interview with author, March 20, 2013. Quoted also in Monica Marks and Omar Belhaj Salah, "Uniting for Tunisia?" *Sada*, Carnegie Endowment, March 28, 2013.

36. Author interview with Mohsen Marzouk, March 13, 2013. Marzouk left Nidaa Tounes to form his own party, Hizb Meshru'a Tunis (Tunisia Project Party), in March 2016, citing a lack of internal democracy and the outsized role of Essebsi's son, Hafedh Caid Essebsi, within the party.

37. See Marks, "Tunisia Opts for an Inclusive New Government."

38. Hamadi Redissi, "Ennahdha entre au gouvernement. Les politiques ont trahi le peuple," *Leaders*, February 7, 2015.

39. Sophie Bessis, "Khadija Cherif, la femme qui fait peur au pouvoir tunisien," *Le Monde*, February 9, 2015. Though Latifa Lakhdar was among the signatories of "A propos d'une dérive," she did not publically oppose Ennahda's inclusion in the 2015 coalition government.

40. Author interview with Taieb Baccouche, July 2015.

41. Ennahda leaders have sometimes claimed they had the option of refusing to enter into coalition with secular parties following the October 2011 election but that they wisely opted to do so because they were genuinely committed to cross-ideological dialogue and democratic institution building. This is technically correct. Following the 2011 election, Ennahda could have created a highly fragile two-party coalition comprising itself and the populist party Aridha Chaabia, which won twenty-six seats and whose members, while not perceived as Islamist, frequently voted to the right of Ennahda in the National Constituent Assembly. Together, that two-party coalition would have had 115 votes—six more than needed to secure a majority. However, Aridha's unpredictably volatile nature—combined with its reputation as an unserious upstart—rendered that option all but absurd for Ennahda.

42. For more on explanations for Ennahda's strategy of minimalism, see Monica Marks, "Tunisia's Ennahda: Rethinking Islamism in the Context of ISIS and the Egyptian Coup," Brookings Institution, August 2015. See Monica Marks, "Why Do Tunisia's Islamists Support an Unpopular Law Forgiving Corruption?" *Washington Post*, May 5, 2017, https://www.washingtonpost.com/news/monkey-cage/wp/2017/05/05/why-do-tunisias-islamists-support-an-unpopular-law-forgiving-corruption/.

43. The Islamic Salvation Front's (FIS) dominance in municipal and the first round of parliamentary elections spooked the Algerian regime, which cancelled elections and initiated a broad crackdown against Islamists. I have referred to Algeria's experience as a "touchstone moment" shaping Ennahda's minimalism. See Marks, "Tunisia Opts for an Inclusive New Government." For more on Algeria's 1990–1991 elections and Tunisia's 1989 elections, see Francois Burgat and William Dowell, *The Islamic Movement in North Africa* (Austin: University of Texas Press, 1997); Emma Murphy, *Economic and Political Change in Tunisia: From Bourguiba to Ben Ali* (New York: Palgrave Macmillan, 1989).

44. See Monica Marks, "Islamism in Transition: Compromise and Contention Inside Tunisia's Ennahda After the Revolution," doctoral dissertation, Oxford University.

45. Ibid. See also Marks, "Tunisia's Ennahda."

46. See Marks, "Tunisia's Ennahda."

47. See Monica Marks, "Convince, Coerce, or Compromise? Ennahda's Approach to Tunisia's Constitution," Brookings Institution, February 10, 2014.

48. Ibid. See also Rory McCarthy, "Protecting the Sacred: Tunisia's Islamist Movement Ennahda and the Challenge of Free Speech," *British Journal of Middle Eastern Studies* (2015).

49. Marks, "Convince, Coerce, or Compromise?"

50. This language exists in Article 6 of the final constitutional draft, completed in January 2014. Rights groups allege the language could allow Tunisia's leaders constitutional justification in silencing free speech, censoring supposedly "blasphemous" statements which it feels endanger the so-called sacred things.

51. This story of internal contention, compromise, and evolution—namely, the story of how Ennahda leaders managed to make core compromises on religious and revolutionary issues while preserving party cohesion—is in large part the focus of my PhD dissertation, cited above, which I am currently completing at Oxford University.

52. See Monica Marks, "Why Do Tunisia's Islamists Support an Unpopular Law Forgiving Corruption?" *Washington Post*, May 5, 2017; Monica Marks, "Letting Go of Every Principle: Tunisia's Democratic Gains Under Threat," *Middle East Eye*, July 23, 2017.

53. Author interviews with Ennahda leaders, 2011–2016.

54. Jürgen Habermas, "Religion in the Public Sphere," *European Journal of Philosophy* 14, no. 1 (2006).

55. See Alfred Stepan, "The Multiple Secularisms of Modern Democratic and Nondemocratic Regimes," paper presented at the American Political Science Association (APSA) meeting in Washington, D.C., September 2–5, 2010.

56. Author interviews with Rached Ghannouchi and other Ennahda leaders, 2011–2016.

57. Secularism (*al-'almaniya*) possesses controversial connotations in Arabic, as it is frequently associated both with atheism and with what are perceived to be Western or colonially imported ideas, often understood as denigrating religion. Secularists in Tunisia often use the word "modern" or "modernity" instead. Nidaa Tounes, for instance, used this word frequently in its electoral campaigns during the fall of 2014.

58. See John Rawls, *Political Liberalism* (New York: Columbia University Press, 1993).

6

PATTERNS OF CIVIL-MILITARY RELATIONS AND THEIR LEGACIES FOR DEMOCRATIZATION

Egypt Versus Tunisia

HICHAM BOU NASSIF

S EVEN YEARS AFTER the 2011 Arab uprisings, the transition to democracy has stalled in Egypt, whereas it appears to be consolidating in Tunisia. After a year of civilian rule under the Muslim Brotherhood, the 2013 military coup brought the generals back to power in Cairo. By contrast, the Tunisian generals refrained from threatening the fledgling democratic experience in their country. When the Zine al-Abidin Ben Ali regime collapsed, the top brass did not rush to fill the void. Nor did the generals use Ennahda's Islamist triumph in the first post–Ben Ali democratic elections as an alibi to annul the popular vote and seize power, thus eschewing the 1992 Algerian model. Finally, despite persisting tension throughout Ennahda's years in power, the military remained neutral and allowed Tunisia's political dynamics to unfold freely. This chapter revolves around the following question: Why did the military in Egypt stage a coup that ended the post-Mubarak experience with democracy whereas it remained supportive of democratization in Tunisia? To explain this difference, I compare civil-military relations in both Egypt and Tunisia and argue that legacies predating the Arab Spring structured the political role of the armed forces in the wake of the 2011 turning point.

In his classic work on the Brazilian military, Alfred Stepan argued that coups must be studied within the larger framework of the overall political system because armed forces are not an autonomous actor but a subsystem not immune to the influence of dynamics unfolding on the political scene.[1] This means in effect that greater degrees of polarization among a society's leading political factions should be correlated with higher risks of military interventionism. Consequently, probing why the military intervened in post-Mubarak Egypt but not in post–Ben Ali Tunisia requires investigating the interaction between, on the one hand, the Islamist and the non-Islamist parties in Egypt and Tunisia and, on the other, the correlation of force and mutual perceptions between civilian and military actors. In this volume, Rached Ghannouchi, Alfred Stepan, and Monica Marks document substantive and continuous dialogue between Ennahda and two important secular parties, the Congress for the Republic and Ettakatol, involving mutual accommodation, enduring coalition building, and growing agreement about how to create a consensual democracy. Nothing comparable to this happened in Egypt, as the chapters by Carrie Wickham and Nathan Brown in this volume make clear. This divergence should be kept in mind as we ponder the agency of the armed forces in both countries. Clearly, the extreme polarization pitting secular liberals and leftists against the Muslim Brotherhood contributed to setting the stage for the 2013 coup by signaling to the military that a putsch would be applauded by Egyptian factions with undeniable popular legitimacy. By contrast, Ennahda's ability to build a coalition with secular forces indicated to any potential coup maker that a putsch would lack the support of any significant Tunisian party. That said, while we cannot study putsches absent the political conditions surrounding them, neither can we neglect patterns of civil-military relations, military institutional cultures, and their effects on coup making. The aim of this contribution is to complement the previously mentioned chapters in this volume by contrasting the radically different legacies of civil-military relations in Egypt and Tunisia. I argue that entrenched self-perceptions within the armed forces contributed to renewed military authoritarianism in Egypt and democratic consolidation unimpeded by the military in Tunisia.

From the early independence years until 2011, democracy remained elusive in both Egypt and Tunisia. Yet the type of autocratic rule in the two countries differed fundamentally. Egypt was a classic case of Third World military dictatorship for almost two decades under Gamal Abdul Nasser (1952–1970). Whereas some civilianization began progressively in the late 1960s and later reached an advanced stage under Mubarak, the military nonetheless remained the fundamental pillar of the successive Egyptian regimes. That the Ministry of the Interior rose in power during the last years of Mubarak's rule is true, but the security establishment never overshadowed the armed forces. Tunisia, by contrast, was a civilian dictatorship. From al-Habib Bourguiba to Ben Ali, the power brokers were the ruling party and the security services under the control of the Ministry of the Interior. To be sure, the top brass did hope to become less marginal when Ben Ali, a former military general, seized power in 1987, but their optimism quickly proved baseless.[2] These divergent trajectories setting military politics apart in Egypt and Tunisia spawned distinct corporate ethos: the institutional culture entrenched among Egyptian officers is militaristic and paternalistic; that of their Tunisian counterparts is professional and republican. This distinction is fundamental to understanding the divergence of the militaries' political agency in post-2011 Egypt and Tunisia.

First, I begin with a brief comparison of civil-military relations in Egypt and Tunisia throughout the foundational postindependence years. The legacies of civil-military relations in both countries have proved path dependent; probing military politics during the tenures of Nasser and Bourguiba respectively in Egypt and Tunisia is essential to understanding their subsequent evolution. Second, I contrast the material privileges of the Egyptian military elite with the financial distress of their counterparts in Tunisia and the Tunisian armed forces at large. Finally, I study the positive incentives behind the 2013 coup in Egypt and contrast them to the absence of such incentives for a coup in Tunisia.

NASSER, BOURGUIBA, AND THE MILITARY: THE ROOTS OF DIVERGENCE

Nasser used the armed forces to consolidate his rule; Bourguiba relegated the military to the political margins. This observation may seem too obvious, but it is the primary point of departure for the contradistinction between the Egyptian and Tunisian armed forces. Three fundamental factors need to be taken into consideration in this regard: (1) Nasser was an officer; Bourguiba was a civilian with strong antimilitarist views. (2) As an obscure midranking officer in the armed forces, Nasser had no popular legitimacy when he seized power in 1952; the armed forces were his only support base. By contrast, Bourguiba was highly popular as the prominent figure of his country's struggle for independence by the time he became president in 1957. (3) Nasser had no political machinery to mobilize support, whereas Bourguiba led a relatively well-organized party, the Neo-Destour.

These factors combined to free Bourguiba, but not Nasser, from dependency on the armed forces as they struggled to consolidate their respective regimes. The Tunisian leader used his leeway as his country's popular first president to subdue the officers, enforce obedience to civilian rule, and keep the military away from politics. In the crucial issue of development—the central concern of newly independent nations following decolonization— Bourguiba gave the military no role to play; pushing Tunisia forward was the mission of the party, not the armed forces. Nor did Bourguiba promote the economic interests of Tunisian generals. Finally, Bourguiba adamantly refused to send Tunisian officers to train in Egypt and Iraq, the leading Arab countries of the time, let alone states from the former Soviet bloc. Rather, he dispatched cadets to military schools in France and the United States. Bourguiba worried about military activism, and the participation of a small group of officers in a plot to overthrow his regime in 1962 seemed to corroborate his suspicions.[3] Still, the ethos pervasive in the Tunisian armed forces throughout the formative years of Bourguiba's long tenure was inherently apolitical.[4]

Nasser's model of civil-military relations was radically different. Under the monarchy, the armed forces' intervention in political matters was strictly forbidden. King Farouk was keen on being popular among his soldiers, but he gave the military no political role to play. In addition, the liberal Wafd Party, Egypt's premier political organization until 1952, was a staunch opponent of officers' intervention in politics. Thus, the two centers of power in prerevolutionary Egypt agreed on keeping the military outside the political arena, even though they frequently disagreed on practically everything else. This picture was turned upside down when Farouk was toppled. The populist orientation of Egypt's new rulers was strategically aimed at giving them the legitimacy they lacked while simultaneously providing an alibi to remain in power. More importantly, it wedded the military to their rule by transmuting the armed forces into a tool of social transformation. Agrarian reform was a case in point: scores of officers were active within the bureaucracy charged with implementing governmental policies aimed at ameliorating the lot of the Egyptian peasantry. In fact, the Higher Committee for the Liquidation of Feudalists set up in 1966 to confiscate and redistribute properties belonging to the landed upper class, the backbone of the ruling elite under the monarchy, was headed by none other than Field Marshall Abdel Hakim Amer, commander of the armed forces.[5] Officers also occupied positions in the bureaucracy that built the Aswan Dam, probably the greatest state-led project in the recent history of Egypt.[6] As the state embarked on comprehensive development programs, including industrialization projects and gigantic housing and public transportation plans, it counted on the military to provide technological expertise and bureaucratic supervision. Furthermore, as Nasser became the most prominent Arab leader of his time and the champion of the pan-Arab cause after the nationalization of the Suez Canal in 1956, the armed forces were no longer hailed as the shield of Egypt alone but as that of the whole Arab world. The Nasserite regime derived its legitimacy from narratives of national liberation militancy and interventionism focused on redistribution, all placing the armed forces at the center of the state's efforts to defend Egypt's independence and promote social justice.

In addition, Nasser gave the officers a stake in his regime by actively promoting their privileges. Nasser recruited heavily from the Free Officers to fill ministerial positions; eight of the nine members of the Free Officers' revolutionary council were appointed in the government he formed in 1954.[7] Besides serving as ministers, officers were heavily represented in the diplomatic corps and in governors' positions.[8] They were appointed to top positions in the nationalized enterprises.[9] When Chams Badran became minister of defense in 1966, he sent a memo to all public administrations and companies forbidding them from filling vacant positions absent a prior authorization from the commander of the armed forces, Abdel Hakim Amer. The latter would only agree to appoint civilians only if he had no military candidates in mind for job openings.[10] Throughout Nasser's years in power, a small coterie of high-ranking officers controlled the key positions in the Egyptian state and kept an unchallenged grip on them. The Egyptian political scientist Anouar Abdel-Malek maintains that 1,500 former officers were appointed in top nonmilitary positions between 1952 and 1964.[11] According to Eliezer Be'eri, the number is closer to one thousand.[12] Either way, it is clear that a military career remained the most privileged route for recruitment into ministerial and bureaucratic elites from the beginning of the Nasserite era to its demise.[13]

To be sure, after the 1967 debacle, an effort was made to professionalize the armed forces and shield them from the worst consequences of the extreme politicization of the 1950s and 1960s. Depoliticization continued under the Sadat and the Mubarak regimes, both of which were more civilianized than Nasser's. That said, two features inherited from the Nasserite era persisted. First, the messianic corporate ethos of the military became entrenched. The Nasserite discourse sanctified the armed forces as the custodians of the nation and the reservoir of Egyptian nationalism. Officers were taught that the military is the spinal column of Egypt.[14] When a decadent king and corrupt political parties had brought the country to its knees, the armed forces believed that they acted in 1952 to set Egypt on the path of modernization at home and glory abroad. But though they intervened in politics, they believed that they remained in fact above politics because they are dedicated to the nation's higher purposes. By contrast, politicians act upon short-term political exigencies. As such, the armed forces cannot remain neutral when political and social conflicts threaten a nation of which they perceive themselves to be the ultimate curators; rather, they do what they deem necessary to neutralize the menace. A corollary to this perception is the right of the armed forces to choose from within their upper echelons Egypt's presidents. Since the military is the custodian of the nation, it is only consistent with the armed forces' calling that the president hails from its ranks. Second, the economic interests of the top brass were upheld by Sadat and Mubarak, just as they were by Nasser. From the officers' perspective, their privileges are a natural entitlement; whatever serves the officer corps serves the armed forces and is good, by extension, for the Egyptian state.

THE EGYPTIAN AND THE TUNISIAN MILITARIES IN 2011

A detailed study of the Egyptian military elites' privileges in opposition to the distress of the Tunisian armed forces goes beyond the limits of this chapter. Suffice it to pinpoint three fundamental dimensions pertaining to financial health, regime patronage, and the armed forces' relationship to the presidency—the center of power in both countries. For all the talk of the security services rising in prominence in Egypt, the part allocated to the Ministry of the Interior in the national budget remained inferior to that of the Ministry of Defense. In other words, the armed forces as an institution were never financially eclipsed by their competitors in the coercive apparatus under the Mubarak regime, as shown by figure 6.1.

The opposite is true in Tunisia, where the armed forces were starved for resources. Officers complained bitterly about their equipment becoming obsolete; the lack of basic necessities, such as sleeping bags for their troops; and an overall insufficient number of recruits—all to no avail.[15] Throughout the Ben Ali years, the military was never provided with the financial resources it lobbied the regime for. In the interinstitutional squabble for greater shares of the budget, the military was systematically outshone by the Ministry of the Interior and its myriad security agencies, as shown by table 6.1.

Two additional factors beyond budgets need to be taken into consideration. First, the armed forces in Egypt run an economic empire. The major military bodies engaged in economic activities—that is, the Ministry of Military Production, the Arab Industrial Organization (AIO), and the National Service Projects Organization (NSPO)—operate, together,

Annual Defense Budget

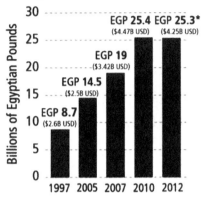

Annual Interior Ministry Budget

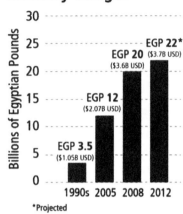

FIGURE 6.1

The Annual Defense Budget of the Ministry of Defense and
the Ministry of Interior in Egypt

Source: Yezid Sayigh, "Above the State: The Officers' Republic in Egypt,"
Carnegie Report, August 2012.

thirty-five factories and farms. Retired officers occupy hundreds of mana-
gerial positions in what Robert Springborg labels "Military, Inc.," and
thus have ample opportunities to enrich themselves unhindered by moni-
toring agencies—allegedly, because military-controlled business is a matter
of national security. No such privilege is bestowed upon the Tunisian armed
forces. A comparison of military elites' postretirement careers in both
countries shows the extent to which the Egyptian top brass benefited from
the largesse of the Mubarak regime, whereas their Tunisian counterparts
were neglected by Ben Ali's. The highly sought-after gubernatorial appointments were a case in point. Tables 6.2 and 6.3 pertain to the professional
backgrounds of governors appointed under Mubarak and Ben Ali; whereas
Egyptian officers reaped the lion's share of such appointments, the number
of Tunisian governors with military backgrounds was close to zero. Tables
6.4 through 6.8 contain data on the second careers of some of Egypt's and

TABLE 6.1 ANNUAL DEFENSE BUDGET OF THE TUNISIAN MINISTRY OF DEFENSE AND MINISTRY OF INTERIOR

YEAR	TOTAL BUDGET (MILLIONS OF TUNISIAN DINARS)	BUDGET ALLOCATED TO THE MINISTRY OF INTERIOR (MILLIONS OF DINARS)	PERCENTAGE OF TOTAL BUDGET ALLOCATED TO INTERIOR	BUDGET ALLOCATED TO THE MINISTRY OF DEFENSE (MILLIONS OF DINARS)	PERCENTAGE OF TOTAL BUDGET ALLOCATED TO DEFENSE
2000	10,510	623	5.9%	435	4.1%
2001	10,820	621	5.7%	453	4.1%
2002	11,533	650	5.6%	478	4.1%
2003	11,410	697	6.1%	510	4.4%
2004	12,730	739	5.8%	542	4.2%
2005	12,990	718	5.5%	469	3.6%
2006	13,552	817	6%	582	4.2%
2007	14,360	858	5.6%	612	4.2%
2008	15,242	869	5.7%	559	3.6%
2009	17,106	1,031	6%	720	4.2%
2010	18,235	1,106	6%	772	4.2%
2011	19,067	1,245	6.5%	828	4.3%

Tunisia's most prominent officers under Mubarak and Ben Ali. They convey the same message as tables 6.2 and 6.3.

The armed forces' institutional cultures and self-perceptions in Egypt and Tunisia differed fundamentally. The two militaries also diverged in terms of access to prized civilian appointments and financial resources. I now probe how this divergence shaped the political agency of the militaries in both countries.

THE GENERALS AND THE POST-2011 DEMOCRATIC EXPERIENCE

That the Tunisian military would not seize power after the fall of the Ben Ali regime is in accordance with its corporate ethos. Every officer I met

TABLE 6.2 THE PROFESSIONAL BACKGROUND OF GOVERNORS UNDER MUBARAK AND BEN ALI BY DECADE

	MUBARAK: 1981–1989	BEN ALI: 1987–1990	MUBARAK: 1990–1999	BEN ALI: 1991–2000	MUBARAK: 1990–2011	BEN ALI: 2001–2010	TOTAL
Military officers	9/30 (30%)	1/20 (5%)	28/67 (42%)	2/64 (3%)	26/59 (44%)	0/52 (0%)	40% vs. 2%
Police officers	11/30 (37%)	0/20 (0%)	11/67 (16%)	1/64 (2%)	12/59 (20%)	0/52 (0%)	22% vs. 1%
Civilians	10/30 (33%)	19/20 (95%)	28/67 (42%)	61/64 (95%)	21/59 (36%)	52/52 (100%)	38% vs. 97%

TABLE 6.3 SECOND CAREERS OF NAVY COMMANDERS
UNDER MUBARAK BY DECADE

1981–1989		1990–1999		2000–2011	
NAME	POSITION AFTER RETIREMENT	NAME	POSITION AFTER RETIREMENT	NAME	POSITION AFTER RETIREMENT
Farouq Younes	No civilian position after retirement	Ahmad Fadel	President of the Suez Canal Authority (1996)	Tamer ʿAbd al-ʿalim	President of the National Navigation Company (2008)
Cherif al-Sadiq	No civilian position after retirement	Ahmad Saber	President of the National Navigation Company (2001)	Mohab Mimich	Active duty as of February 2011, Commander of the Navy

TABLE 6.4 SECOND CAREERS OF THIRD FIELD ARMY COMMANDERS UNDER MUBARAK BY DECADE

1981–1990		1990–2000		2000–2011	
NAME	POSITION AFTER RETIREMENT	NAME	POSITION AFTER RETIREMENT	NAME	POSITION AFTER RETIREMENT
Qadri 'Othman Badr	Governor, Aswan (1984)	Kamal Ahmad 'Amer	Governor, Matrouh (1997) and Aswan (1999)	Ahmad Moukhtar Fathi Salama	Governor, al-Wadi al-Gidid (2008)
Hassan al-Zayyat	No civilian position after retirement	Abou Bakr al-Richidi	Governor, al-Wadi al-Gidid (2004) and Red Sea (2006)	Sa'ad Mouhammad Khalil	Governor, al-Wadi al-Gidid (2006) and Matrouh (2008)
'Ali Ahmad Saleh	No civilian position after retirement	Abou Bakr al-Gindi	Director of the National Statistics Bureau (2005)	'Adel Amara	Active duty as of February 2011, SCAF
'Adel al-Kadi	No civilian position after retirement			Mohammad Saber 'Atiah	Active duty as of February 2011, Chief of Operations
Salah Halabi	Retired as Chief of Staff			Soudki Soubhi	Active duty as of January 2011, Commander of the TFA

TABLE 6.5 SECOND CAREERS OF AIR FORCE COMMANDERS UNDER MUBARAK BY DECADE

1981–1990		1990–2000		2000–2011	
NAME	POSITION AFTER RETIREMENT	NAME	POSITION AFTER RETIREMENT	NAME	POSITION AFTER RETIREMENT
Mahmoud Chabana	Ambassador to Switzerland (1982)	Ahmad 'Abdel Rahman Nasr	No civilian position after retirement	Magdi Jalal Cha'araoui	Ambassador to Switzerland (2008)
Mohammad 'Abdel Hamid al-Chahat	Governor, Matrouh (2001–2006)	Ahmad Chafiq	Minister of Civil Aviation (2002); Prime Minister (2011)	Rida Mahmoud Hafiz	Active duty as of February 2011, Commander of the Air Force
'Alaa' Barakat	Ambassador to Spain (1990)				

TABLE 6.6 SECOND CAREER OF THE TUNISIAN NAVY CHIEFS OF STAFF UNDER BEN ALI BY DECADE

1987–1990		1990–2000		2000–2011	
NAME	POSITION AFTER RETIREMENT	NAME	POSITION AFTER RETIREMENT	NAME	POSITION AFTER RETIREMENT
Chadli Cherif	No civilian position after retirement from the military	Ibrahim Barrak	No civilian position after retirement from the military	Tarek al-'Arabi	Active service as of January 2011

TABLE 6.7 SECOND CAREER OF THE TUNISIAN AIR FORCE CHIEFS OF STAFF UNDER BEN ALI BY DECADE

1987–1990		1990–2000		2000–2011	
NAME	POSITION AFTER RETIREMENT	NAME	POSITION AFTER RETIREMENT	NAME	POSITION AFTER RETIREMENT
Rida 'Attar	No civilian position after retirement from the military			Mahmoud Bin Mohammad	No civilian position after retirement from the military
				Attayib Aloujeimi	Active service as of January 2011

while researching the Tunisian armed forces expressed pride in *la spécificité tunisienne*, the tradition of a republican military respectful of civilian rule in a region plagued with military interventionism.[16] Simply put, the Tunisian officers perceive putsches to be incompatible with military honor. In addition, as previously made clear, the members of the top brass do not

TABLE 6.8 SECOND CAREER OF THE TUNISIAN ARMY CHIEFS OF STAFF UNDER BEN ALI BY DECADE

1987–1990		1990–2000		2000–2011	
NAME	POSITION AFTER RETIREMENT	NAME	POSITION AFTER RETIREMENT	NAME	POSITION AFTER RETIREMENT
Mohammad Sa'id al-Kateb (1987–1990)	Ambassador to Cameroon	Mohammad al-Hadi Bin Hassine (1990–2001)	Director of the National Security Agency	Rachid 'Ammar (2002–Present)	Active duty as of January 2011, Chief of Staff of the Army
		Abd al-Aziz Skik (2001–2002)	Died in helicopter crash		

have an economic agglomerate or prized appointments in the bureaucracy to protect. Nor could the military count on civilian support to topple Ennahda. The combination of all these factors meant that the military would confine itself to the barracks while Tunisia labored to consolidate its nascent democracy.

The dynamics at play in Egypt were more complicated. Following Mubarak's fall from power, the Egyptian military elite sought to enshrine three corporate privileges in the constitution. First, the top brass wanted to ensure the independence of the military from civilian oversight agencies. In effect, this demand meant that the military rejected parliamentary control over the military-run economic sector and the military budget. Nor would they accept the appointment of a civilian as minister of defense. Second, the military sought the establishment of a National Defense Council, with wide prerogatives on matters pertaining to national security and stacked with top brass. Third, the generals aimed to consolidate the power of the armed forces to try civilians in military tribunals. These demands were present in one form or another throughout the different attempts at constitutional engineering during the transitional period that followed the fall of Mubarak in February 2011 and preceded the election of the Brotherhood's Mohammad Morsi to the presidency in June 2012, when the Supreme Council of the Armed Forces (SCAF) was in direct control of Egypt.[17] They were endorsed by the December 2012 constitution approved under Morsi.[18] The Muslim Brothers believed that accommodating the generals' corporate demands would facilitate the military's exit from politics and, by doing so, promote civilian control of the armed forces. Following its concessions to the top brass, the Brotherhood was convinced that the military elite would remain henceforth politically neutral, "having accepted a 'professional' role in a civilian-led political system."[19] So cordial was the newly found entente between the generals and the Brotherhood during the first weeks under Morsi that opposition activists and writers scolded the top brass for selling out to the Brotherhood after securing their own interests.[20] But considering how accommodating the Brotherhood proved to be, why did the military stage a coup a year later?

A MATERIAL INCENTIVES–BASED EXPLANATION OF THE 2013 MILITARY COUP

Did the generals feel threatened by the Brotherhood even after the vote on the constitution enshrined their core demands? This is a legitimate question, bearing in mind that the Brotherhood's electoral prowess allowed them to score one victory after another and to dominate the post-Mubarak political scene. By the time Morsi formed his first government in August 2012, the Brotherhood had come to control the two chambers of parliament, the presidency, and the premiership. A Brotherhood onslaught on the bureaucracy appeared inevitable, and Egypt was awash in talk about *Akhwanat al-dawla*, the "Brotherization of the state." The rumors were not unfounded. The Brotherhood did open the doors of the bureaucracy to their adherents; hundreds of members and supporters were appointed in different sectors of the bureaucracy, including in the upper echelons.[21] But the question of interest to this study is whether the Brotherhood expanded at the expense of the generals.

My findings pertaining to appointments in local government suggest that the Brotherhood did not significantly reduce the senior officers' share of governors' appointments. Fifteen of the forty-three (that is, 35 percent) governors appointed under Morsi hailed from the armed forces.[22] Nor did the share of the generals' appointments in the bureaucracy suffer, although the Brotherhood captured many top bureaucratic positions in several ministries, namely, the Ministry of Finance, Higher Education, Transportation, Commerce, Health, and Housing and Urban Development.[23] It is beyond the purpose and limits of this study to expand on the data I gathered pertaining to the Brotherhood's appointment strategy in the bureaucracy. Suffice it to say that the Brotherhood tended prudently to place their supporters in positions already occupied by civilians rather than replace generals-turned-bureaucrats with their own adherents. The Ministry of Transportation is a case in point. Both technocrats who headed the ministry under Morsi were senior members of the Muslim Brotherhood; they appointed tens of fellow Brotherhood affiliates as councilors and directors in the ministry.[24] Yet the Brotherhood did not encroach on the military elite's sinecures in maritime transport, famous for being the traditional fiefdom of admirals and generals retired from the Egyptian navy. The most senior positions traditionally allocated to the military elite are the chairmanships of the Maritime Transport Sector, the Maritime Security Committee, the Suez Canal Authority, the Alexandria Port, the Damietta Port, the Port-Said Port, and the Red Sea Port. All these positions were still occupied by retired officers throughout Morsi's tenure, namely, Major General al-Sayed Hidaya, Major General Ibrahim Fleifel, Vice Admiral Mohab Mmich, Major General 'Adel Yassin Hammad, Major General Sami Mahmoud, Major General Ahmad Sharaf, and Major General Mohammad 'Abdul Qader Jab Allah.[25] The overall picture of *Akhwanat al-dawla* versus militarization of the public sector shows that the Muslim Brotherhood's appointees were advancing in both local government and the bureaucracy while the generals were keeping their bureaucratic strongholds nearly intact.

Nor did the Brotherhood threaten the armed forces' economic empire or appear determined to prosecute corrupt generals. The data I collected so far tentatively suggests that nothing in the Brotherhood's governance style posed an immediate menace to the generals' financial interests. In effect, the Brotherhood did not act as a reformist party but as a newcomer eager to accommodate the power elite—and thus be allowed to join their circle. It could be argued, of course, that the top brass acted preventively by undercutting the Brotherhood before they mustered enough power to pose a threat. Or it may be that political and ideological considerations played a greater role in pushing the generals to act than financial incentives.

AN IDEOLOGICAL INCENTIVES–BASED EXPLANATION OF THE 2013 MILITARY COUP

Authoritarian breakdowns are not necessarily correlated with the armed forces' subordination to civilian rule. Just as military elites can lose power, they can claim it back when the correlation of force favors them again. The contemporary history of Thailand is a case in point. At the same time, it is also not inevitable that the armed forces would be adamant on restoring military rule after the transition to democracy. The experience of direct political involvement can be damaging to the military by undermining its fighting capacity, undercutting its national standing, and, above all, threatening its internal cohesion. The Argentinean officers, for instance, lost their appetite for power after the traumatizing experience of military rule (the *proceso* years, 1976–1983), during which they fared poorly as economic managers and suffered a devastating defeat in the Falklands/Malvinas War. The same could be said of the generals in Brazil. If students of Latin American civil-military relations concur that armed forces in the continent no longer threaten democracy, it is fundamentally because their institutional cultures have moved beyond interventionism.[26]

Self-image and the perception of civilian political forces shape the essence of the military corporate ethos. These two variables are related: the more messianic a military self-image, the less the perception of civilian forces is likely to be positive, and the opposite is also true. Officers who perceive themselves to be necessarily more competent and more patriotic than civilians because they believe that their military background provides them with better knowhow and technological training as well as greater devotion to their country will be more difficult to subdue to civilian rule. By contrast, officers who learn to accept their limitations as rulers and cease to dismiss all political forces as corrupt and exclusively focused on petty partisan bickering are more likely to accept civilian authority. Note that authoritarianism is not necessarily correlated with interventionist militaries. Armed forces have been subordinate to civilian authorities in dictatorships (the Soviet Union, Cuba) or pervaded with interventionism in countries struggling to democratize (Turkey). One thing is certain, however: No country can become a stable democracy as long as the military's corporate ethos has not shed messianism and accepted the popular vote as the ultimate maker of the power elite, even if that means bringing politicians perceived to be corrupt or incompetent to power.

In that regard, the ethos pervasive within the Egyptian officer corps remains problematic. First, its self-perception is still messianic. In three stints of fieldwork in Egypt in 2011, 2012, and 2014, Egyptian officers whom I interviewed presented a glorified vision of the military's role in the formation of modern Egypt, from the reign of Mohammad Ali forward. In their historical worldview, the creation of the modern Egyptian armed forces preceded the creation of the modern Egyptian state; whereas other states build a military, the latter, in Egypt, built the state. In addition, by triggering the 1952 coup, the armed forces toppled a corrupt dynasty, secured the independence of Egypt from Britain, and put Egypt on the path of modernization. The military shed blood for Egypt in four wars with Israel and rose out of the defeat of 1967 to redeem national honor in 1973 and reclaim Sinai. Finally, the armed forces have developed an industrial-economic sector that, according to a majority of my interviewees, makes the military financially autonomous and thus relieves the budget from its burden. In addition, the agencies created by the military's industrial sector are actually more efficient than their civilian equivalents and thus better at delivering public-sector projects. Undoubtedly, the generals knew that millions of their countrymen lived below the poverty line by the time I was interviewing them. Yet my interviewees seemed quite convinced that ordinary Egyptians should be grateful for what the armed forces and the military-backed regimes have done for them. I said earlier that Argentinean officers questioned their ability to rule in the wake of the *proceso*; my conclusion after months of fieldwork in Egypt is that nothing of the sort has happened in the Egyptian officer corps—certainly not among its upper echelons.

A corollary of the previous observations is the prevailing view within the military elite pertaining to their relationship with the presidency. A solid majority of my interviewees favored a president hailing from their ranks; many referred to the military background of Egyptian presidents as a "time-honored Egyptian tradition"—one that they were clearly bent on perpetuating. At a time when Egypt was awash with talk about Mubarak-era corruption scandals, the generals tended to pinpoint perceived positive aspects of Mubarak's tenure—especially, the rehabilitation of Egypt's infrastructure—and accused civilians around Mubarak, not the former president himself, of potential wrongdoings. My interviewees tended to be bitter about Mubarak's imprisonment. They still considered the regime that crumbled to be theirs, despite their reservations about Gamal Mubarak and the security services.

Contra a very flattering self-perception, the top brass views political forces with suspicion. The theme of a foreign conspiracy against Egypt is something of a leitmotif within military circles, centering on civilians' alleged "links to outside powers." In addition, the political parties were allegedly benefitting from the "lack of democratic preparation" among Egyptians at large to promote self-centered agendas at the expense of public interests. The list of accusations against the Muslim Brotherhood, in particular, is so long and complex it goes well beyond the limits of this chapter. According to my interviewees, the Brotherhood was conspiring with Hamas against the armed forces and with Sudan to undermine the territorial integrity of Egypt. Ever loyal to a transnational *umma* (nation) of Muslims and ever seeking to reestablish the caliphate under which all Muslims will be joined, the Brotherhood's very ideology is anti-Egyptian and their presence in power a grave threat to the Egyptian state and its identity.[27]

These matters transcend who-should-get-what quarrels. They could, of course, be dismissed as mere alibis or frames under which the generals were cloaking petty material concerns. However, the impression I got from my stints in the field is that underestimating the ideological component of the 2013 coup would be a mistake. First, the generals expressed open animosity to the 2011 uprising—their political sympathies were clearly counterrevolutionary. The members of the top brass were unable to uphold the status quo in 2011, lest they trigger an open revolt among the midranking and junior officers, who were reluctant to open fire on their countrymen to save Mubarak's regime.[28] In other words, the generals lacked the capacity, not the will, to defend Mubarak, and democratic transition was simply unwelcome. The breakdown of the Mubarak regime was forced on the military elite by a series of quick events they were unable to stop; change was never preceded by an alteration in military culture similar to the one that progressively shifted the corporate ethos of Latin American militaries in more democracy-friendly directions. On the other hand, animosity between the military and the Brotherhood stretches back to the 1950s. For a brief while, the two forces did collaborate after the overthrow of the monarchy, but they quickly identified each other as a mortal threat. From the time they clashed bitterly in 1954 until 2011, Nasser violently suppressed the Brotherhood, Sadat tried to use them instrumentally against the left, and Mubarak restricted and strictly monitored their participation in the political process. In brief, the friction between the two institutions has been a permanent feature of Egypt's contemporary history, and it is thus no stretch of the imagination to believe that the generals' deeply felt animosity vis-à-vis the Brotherhood was genuine. In short: The Egyptian top brass was not ready in 2011 for a civilian in power; that Egypt's first nonmilitary president hailed from the Muslim Brotherhood reduced whatever slim chance there was to establish civilian control over the armed forces to zero.

Incentives are not enough to trigger a putsch, however; coup planners must also have the capacity to execute it successfully. The Egyptian top brass failed to save Mubarak and mismanaged the transition period following his downfall. How did they prove capable of overthrowing Morsi and reversing what briefly appeared like an inexorable decline? The answer lies with the newly found cohesiveness of SCAF reconstituted under Abdul Fattah Sisi—the director of military intelligence whom Morsi appointed commander of the armed forces and minister of defense—combined with the extreme polarization pitting Egypt's main political forces against one another and the ensuing strong civilian support for a military takeover.

Throughout the transitional period, SCAF had been divided along political and generational lines. First, the presidential ambitions of Lieutenant General Sami Anan, then chief of staff, progressively drove a wedge between him and the then commander of the armed forces, Field Marshal Tantawi, who opposed Anan's presidential bid. By the end of the transitional period, Tantawi had become distrustful of Anan.[29] Second, Anan himself was worried about the progressive rise in prominence of the head of military intelligence, Major General Abdel Fattah al-Sisi, who secured Tantawi's backing. Anan tried to block Sisi's advancement by leaking information to the press about Sisi's involvement in the assassination of civilian protesters in Tahrir Square during the January 2011 uprising, which poisoned their relationship.[30] Third, the SCAF's younger generals were eager for promotion, which was blocked by older generals who had occupied their positions for years.[31] These lines of fracture gave leeway to the Muslim Brotherhood to capitalize on the officers' rivalries. The generational divide was particularly instrumental. Observers of Egyptian military politics generally concur that Morsi would not have been able to sack Tantawi and Anan in August 2012 had the younger generals not been willing to move against their superiors in the military hierarchy.[32] The generational fracture also gave Morsi the ability to frame his move against Tantawi and Anan, which essentially aimed at securing control over the SCAF, as a well-intentioned attempt to "rejuvenate" the armed forces.[33]

Sisi's SCAF was more cohesive than Tantawi's. Shortly after being nominated minister of defense, Sisi retired seventy senior officers from the armed forces, including six SCAF members who had served under Tantawi; promoted others; and reshuffled the higher echelons of the officer corps.[34] The reconfigured SCAF was essentially made up of relatively young officers who owed their ascendancy to Sisi.[35] The latter graduated from the military academy in 1977. Most of the new SCAF members graduated between 1973 and 1977, meaning that they have been Sisi's friends or classmates since his early days in the armed forces.[36] Sisi's choice for the sensitive position of chief of staff, the commander of the Third Field Army, Major General Sobhi Sodki, is a case in point. Sodki graduated in 1976 and is said to be Sisi's lifelong friend.[37] In at least one case, familial bonds were also at play: the daughter of the new director of military intelligence, Major General Mahmoud Hejazi, who, like Sisi, graduated in 1977, is married to one of Sisi's sons.[38] In brief, the SCAF's generals, all handpicked by Sisi, were no longer divided along generational lines, and this strengthened their position in the overall political system. Sisi's unassailability as commander of the armed forces was demonstrated twice under Morsi. First, when rumors circulated in February 2013 that Morsi was determined to dismiss Sisi, an authorized source in the armed forces leaked to the Egyptian press that the military institution would not tolerate a replay of the ouster of Tantawi and Annan, warning that any move against Sisi would be tantamount to the "whole political system committing suicide."[39] Second, in June 2013, shortly before being overthrown, Morsi decided to replace Sisi with Major General Ahmad Wasfi, the commander of the Second Field Army, but Wasfi declined Morsi's offer and warned Sisi that the president was trying to replace him.[40] Had the Brotherhood unified Egypt's political factions by forming a coalition government, they would have created an environment unfavorable for coup making. But in the summer of 2013, a cohesive military was facing a completely polarized civilian sphere. The putsch came in the wake of a palpable shift in the correlation of force favoring military actors over civilians.

* * *

In conclusion, the political quiescence of the Tunisian military facilitated democratic transition in Tunisia. The Egyptian armed forces, by contrast, restored autocracy after only a year of civilian rule. Behind the variation in the officers' political agency lies divergent historical trajectories and perceptions. The republic in Tunisia was founded by al-Habib Bourguiba, who, as the most prominent figure of the country's struggle for independence, did not need the armed forces to survive politically. Bourguiba kept the Tunisian military small, counterbalanced it with security services and the ruling party, and sent his officers to train in France and the United States, where they internalized the Western model of civil-military relations. In Egypt, military officers simultaneously established a republic and a military regime under Gamal Abdul Nasser. Though the Egyptian regime eventually became civilianized, the special link between the armed forces and the presidency endured, and with it a deep sense of personal and institutional entitlement became entrenched among the military elite, against the backdrop of paternalistic attitudes and a messianic institutional culture. The Egyptian generals were not ready in 2011 to see a civilian in the presidency, let alone a member of the Muslim Brotherhood; only a pact among civilian forces to keep the military at bay could have prevented renewed military interventionism. The extreme polarization between the Muslim Brotherhood and their political opponents inhibited civilian unity and thus invited the 2013 coup. In Tunisia, tension between Islamists and their political rivals was palpable. But there was enough cooperation between the different formations to avoid the gridlock characteristic of the Egyptian transitional scene. It is particularly interesting in this regard to compare the Tamarrod movement in both countries. In Egypt, millions took to the streets and called openly for the overthrow of the Brotherhood's administration. When a group of Tunisian activists announced the creation of a copycat Tamarrod movement in Tunisia, Arab media was awash with speculations about a potential overthrow of the Ennahda-led government and a repetition of the Egyptian scenario in Tunis. Yet it quickly became clear that Tunisia's Tamarrod movement was a failure. On the one hand, it never enjoyed the backing of major Tunisian political forces, including secularists opposed to Islamist rule. On the other hand, though the organizers of the movement claimed to have collected 175,000 signatures supporting their call for overthrowing the Islamists, the popular muscle they could muster in the Tunisian street remained feeble. Civilian support for an extrainstitutional showdown with Ennahda was simply lacking in Tunisia.

I highlighted in this chapter the importance of ideological variables in shaping the agency of Egyptian generals. Nothing in this argument underplays the importance officers attach to their material privileges and corporate interests. But the generals' sinecures and military economic agglomerate were not under threat by the Brotherhood. The chief motivations for the 2013 coup lay elsewhere. Though institutional cultures endure when they become entrenched, they can also change. The military may reach the conclusion that it is not fit to rule and thus lose the appetite to govern. Or if military rulers are overthrown and the armed forces stay out power for an extended period of time, new generations of officers may become reconciled with being subordinate to elected officials. However, the antidemocratic institutional culture of the Egyptian officer corps is not likely to undergo change soon; if anything, the ongoing confrontation with extremist organizations can only make the generals even more convinced of their indispensability to Egypt as saviors and rulers. Egypt's road toward democracy appears once again long and tortuous. And until Egypt's Muslim Brotherhood and its liberal and leftist opponents finally decide that they hate the officers more than they hate one another, military rule in Cairo will remain secure.

NOTES

1. Alfred Stepan, *The Military in Politics: Changing Patterns in Brazil* (Princeton, N.J.: Princeton University Press, 1971). Stepan contended, "If politicians, for example, believe that the regime is unworkable, the question of who should receive political power following the removal of the president becomes much more difficult. The way clearly opens for the military to assume a new political role in society: that of director instead of moderator of the political system. If the military themselves feel that a new set of measures must be implemented, the military role may shift from that of system-maintenance to system-change" (134).

2. Hicham Bou Nassif, "A Military Besieged: The Armed Forces, the Police, and the Party in Ben Ali's Tunisia, 1987–2011," *International Journal of Middle East Studies* 47 (2015): 65–87.

3. For a firsthand account on the 1962 plot, see Moncef el Materi, *De Saint-Cyr au peloton d'execution de Bourguiba* (Tunis: Arabesques, 2014).

4. Interview with retired colonel-major in the Tunisian army, Muhammad Mizughi, former director of the Haute Ecole de Guerre (Tunisian War College) and military attaché in France. Tunis, June 5, 2013. The best available account on the early years of the Tunisian military under Bourguiba is Boubaker Benkraiem, *Naissance d'une armeé nationale, la promotion Bourguiba* (Tunis: Maision d'edition de Tunis, 2009).

5. Anouar Abdel-Malek, *Egypt: Military Society, the Army Regime, the Left, and Social Change Under Nasser* (New York: Random House, 1968), xxxiv.

6. Muhammad 'Abd al-Ghani al-Gamasi, *Mudhakkirat al-Gamsi: Harb Uktubr 1973* [Gamasi's memoirs: the October 1973 war] (San Francisco: Dar Buhuth al-Sharq al-Awsat al-Amayrikiyya, 1977), 132.

7. Gamal Hammad, *Asrar Thawrat 23 Yuliyu* [Secrets of the July 23 revolution] (Cairo: Dar al-'Ulum, 2011), 1166. The percentage of officers occupying ministerial positions

remained high from the early years of the Nasser regime until its demise. It oscillated between 40.9 percent in the 1953 cabinet to 36.3 percent in the 1956 cabinet and 55.2 percent in the 1966 cabinet. The military presence reached an unprecedented 65.4 percent in the first government formed after the 1967 debacle under Nasser's premiership before dropping to 39.4 percent in the 1968 cabinet. Officers were heavily represented even in civilian-led ministries, where they typically occupied number-two positions as deputy ministers and undersecretaries. The rise of the officer-technocrat rendered the militarization of the administration easier. These were officers who were trained in nonmilitary fields such as engineering, medicine, law, journalism, and so forth. They were appointed to ministries requiring technical knowledge, namely Public Works, Irrigation, Agriculture, Justice, and Commerce. Hrair Dekmejian, *Egypt Under Nasser: A Study in Political Dynamics* (Albany: SUNY Press, 1971), 172–178.

8. Twenty-five of the fifty-eight Egyptian ambassadors were retired officers in 1952, and forty-three out of seventy-three in 1964. Amos Perlmutter, *Egypt: The Praetorian State* (New Brunswick, N.J.: Transaction, 1974), 116.

9. Eliezer Be'eri, *Army Officers in Arab Politics and Society* (New York: Praeger, 1970), 247.

10. 'Abd al-Latif al-Baghdadi, *Mudhakkirat* [Memoirs] (Cairo: al-Maktab al-Misri al-Hadith, 1977), 172.

11. Abdel-Malek, *Egypt*, xix.

12. Be'eri, *Army Officers in Arab Politics*, 429.

13. In addition to receiving privileged access to civilian jobs, officers were given priority for being allocated low-rent housing and being able to purchase cars. Their salaries were increased. Scores were able to acquire sequestered properties that had previously belonged to the Egyptian upper class under the monarchy or to foreign nationals driven out of Egypt after 1952. George Haddad, *Revolution and Military Rule in the Middle East: The Arab States*, vol. 2: *Egypt, the Sudan, Yemen, and Libya* (New York: Robert Speller and Sons, 1973), 79.

14. Probably the best account on the Nasserite ideology and propaganda, including that pertaining to the military, is Sharif Youness, *Nida' al-Shaab. Tarikh Naqdi li al-ideologia al-Nasiriya* [The call of the people. A critical history of the Nasserite ideology] (Cairo: Dar al-Shourouq, 2012).

15. Bou Nassif, "A Military Beseiged," 73.

16. Ibid., 80.

17. See Articles 9 and 10 of the November 2011 Document for Fundamental Constitutional Principles, known as the "Selmi Document" (*Wathikat al-Selmi*). See also Articles 53 and 54 of SCAF's Constitutional Declaration as modified by the June 2012 Constitutional Addendum.

18. See in particular Articles 193, 195, 197 and 198 of the December 2012 constitution, at http://niviensaleh.info/constitution-egypt-2012-translation/.

19. "Marching in Circles," Crisis Group Interview with Muslim Brotherhood member and advisor to the presidential team, Cairo, May 25, 2013, http://www.crisisgroup.org/en/publication-type/media-releases/2013/mena/marching-in-circles-egypts-dangerous-second-transition.aspx.

20. See Abdel Azim Hammad, *Al-Thawra al-Taiha. Siraa al-Khouza wa al-Lihya wa al-Maydan. Rou'yat Chahid Ayan* (Cairo:Markaz al-Mahroussa, 2013), 141; Chahata Siyam, *Al-'Askariyoun wa al-Thwara al'Mankousa* (Cairo:Rawafad lil Nachr wa al'Tawzi,' 2013), 291; Nachwa al-Houfi, *Ya Nokhba Ma Tammit* (Cairo: Dar Dawwin, 2013), 73. See also Ibrahim al-Hidibi's article in the Egyptian daily *al-Shouroq*, "'An Motalabat 'Awdat al-Jeish," March 8, 2013.

21. See the Egyptian daily *al-Shourouq*, August 8, 2013, for reports on the "Ikhwanization" of the bureaucracy: http://www.shorouknews.com/news/view.aspx?cdate=08072013&id=4be bc7e2-c41b-4852-962d-2af61073601b. See also the Egyptian website *al-Bawaba*, March 8, 2013: http://www.albawabhnews.com/21286.

22. See Hicham Bou Nassif, "Coups and Nascent Democracies: The Military and Egypt's Failed Consolidation," *Democratization* 23, no. 5 (2016).

23. See Ibrahim Gad, *Tamarrod . . . Wal Tarik ila 30 Youlyou* (Cairo: Markaz al-Mahroussa, 2014), 137–146.

24. See the report on the Ministry of Transport under the Muslim Brotherhood published by the Egyptian daily *Akhbar al-Youm*, December 31, 2013.

25. Interview with two retired major generals in the Egyptian navy, in Cairo, on February 18 and March 25, 2014.

26. David Pion-Berlin, ed., *Civil-Military Relations in Latin America: New Analytical Perspectives* (Chapel Hill: University of North Carolina Press, 2001).

27. For more on the perceptions and self-perceptions structuring the politics of the Egyptian military elite, see Bou Nassif, "Coups and Nascent Democracies."

28. On the unwillingness of officers in Tahrir Square to open fire on civilians, see Wendell Steavenson, *Circling the Square: Stories from the Egyptian Revolution* (New York: Harper Collins, 2015), 17–18; see also Hazem Kandil, *Soldiers, Spies, and Statesmen: Egypt's Road to Revolt* (London: Verso, 2012), 160; Christopher Read, *Allegiance: Egypt Security Forces*, MA thesis, Naval Postgraduate School, 2013, 34, https://calhoun.nps.edu/bitstream/handle/10945/38998/13Dec_Read_Christopher.pdf?sequence=1.

29. Interview with Abdullah Sinnawi, Cairo, March 9, 2014. For more on the interaction between Tantawi and Annan, see Mohammad al-Baz, *al-Mouchir wa al-Fariq, al-Malaffat al-Siyassia li Tantawi wa Annan* (Cairo: Konouz, 2013); see also Mohammad al-Baz, *al-Aqrab al-Sam. Omar Suleiman, General al-Moukhabarat al-Ghamid* (Cairo: Konouz, 2013).

30. See Sinnawi's article in the Egyptian daily *al-Shourouk*, on August 20, 2012: http://www.shorouknews.com/columns/view.aspx?cdate=20082012&id=078ef184-b91f-4ee5-b902-6a2857929a61.

31. See Yassir Thabit, *Rais al-Fouras al-Dai'a, Morsy Bayna Masr Wal Gama'a* (Cairo: Dar Okotob Lil Nachr Wal Tawzi', 2013), 73.

32. Ibid. See also Gad, *Tamarrod*, 32.

33. For details on Sisi's permutations, see the Egyptian daily *al-Ahram*, August 13, 2012: http://gate.ahram.org.eg/UI/Front/Inner.aspx?NewsContentID=240555; the Egyptian daily *al-Masry al-Youm*, September 3,2012: http://www.almasryalyoum.com/news/details/161115; the Egyptian daily *al-Shourouk*, August 18, 2012: http://www.shorouknews.com

/news/view.aspx?cdate=18082012&id=4153ae96-a2a9-49d5-8767-3f251257dce6; and the Egyptian news site *Moufakkirat al-Islam*, September 2, 2012: http://islammemo.cc/akhbar /arab/2012/09/02/155029.html#1.

34. See the Egyptian daily *al-Shourouk*, August 15, 2012: http://www.shorouknews.com /news/view.aspx?cdate=15082012&id=68dc55f1-96a9-4561-b8f4-93ac82e5ff96.

35. Two exceptions are Major General Mamdouh Chahin and Major General Mohammad al-Assar, respectively the assistant to the minister of defense for legal affairs and the assistant to the minister of defense for armaments affairs. They occupied the same positions under Tantawi.

36. Interview with a retired major general (army). Cairo, April 1, 2013.

37. Ibid. Note that Sobhi Sodki later replaced Sisi as minister of defense.

38. See Lee Keath and Maggie Michael's report in the Associated Press, January 30, 2014: http://news.yahoo.com/popular-wave-could-lift-egypt-army-chief-office-223857617.html. See also Hejazi's profile, published by the Egyptian daily *al-Masry al-Youm*, March 27, 2014: http://www.almasryalyoum.com/news/details/418190. Note that Hejazi replaced Sobhi Sodki as chief of staff of the armed forces when Sodki was appointed minister of defense.

39. See, generally, Egyptian newspapers published on February 19, 2013.

40. Gad, *Tamarrod*, 131.

7

THE FAILURE OF THE INTERNATIONAL COMMUNITY TO SUPPORT TUNISIA

RADWAN MASMOUDI

And tonight, let us be clear: the United States of America stands with the people of Tunisia, and supports the democratic aspirations of all people.

—PRESIDENT BARACK OBAMA, STATE OF THE UNION SPEECH, JANUARY 25, 2011

A MERE NINE DAYS after Ben Ali fled Tunisia, President Obama made this declaration in front of Congress and expressed his support, and that of the American people, to the people of Tunisia in their quest for freedom, dignity, and democracy. Countless such statements of support were made by President Obama, secretaries of state Clinton and Kerry, and leaders and members of the House and the Senate. A typical statement of support for and appreciation of Tunisia's democratic transition can be found in a speech by Secretary Kerry at the Carnegie Endowment for International Peace on October 28, 2015, where he said: "To skeptics who say that democracy can't make it in the Middle East and North Africa, I reply with one word: *Tunisia*."

At the first G8 meeting in June 2011 following the Arab revolutions, the G8 leaders promised an assistance package of $80 billion to the countries of the Arab Spring, including $25 billion for Tunisia, to help ensure the success of these difficult and challenging transitions to democracy.[1] Yet the wonderful statements and promises of support emanating from European and American heads of governments and members of parliament have not translated into action. In fact, Tunisia has not received *any* additional support for its democratic achievements. Instead, the governments of Europe and the United States are occupied by crises in Iraq, Syria, Egypt, Yemen, and Libya and continue to fund governments that are semi- or outright authoritarian. In 2016, Tunisia received the best possible score for political rights given by the NGO Freedom House. Although Jordan received a very low score (and its population is half that of Tunisia), it garnered more than ten times as much aid, $1.4 billion, as Tunisia. The Egyptian military regime has a terrible political rights score, given its origins in a coup and its unprecedented levels of repression, but in 2016 it was nonetheless rewarded with its annual $1.5 billion dollars in U.S. aid. The West has long supported authoritarian countries in the Middle East for geopolitical reasons, instead of rewarding democratic success. This pattern of support threatens the promise that a democratic Tunisia offers to the MENA region and the world.

Since 2011, Tunisia has made amazing and impressive progress on the political front. Yet its economy is in shambles. Lack of stability, corruption, and mismanagement inherited from Ben Ali's regime; rising social demands and strikes; and terrorist attacks on politicians have all taken their toll. Perhaps worse, the 2015 attacks on tourist sites including the Bardo Museum in Tunis and attacks in Sousse devastated Tunisia's tourist industry, which employs over four hundred thousand people in a country of only ten million. Between 2011 and 2015, nearly two thousand companies closed shop and moved to Morocco, laying off tens of thousands of workers and employees.

The economic situation has recently reached alarming levels; in 2015 economic growth was about 0.5 percent, the lowest in nearly forty years. At Reuters' Middle East Investment Summit on October 26, 2015, Tunisia's finance minister Slim Chaker pleaded for assistance: "Tunisia is asking the G8 for a rescue programme or Marshall Plan of $25 billion over five years to finance development of infrastructure, support social peace, strengthen security and reduce the budget deficit." He added: "We are very frustrated with the international community over the lack of support of our special democratic experience." His appeal was unsuccessful.

The whole world knows that the success of Tunisia's democratic transition is crucial for peace and stability in the MENA region. If democracy does not succeed in Tunisia, it will not succeed in any other country in the region. Failure in Tunisia will be devastating: everyone, especially young Arabs across the region, will conclude that democracy is not possible and will turn in much greater numbers to violence, extremism, and radicalism to rid themselves of corrupt and oppressive regimes. After the Arab Spring, millions of Arab citizens tasted freedom, and there is no way they will go back to the old "order" of "stability" under corrupt and tyrannical regimes. The alternative to democracy will not be dictatorship but chaos and civil war, as we currently see happening across the region, in Libya, Yemen, and Syria.

THE COUNTERREVOLUTION OF THE ARAB GULF STATES

In the beginning of 2012, immediately following the 2011 elections in Egypt and Tunisia, the United Arab Emirates and other Gulf states started to coordinate their efforts to derail democratic transitions in the countries of the Arab Spring. UAE government officials and leaders of other Gulf states made their position against democracy and the democratic process very public in the media, especially against the Islamic parties that won the elections, including the Muslim Brotherhood in Egypt and Ennahda in Tunisia. The UAE dedicated billions of dollars to overthrow these nascent democracies by supporting the military coup in Egypt and by urging or supporting similar coups in Tunisia, Libya, and Yemen. A few days after the military coup in Egypt, the UAE, Saudi Arabia, Bahrain, and Kuwait announced an assistance package to Egypt worth over $45 billion to "stabilize and support the economy."[2]

The UAE particularly focused on Libya by allying with General Khalifa Haftar, who announced a "takeover" of the elected government in Tripoli in February 2014. Haftar's coup attempt was more theatrical than real. He appeared on the UAE-based television channel Al-Arabiya, in military uniform, to demand the dissolution of parliament and an interim government, claiming his forces had seized control of strategic sites around the country. Al-Arabiya also quoted eyewitnesses who claimed that the UAE's air force had joined Haftar's group and bombed a barracks occupied by the revolutionary "17 February Battalion," described by the channel as an "Islamic militia." General Haftar has also coordinated militarily with the government in Egypt. Air strikes in August and October 2014 on pro-Tripoli government positions are believed to have been launched from Egypt.

In Tunisia, the UAE provided huge amounts of money to pro–Ben Ali journalists and to opposition groups across the political spectrum during 2013 and 2014. This was part of a plan concocted by Mohamed Dahlan, a former PLO official accused by the PLO of being an Israeli spy and of poisoning Yasser Arafat, to create a chaotic situation that could lead to destabilization and possibly to a military coup, just like what happened in Egypt.[3] In fact, newly formed and UAE-financed groups, the National Salvation Front and Tamarrod, have exactly the same names as those groups behind the June 30 demonstrations that led to the military coup in Egypt, on July 3, 2013.[4] There is also plenty of evidence that the leaders of the two Tunisian and Egyptian branches of Tamarrod trained together in Egypt and in the UAE.[5]

Beginning in early 2013, with the assassination of the leftist Tunisian political leader Chokri Belaid on February 6, it became clear that both external and internal forces were mobilizing to abort the democratic experiment. Salafi forces, notoriously supported by several of the Gulf countries, were spreading ideas that democracy was against Islam, and they were furious that the ruling Islamist party—Ennahda, or "Renaissance"—had not insisted on infusing Islamic law, or sharia, into the new constitution.

Tunisia's ruling coalition of Islamist and secularist parties—known as the "Troika"—found great difficulty in implementing the necessary reforms in government, media, and economic sectors. Not only did they have little experience in governing, but opposition from remnants of Ben Ali's "deep state," still holding great influence in the judiciary and security apparatuses, obstructed reform. The most obvious and unfortunate loss was the Law of Transitional Justice, which, had it been passed early on, would have set in motion a culture and system of transparency, accountability, and justice that could have ultimately marginalized and diminished the capacity of the antirevolution forces to impede much-needed democratic reforms, both on the economic and political fronts. Instead, it only passed after two long years of "negotiations," and its implementation remains spotty at best.

The constitutional drafting process took longer than had been projected, a fact that was used by opposition parties and old-regime actors alike to demand the dissolution of the National Constituent Assembly on the grounds that its legitimacy had expired. Feeling "empowered" by the military coup in Egypt, they sought to achieve the same thing in Tunisia.

On July 25, 2013, a political assassination sent Tunisia's transition into disarray, and fifty members of the Assembly decided to "freeze" their participation in that body and join the National Salvation Front, which was at least partially funded by the UAE and Mohamed Dahlan.[6] On August 6, the president of the Assembly, Dr. Mustapha ben Jaafer, announced that he would suspend the work of the Assembly until a national dialogue could convince those members to return (who, by the way, constituted only a fourth of the 217-member elected body).

From August 6 until December 15, 2013, all the main ruling and opposition parties engaged in a national dialogue to negotiate a resolution to the political crisis. The opposition insisted that the members would return to the Assembly only after the government resigned. The Troika coalition agreed in principle with resignation, but would do so only after the new constitution was ratified and a date set for the next elections. Intransigent demands by the opposition National Salvation Front and Tamarrod could have easily derailed the whole process, but the Tunisian army and military refused to intervene in the country's political affairs. Reaching an agreement on the makeup of the new government, especially on the new technocratic prime minister, who would lead the country through this critical interim period, proved to be the most difficult challenge.

The national dialogue process lasted approximately four months and was finally concluded with an agreement between all the parties on (1) finishing and ratifying the new constitution, (2) resignation of the Laaryedh/Nahdha-led government, (3) formation of a new independent/technocratic government led by Mehdi Jomaa, (4) agreement on the leadership and membership of the Independent Election Commission (ISIE) to organize and supervise the new elections, and (5) agreement on the dates of the new parliamentary and presidential elections to take place within a year (that is, before the end of 2014).

Despite these challenges and roadblocks, Tunisia succeeded in keeping the political process on track, and the country is and remains the best hope and the best chance for democracy—an inclusive democracy that does not exclude anyone—to take root in the Arab world. Following the second round of free and fair legislative and presidential elections in 2014, Nidaa Tounes (secular) and Ennahda (moderate religious) emerged as the largest two blocs in parliament and agreed to work together, forming a coalition government with two other secular but smaller parties.

During the campaign for the parliamentary and presidential elections of 2014, both Beji Caid Sebsi and Mohsen Marzouk, the two founding leaders of the secular-leaning Nidaa Tounes movement, repeated publicly that they had received promises of economic support from the UAE of at least $125 billion over five years if Nidaa Tounes won the elections. The implication was of course that citizens should elect Nidaa Tounes because Tunisia would receive a huge assistance package. However, the unstated condition, revealed after the elections, was that Nidaa was supposed to govern alone and not include the Ennahda party in its government.[7] However, following the elections, Nidaa and Ennahda agreed to form a coalition government, in an alliance with two other parties. Relations with the UAE quickly deteriorated, and none of the economic support promised before the elections was delivered to Tunisia. President Sebsi told journalists (as reported by Sofiane Ben Farhat) that the UAE conditioned its economic support on "repeating the Egyptian scenario," which he said he refused because it was not in Tunisia's interests.[8]

Tunisia, which has managed to make significant and historic political progress in its march to consolidate its nascent democracy, is not immune to the turbulence of the region. It has been the site of persistent economic and security challenges that threaten to overshadow and ultimately derail its democratic process. The two high-profile political assassinations of 2013 and ongoing terrorist attacks on civilians and security forces alike present the most obvious and immediate test of the endurance of the forces of democracy. This violence and extremism are both products of the tyranny of the Ben Ali regime and the largely porous national borders that have allowed extremists and weapons to flow in and out with relative ease; at the same time, it is an unfortunate yet entirely foreseeable byproduct of revolutions that usher in unprecedented freedom and then struggle to balance that freedom with the institution of a democratic yet tough security apparatus.

It was only with the presidential and parliamentary elections from October to December 2014 that the government was able to begin addressing the structurally deficient and corrupt economic model it had inherited. This process is an inherently complex and long-term one, the product of difficult compromises that must balance the priorities of the government, businessmen and employers, existing and future workers, and the public at large; it will take at least five, if not ten, years to bear any fruit. In the meantime, job-creation initiatives have been very slow and disappointing, the economy has seen negative growth in the last year, more young people are graduating with advanced degrees from universities than are entering the workforce, and the tourism industry, the second-biggest industry in the country, has come to a screeching halt.

Tunisians are growing increasingly restless, desperate for a stable and strong economy that would provide meaningful and competitive employment opportunities and restore dignity to their lives. It was, after all, in the name of freedom and dignity that the Tunisian people rose up, sacrificed, and persevered. To continue to sacrifice and persevere patiently with no semblance of hope for an improving economy is too much of a burden to demand the Tunisian people continue to shoulder. For the government and parliament to continue in their difficult work without the Tunisian public reaching a breaking point, immediate and decisive action must be taken. Rhetorical support for democracy must now translate into deeds, not only for the sake of Tunisia but for the entire region.

To inject stability into the frail and failing Tunisian economy today would effectively support the consolidation of the nascent Tunisian democracy. A Support Tunisian Democracy Act has been discussed by the Tunisian government and seeks to raise five billion U.S. dollars annually for five years not only from the United States, the European Union, Turkey, and Qatar but also from all nations and private, individual donors who see the importance of supporting this democratic experiment in the Arab world. This request precipitated an international investment conference, Tunisia 2020, organized by the Tunisian government in November 2016, which sought to encourage international investment and economic development.

Tunisia has received much praise and attention—even the Nobel Prize—as it continues its democratic path founded on dialogue, moderation, and a unique political model of consensus, led by Tunisia's party of Muslim democrats, Ennahda. But Tunisia has also become a victim of its own success. Many think its democratic journey is complete, rather than just starting, and, despite global appreciation, very few resources have been allocated to sustain this lone surviving model of democracy in the region.

The West presumes that a tiny Arab country—with roughly half of its population under thirty; a distressed economy resulting from decades of cronyism, centralization, social exclusion, and corruption; and surrounded by a region in chaos—will be able to succeed on its own. That expectation is misfounded—and, in January 2016, this became evident after a new wave of unrest spread across Tunisia, sparked once again by the recent death of a young man, this time protesting his exclusion from a list of government jobs.[9]

Youth in Tunisia, who expected democracy to provide prosperity and dignity, are desperate—more than three-quarters of the unemployed in the country are eighteen to thirty years of age. Some have already been lured into extremism—Tunisia endured three horrific terrorist attacks in 2015 and 2016, shattering the vital tourism sector and compounding its poor economic situation—and more will be tempted to do so as groups like ISIS tap into their growing frustration and resentment. That would be a tragedy, one that can and must be avoided.

Tunisians are aware they are the sole representatives of something great in the region—they have held free and fair elections and have had two peaceful transfers of power. Tunisia has strong women leaders, a resilient civil society, and, most importantly, the most progressive constitution in the Arab world, one passed by 94 percent of the National Constituent Assembly.

But they also understand how precarious their situation is. They see the bloodshed in Syria, as both Bashar al-Assad's army and ISIS indiscriminately and mercilessly decimate towns and villages; they see Libya sinking into the nightmare of civil war; and they see Yemen becoming a bloody playground for the region's proxy wars. Worse, they see porous national borders that have allowed extremists and weapons to flow between Libya and Tunisia with relative ease; they see poor infrastructure, especially in the interior regions of the country, and a lack of foreign aid and investment that cripples job growth; and they see terrorist activity bringing the economy to its knees.

This is not what Tunisians want, and this is not what the United States and other democracies around the world should want either. Tunisians hear Western leaders talk about their country being the shining light of Arab democracy, but they need more than talk. They are growing increasingly restless, desperate for a stable and strong economy that would provide meaningful and competitive employment opportunities and restore dignity to their lives.

Just as the United States and the European Union provided tens of billions of dollars in direct support to post-Soviet Eastern Europe or to the Marshal Plan to rebuild Germany after World War II, the United States must similarly help Tunisia. Those concerned with the prospects of Tunisian democracy should work with the Tunisian government to champion its fundraising and economic development efforts. Tunisia desperately needs these funds to support large-scale infrastructure projects in the interior of the country—highways, roads, railways, hospitals, schools, and universities—that will facilitate job creation and bring investors. In the short term, this shot of international assistance will spur economic growth in the historically disenfranchised interior regions and keep hope alive for thousands of young Tunisians. Over the long term, it will stimulate economic activity and attract investments.

In turn, the United States should push the Tunisian government to establish a donor fund, administered by an eminent board of public- and private-sector leaders, to manage these funds in a transparent manner and enable investors and donors to contribute directly to urgently needed infrastructure projects. This fund must also be granted fast-track authority to implement large-scale projects quickly and bypass the notoriously slow administrative and legal web of "required procedures."

The United States must also help build Tunisia's institutional capacity so it can counter corruption, strengthen its democratic institutions, and facilitate decentralization and local governance. Importantly, the U.S. government must also provide its promised military support to combat and defeat the terrorist threat. For example, it will take four years for the United States to deliver twelve military helicopters to Tunisia to handle surveillance and counterterrorist activities. Expediting delivery of these helicopters, without requiring Tunisia to pay for them, should be a top priority.

Make no mistake about it: Tunisia is on the brink once again. Whether it succeeds largely depends on the role and the support of the international community. If we are serious about ending the cycle of oppression and extremism in the Arab region, we must usher in peace and security firmly grounded in democracy, freedom, and human dignity. In the Arab world today, there is no country better poised than Tunisia to prove that democracy is not only possible but that it delivers a better life to its citizens. It must be supported, now, before it is too late.

NOTES

1. Margaret Besheer, "G8 Commits $80 Billion to Arab Spring Democracy," *Voice of America*, September 19, 2011, http://www.voanews.com/content/g8-commits-80-billion -to-arab-spring-democracy-130242553/158882.html.

2. "Egypt Got $23 Billion in Aid from Gulf in 18 Months—Minister," *Reuters*, March 2, 2015, http://uk.reuters.com/article/uk-egypt-investment-gulf-idUKKBNoLYoUT20150302.

3. Simona Sikimic, "Profile: Mohammed Dahlan, Gaza's Comeback Kid," *Middle East Eye*, April 7, 2014, http://www.middleeasteye.net/news/profile-mohammed-dahlan-gazas -comeback-kid-1305037516.

4. "Tunisia Follows in Footsteps of Egypt: 'Tamarrod' to Challenge Ennahda's Constitution," *Middle East Online*, July 3, 2013, http://www.middle-east-online.com/english/ ?id=59870.

5. "UAE Threatens to Destabilise Tunisia for Not Acting in Abu Dhabi's Interests," *Middle East Eye*, November 30, 2015, http://www.middleeasteye.net/news/uae-threaten -destabilise-tunisia-not-acting-abu-dhabis-interests-1261316730#sthash.jCvzKdsO.dpuf.

6. Monia Fadel, "The Hands of the Gulf in Tunisia," *Gulf House for Studies and Publishing*, October, 18, 2015, http://gulfhsp.org/en/posts/1322/.

7. "Tunisie: Crise diplomatique entre la Tunisie et les Emirats Arabes Unis: Dessous et enjeux," *Tunisie Numerique*, September 21, 2015, http://www.tunisienumerique.com/tunisie -crise-diplomatique-entre-la-tunisie-et-les-emirats-arabes-unis-dessous-et-enjeux/266972.

8. "Row in Tunisia Over Claims That UAE Is Buying Political Influence," *Middle East Eye*, May 24, 2015, http://www.middleeasteye.net/news/row-tunisia-over-claims-uae-buying -politic al-influence-1185267817#sthash.KA6tfRik.dpuf.

9. Callum Paton, "Tunisia: Violence on the Streets of Kasserine as Youth Return to Protest Incomplete Revolution," *International Business Times*, January 21, 2016, http://www .ibtimes.co.uk/tunisia-violence-streets-kasserine-youth-return-protest-incomplete-revo lution-1539357.

PART II

RETHINKING OTHER DEMOCRACIES WITH LARGE MUSLIM POPULATIONS

What Policies Helped in Indonesia and India?

8

CRAFTING INDONESIAN DEMOCRACY

Inclusion-Moderation and the
Sacralizing of the Postcolonial State

JEREMY MENCHIK

Rule of law in Indonesia must be understood through the viewpoint of the 1945 Constitution, namely a constitutional state which places the ideal of Belief in God as its foremost principle as well as religious values underlying the movements of national and state life, and not as a country that imposes separation of state and religion or merely holds to the principle of individualism or communalism.

—INDONESIAN CONSTITUTIONAL COURT (2010), DECISION 140/PUU-VII/2009, §3.34.10

INTRODUCTION

Indonesia is the largest Muslim-majority country in the world and a stable, consolidated democracy, according to most scholars as well as indicators from Polity.[1] The centrality of Islamic organizations to Indonesia's successful democratic transition and consolidation has affirmed scholars' view that the inclusion of antisystem parties in the political process fosters their moderation. Over the course of the twentieth and early twenty-first century, the Indonesian Islamic organizations that have participated in crafting the policies of the state have implicitly or explicitly moderated their views. Their ideologies have shifted from pan-Islamists who seek a global caliphate to Indonesian Islamists who aim to create an Indonesian Islamic state, Indonesian Muslim pluralists who actively work with other religious and ideological groupings and promise to safeguard their rights, and post-Islamists who view Islam as complementary to other ways of organizing politics and society. In other words, they have moderated through participation. While there are exceptions to this trend, most notably the "new Islamists," who generate dramatic headlines but possess little electoral influence, the overall trend toward moderation is clear: include Islamists in the political process, and over time their ideologies and tactics will moderate toward support for democracy and the religious tolerance demanded by its institutions.

Most analyses of Indonesian Islam end at this normatively celebrated juncture. What this vantage point ignores, however, is that the inclusion of Islamic actors changes the political system even as it fosters their moderation. The inclusion of Islamists in the democratic bargain means that the negotiating partners of Islamists, most often secular nationalists and the secular institutions of the postcolonial state, must cede ground on important policy issues. Islamic society and the state coevolve.

This chapter demonstrates this coevolution through a diachronic case study of the sacralizing of Indonesia's postcolonial state from 1945 to 2014. As a result, the contemporary state is neither secular nor a theocracy but rather somewhere in between, where the government makes religious education mandatory, obliges citizens to declare their adherence to a religion, restricts interfaith marriage, and limits activities that it sees as interfering with communal rights, such as interfaith proselytizing. Theoretically, this case suggests that the sacralizing of the postcolonial state is just as important for democratization in the Muslim world as are inclusion and moderation. As a result, for democratization to succeed in transitional democracies like Tunisia, it is just as important that Islamic actors never fully "lose" as it is that they never fully "win." Additionally, given the salience of religion in contemporary Europe, this chapter suggests that politics in peripheral states like India, Indonesia, and Tunisia, where religious actors are central to the crafting of mutual accommodation, may illuminate aspects of Europe's present, rather than its past.

This chapter proceeds in three sections. The literature review discusses major writings on the participation/moderation tradeoff and then demonstrates how they apply to the Indonesian case. The theory section discusses the neglected counterparts of participation/moderation: the sacralizing of the postcolonial state. The subsequent empirical section highlights four policy areas—education, recognition of religions, marriage law, and proselytizing—that have become sacralized and compares Indonesia's laws to those of other democracies. A brief conclusion reflects on the implications of these twin processes for democratic theory.

LITERATURE REVIEW

Scholars of democracy have long been concerned with the role that radical or antisystem parties play in derailing democratic transitions. Samuel Huntington argued, "Implicitly or explicitly in the negotiating process leading to democratization, the scope of participation was broadened and more political figures and groups gained the opportunity to compete for power and to win power on the implicit or explicit understanding that they would be moderate in their tactics and policies."[2] Such moderation on behalf of the opposition entailed agreeing to abandon violence and any commitment to revolution; accepting existing basic social, economic, and political institutions; and working through elections and parliamentary procedures in order to put through their policies.

Stathis Kalyvas was the first scholar to demonstrate that religious actors are as capable of moderation as any other antisystem party. He argued that socialists and Catholics in nineteenth-century Europe entered the political system in order to make immediate gains to their interests but as a result ended up compromising their goals as they became part of the system. Kalyvas summarizes the moderation of Catholic parties as follows: (1) mass mobilization, (2) an antisystem political discourse, (3) the combination of an appeal to religious sensibilities coupled with a political message of economic inclusion, (4) the transformation of religious practices, and (5) the moderation of Catholic parties and the democratization of the political institutions within which they operated. Drawing on the example of the Islamist movement in Turkey, he argues that liberalization, democratization, and inclusion are more likely where states reward moderation, punish antisystem behavior, and include Islamists in meaningful electoral competition.[3]

Elsewhere, however, Kalyvas has also argued that only religious institutions with hierarchical structures can alleviate the commitment problems necessary for democratization.

> The centralized, autocratic, and hierarchical organization of Catholicism allowed moderate Catholics to solve their commitment problem, while the absence of a comparable structure in Algeria contributed to the inability of the moderate FIS leadership credibly to signal its future intentions. It is indeed ironic that Islam's open, decentralized and more democratic structure eventually contributed to the failure of democratization, while the autocratic organization of the Catholic Church facilitated a democratic outcome.[4]

While Kalyvas's account is useful for highlighting the unintended consequences of participation, his description of Islamic parties as unable to commit credibly runs at odds with the many cases where Islamic parties have maintained such commitments, more specifically the eighty-nine parliamentary elections in twenty-one countries where Islamic parties have repeatedly contested elections.[5] Additionally, subsequent scholarship on the Belgian and Algerian cases has criticized Kalyvas's account for ignoring regime differences in favor of cultural determinism; credible commitments in Algeria were less important to the success of the democratic transition than the regime possessing a secure military apparatus and Western support—and the regime being uninterested in relinquishing power.[6]

More importantly, and similar to the Indonesian case, Kurzman and Naqvi found that since the 1970s Islamic political parties have consistently moderated as a result of their participation. That moderation has been visible on the issues of implementation of sharia, jihad, opposition to capitalism, and hostility toward Israel; the parties have also become more explicitly supportive of religious-minority rights, democracy, and women's rights.[7] In an important review essay, Jillian Schwedler agrees that Islamists are capable of moderation and distinguishes the factors behind the behavioral moderation of groups, the ideological moderation of groups, and the ideological moderation of individuals.[8]

There are, however, important critiques of inclusion-moderation theory. Nancy Bermeo argues that radical mass organizations may not imperil democratic transitions. Drawing on the Portuguese transition of 1974–1975, she shows that the democratization process survived even though capitalist property rights were challenged on a large scale by a mobilized working class. Likewise, the armed wing of the Basque separatist movement, Euskadi Ta Askatasuna, failed to moderate its demands during the Spanish transition of the late 1970s, nor did its use of violence decrease during the successful democratic transition. Furthermore, using comparative data on labor strikes during the democratic transitions in Brazil, Chile, Ecuador, South Korea, Peru, and the Philippines, she shows that the politically mobilized working class did not moderate their demands during those transitions. Her conclusion is worth repeating: "Moderation is not a prerequisite for the construction of democracy; the parameters of tolerable mobilization are broader than we originally anticipated. In many cases, democratization seems to have proceeded alongside weighty and even bloody popular challenges."[9] Additional critiques come from Güneş Murat Tezcür and Schwedler, both of whom argue that behavior moderation may serve to hamper democratic transitions and bolster authoritarian regimes that co-opt Islamists rather than engage in substantive reform of political institutions.[10] Schwedler challenges scholars to unearth their normative preference for moderation, since democratization may demand *immoderate* behavior in order for social actors to topple Middle Eastern dictators. This chapter attempts to answer Schwedler's important appeal.

The Indonesian case affirms the argument that the inclusion of antisystem parties in the political process fosters their moderation. Indonesia is home to some of the largest, oldest, and most politically influential mass Islamic organizations in the world. Muhammadiyah is the world's largest Islamic reformist (or modernist, based on the ideas of Mohammad Abduh and Rasyid Ridha) organization, with twenty-five to thirty million members rooted in schools, universities, hospitals, and health clinics. Nahdlatul Ulama (NU) is among the world's largest traditional Islamic organizations, with upward of sixty million members based largely in Java and organized around Islamic boarding schools (*pesantren*) and prominent ulama. Together these two organizations, including their women's wings, run thousands of schools and universities, hundreds of hospitals and clinics, youth organizations, mosques, and prayer circles. Of Indonesia's two hundred million Muslims, 75 percent identify with one or the other.[11] A third organization under review, Persatuan Islam (Persis), is substantially smaller but one of the most intellectually influential Indonesian Islamist organizations, founded before the Muslim Brotherhood in 1923. The three are ideologically varied—Muhammadiyah is modernist, NU traditionalism hews closely to the Shafi'i school of jurisprudence, and Persis is Islamist—yet all three organizations and their political vehicles have undergone significant moderation.[12]

These organizations have moderated from being antinationalist to Islamic nationalist and from Islamic nationalist to inclusive-Islamist. Their ideologies have shifted from emphasizing Islam as the all-encompassing solution to emphasizing the comparative advantage of moral parties for combating corruption, from being opposed to the national ideology of Pancasila on the ground that it was anti-Islam toward reconciling Pancasila and Islam, and from being exclusively Muslim and targeting only Muslim voters to courting secular Muslims and even having token non-Muslims on their election tickets.[13] Indonesian Islamic organizations are not secular or liberal, but they have moderated since they were created in the early twentieth century.

Indonesia provides strong evidence that if you allow Islamic organizations to participate in the political process they will moderate their demands and become part of the system rather than seeking to overthrow it. This has happened in a few steps. First, Islamist movements accepted the boundaries of the contemporary state and became rooted in the interests of the population in that territory. This meant putting aside notions of a global caliphate or a pan-Islamic political union; this happened mostly in the 1930s and 1940s. Second, Islamic organizations accepted elections as the legitimate means to obtaining political power and transforming state and society. Implicit in this move was the recognition of non-Muslim actors as well as more secular Muslims as part of the system. Most Indonesian Islamic organizations accepted elections as a legitimate method of transforming the state in the 1950s and 1960s. Third, Islamic organizations accepted democracy as a value in its own right and not as a process to Islamizing the state. This step involved accepting that society is religiously plural and that the state must cater to the needs of a diverse citizenry. Most mass Islamic organizations underwent this shift in the 1970s and 1980s, with their political vehicles doing the same in the 1990s and 2000s. Table 8.1 provides an overview of the stages of moderation of Indonesia's major Islamic organizations during the twentieth and early twenty-first century.

Table 8.1 details the major shifts toward moderation during the period from 1924 to 2010. There are, of course, inevitable exceptions to the rule in a country as large and diverse as Indonesia. In the 1950s, the Darul Islam rebellion used military force to try to make Indonesia an Islamic state.[14] In contemporary Indonesia there are new, militant Islamists like the terrorist group Jemaah Islamiyah, the vigilante group Front Pembela Islam, and the pan-Islamist political party Hizb-ut Tahrir, which seek to create an Islamic state. These groups are more successful at gaining publicity than social support. The rule is also subject to temporal variation. NU was an early moderator, and Persis has been the last and most incomplete. The new Islamist party PKS has moderated in a shorter time span than the older organizations, owing to its roots in the 1980s *tarbiyah* movement. The rule is also varied across issues. Islamic organizations are more tolerant of Christians today than in the 1920s, but the same cannot be said for their tolerance of communists or Ahmadi Muslims, due to the influence of state policies.[15] Similarly, Islamic organizations are significantly more liberal about women's use of birth control than in the 1930s but are resistant to other forms of birth control, such as nonemergency abortion, as well as to

1924	**PAN-ISLAM**: Representatives from Muhammadiyah, Sarekat Islam, and Abdul Wahab Chasbullah (later the founder of NU) issue a joint call for the creation of a modernized caliphate that will be representative, elected, led by a caliph, funded by the world Muslim community, and based in an independent Muslim country.
1930s	Subsequent attempts to mobilize Indonesian Muslims behind pan-Islamic ideals fail because of doctrinal differences between traditionalists and modernists.
1941	Ahmad Hassan of Persis publishes a pamphlet saying Islam is incompatible with nationalism: "Whoever calls for nationalism is not one of us; whoever fights for the (cause of) nationalism is not one of us; and whoever dies for the (cause of) nationalism is not one of us."
1945	**INDONESIAN ISLAMIC NATIONALISM**: Despite Hassan's argument of 1941, NU issues dramatic call for Indonesian Muslims to join the national revolution as an obligatory jihad.
1945	Muslim representatives on the constitution-drafting committee support a preamble that "all Muslims are obliged to carry out Islamic Law." This "Jakarta Charter" is dropped from the final version of the constitution.
1955	Muslim political parties win 44 percent of the vote. They are unable to pass legislation mandating the state implementation of Islamic law without a majority in parliament.
1970	**INDONESIAN ISLAMIC PLURALISM**: Nurcholish Madjid, Syaafi Maarif, and other influential intellectuals of the *pembaharuan pimikiran* movement call for "desacralizing" political parties and the state: "Islam yes, Partai Islam no" (Yes to Islam, no to Islamic parties) and "Tidakada Negara Islam" (There is no Islamic state).
1983	Abdurrahman Wahid leads NU, returns to its "Khittah of 1926" of social and educational activism, disallows prominent NU officials to lead political parties, and adopts Pancasila as NU's ideology.
1999	**INCLUSIVE INDONESIAN ISLAMIC POLITICAL PARTIES**: NU's PKB and Muhammadiyah's PAN run as inclusive Islamic political parties with non-Muslims, ethnic Chinese, and unaffiliated Muslims on their ticket.
2000–2002	Islamist parties PBB, PK, and PPP support the reintroduction of the Jakarta Charter but receive little support in parliament.

(*continued*)

TABLE 8.1 MODERATION OF MAJOR INDONESIAN MUSLIM
ORGANIZATIONS, 1945–2014 (*continued*)

2004	As a more moderate Islamist party, PKS (previously PK) wins 7.3 percent of the vote and three cabinet seats.
2006–2010	PKS moderates further, embraces Pancasila, allows women and non-Muslims to hold executive positions, and enters into coalition with non-Islamist parties.
2010	In response to new Islamists (*Hizbut Tahrir, Front Pembela Islam*), Persis joins interfaith-dialogue groups and builds bridges with the government. Persis Chair Maman Abdurrahment declares, "Dakwah [Islamic propagation] is more effective when we are close to the palace," and President Susilo Bambang Yudhoyono attends the national congress.

Sources: Robert Elson, "Disunity, Distance, Disregard: The Political Failure of Islamism in Late Colonial Indonesia," *Studio Islamika* 16, no. 1 (2009): 1–50; Martin van Bruinessen, "Muslims of the Dutch East Indies and the Caliphate Question," *Studio Islamika* 2, no. 3 (1995): 115–140; Howard Federspiel, "Islam and Nationalism," *Indonesia* 24 (1977): 39–85; Dirk Tomsa, "Moderating Islamism in Indonesia," *Political Research Quarterly* 65, no. 3 (2009): 486–498.

the use of birth control by unmarried women.[16] All of these exceptions, however, do not negate the general trend. The largest and most influential Indonesian Islamic organizations have undergone ideological and behavior moderation as a result of their inclusion in the political process.

Why have Indonesian Islamic organizations moderated? The literature points to three primary mechanisms underlying moderation.[17] First, while voters care about religious issues, they also care about economic, social, and cultural issues. Political parties competing in successive elections therefore have a strategic incentive to broaden their policy stances beyond the implementation of sharia to other issues, including more secular issues and issues in which cooperation with non-Muslims is necessary.[18] Indonesian political parties have learned this, and those Islamic parties that have moderated have generally performed better in electoral competition than those who have not (this point is discussed below). Second, ideological change often follows behavioral shifts. In order to change policies, Islamic leaders must undergo debate within their organization, cooperate with groups outside their organization, and are often led by charismatic leaders who are capable of shifting their groups' preferences.[19] Charismatic leaders like Abdurrahman Wahid have led similar debates and transformations within Indonesian Islamic organizations and civil society. Third, individuals, rather than groups, have moderated their views through political learning. Wickham, Huntington, and Bermeo see learning as distinct from strategic calculation and see individuals changing their beliefs as a result of interaction with their environment.[20] Nurcholish Madjid and Syaffi Maarif are credited with making similar shifts in Indonesian Islam as a result of their education and relationships with others and then shaping the behavior of mass Islamic organizations.

In addition to the existing mechanisms of moderation, the Indonesian case suggests that two other mechanisms, war and endogenous organizational leadership shifts, provide opportunities for moderation. First, scholars of political development have long recognized that war offers a key moment for changing the relationship between state and society.[21] The 1945–1950 revolutionary war against the Dutch was marked by Christian and Muslim unity in defense of the newly proclaimed homeland. NU and Muhammadiyah declared that defense of the fatherland against the Dutch was a holy war, an obligation for all Muslims. This was in contrast to the 1940s, when they refused a Japanese request to declare World War II a holy war.[22] Similarly, as a result of their participation in the war, Indonesian Christians came to be seen as part of the nation instead of as foreigners backed by Dutch finance and power.[23] And Muslim leaders, including those from Persis, began to see Christians as allies rather than enemies and began working more productively with non-Muslim Indonesians. Second, key changes in Indonesian organizations' policies have been accompanied by an internal leadership shift. While the concept of a leadership shift has not been articulated in the literature on moderation, its occurrence is common in scholarship on other organizations.[24] Quinn Mecham argues that the Welfare (Refah) and Virtue (Fazilet) parties in Turkey moderated their platforms in response to strategic interaction in a political system that rewards political entrepreneurship, the presence of institutional constraints on the Islamist movement's behavior, and incentives for the movement to provide costly signals about its intentions. Key to Mecham's story is the switch from the old parties' elites, Recaï Kutan and Necmettin Erbakan, to the new leaders, Recep Tayyip Erdogan and Abdullah Gül.[25] Likewise, in the Indonesian case Edward Aspinall explains the transformation of the Islamist Darul Islam rebellion into a secular, ethnically Achenese movement on the basis of national identity construction and differentiation. Central to Aspinall's story is the changing leadership of the movement from the chiefly caste, the *uleebalang*, to the Islamic *ulama* and then to more secular Achenese nationalists.[26]

Most analyses of religious parties end at this juncture of the moderation of ideology and behavior.[27] What this stopping point ignores, however, is that the inclusion of Islamic actors changes both the political system and society. The next section lays out the logic of coevolution and its implications for democracy.

THEORY

I define the "sacralizing of the state" as a process of layering laws and administrative regulations onto those of the secular state in order to promote individual adherence to religious values, communal identification with religious communities, and a state that prioritizes religious belief as an important part of national identity and for the functioning of sociopolitical institutions. The goal of sacralizing is not for the state to be the object of worship but rather for the state to be a conduit for individual and collective belief.

The term "sacralizing" is derived from related processes described by sociologists of religion. Peter Berger coined the term "desecularization" to describe the resurgence of religious identities and movements in the world, a process that is occurring alongside secularization.[28] Yet the term desecularization is unhelpful here because it suggests that underneath the Indonesian state is latent sacred content. The Indonesian state did not exist prior to its creation by the Dutch, which makes any discussion of latent content illogical. "Desecular" is also a negative category—*not* secular—which tells us nothing about the *positive* content of the new laws and regulations. Another related process is "Islamizing," which Indonesian scholars use to refer to the conversion of syncretic (*abangan*) and secular Muslims to more orthodox practices.[29] Here, too, the term is unhelpful because the state is not becoming Islamic. Instead, I use the term "sacralizing" because it captures the layering on of laws and regulations designed to imbue the state with a positive commitment to religious values.

Sacralizing of the Indonesian state occurred after independence. The national legislature, office of the executive, political parties, and administrative bureaucracy have all contributed to drafting and implementing laws designed to promote religious values. Key policy areas are education, recognition of religion, marriage laws, building of places of worship, and the regulation of proselytizing. The result is that, as the constitutional scholar Donald Horowitz notes, the contemporary Indonesian constitution is not "100 percent secular."[30]

This trend is also apparent through the changing ideology of Indonesian political parties. Indonesia has held five free and fair national elections since 1955. Here I want to borrow from Anies Baswedan's influential typology of political party ideologies: Islamic-exclusive, Islamic-inclusive, secular-exclusive, and secular-inclusive.[31]

- Islamic-exclusive are parties that want the state to be based on Islamic law: Masyumi, PNU, PPP, PBB, PK, and the Reform Star Party (PBR).

- Islamic-inclusive are the parties that have moderated; they are Islamic but inclusive of non-Muslims in both their membership and policies: PKB, PKNU, PAN, and PKS.

- Secular-exclusive are ardent secularists who argue that the state must not be involved in religious affairs; they include the Indonesian Communist Party (PKI), Indonesian Nationalist Party (PNI), and the Indonesian Democratic Party of Struggle (PDIP).

- Secular-inclusive are parties that follow in the tradition of Golkar under Soeharto during the mid-1980s and 1990s. In the 1980s, Golkar embraced the ideas of Nurcholish Madjid and worked with Islamic leaders who claimed that it is legitimate for Muslims to expect the government to reflect the moral values of Islam. Baswedan contrasts Golkar with the secular-exclusive views of PDIP, whose founder Megawati Sukarnoputri follows in the tradition of her father Sukarno's PNI.[32] The secular-inclusive parties include Golkar as well as Susilo Bambang Yudhoyono's Democrat Party (PD), the Christian Prosperous Peace Party (PDS), and the National Democrat Party (NasDem).[33]

The sacralizing of the state has occurred under the watch of the inclusive-Islamic and the inclusive-secular parties. These parties are the ones that have backed legislation and administrative regulations that promote religious education, the privileging of religious beliefs over heterodox or animist faiths, religious marriage, and limits on proselytizing.

Most Islamic political parties have moderated their policies over the course of successive elections and been rewarded by voters. Those that have not moderated have lost vote share. Meanwhile, the secular parties have also moderated their policies toward inclusion or lost vote share. The big winners have been the two middle groups: inclusive Islamic parties and inclusive secular parties.

The result of these dual processes is that Indonesia is today a democracy that makes the promotion of religious values like belief in god and communal affiliation a major goal for civil society and the state.[34] In this regard, Indonesia is similar to India, Romania, Bulgaria, Greece, some Swiss cantons, and Austria. Like Indonesia, these governments have mandatory religious education, mandatory registration of religions and a multitiered system of recognition, marriage laws based on religious affiliation, communitarian laws regulating the construction of churches, and financial support for corporatist umbrella bodies representing each recognized religion. These are not theocratic polities but rather ones that promote religious values while synthesizing liberal individual rights and group-differentiated rights within a system of legal pluralism. Within Alfred Stepan's framework, the Indonesian government is closest to the model of a "Nonsecular, but Friendly to Democracy" pattern of religious-state relations.[35] Indonesian democracy is based on a combined commitment by the state and civil society to promote religious values but is also plural in providing multiple pathways. As long as citizens belong to one of the state-sanctioned routes to religious belief, they become full members of civil society and receive state protection and other benefits of citizenship.

This comparative perspective illuminates a limitation to Kalyvas's work beyond the critiques leveled by Schwedler, Kurzman and Naqvi, Bermeo, and Brownlee. Kalyvas's account of how Catholics compromised their goals as they became part of the system assumes that the state is always and already secular and is unresponsive to the religious preferences of those who govern. While such a stylized account may be useful for the purpose of producing a formal model, it runs roughshod over the impact of Europe's Christian heritage and its Christian democratic parties on political institutions. That impact may have been latent in the 1990s when Kalyvas was writing, but Europe's Christian identity and institutions are readily apparent, for example, in contemporary discussions about the boundaries of the European Union and the assimilation of Muslim minorities.[36] In that respect, studying peripheral states like Indonesia, where Islamic actors are central to the crafting of mutual accommodation, may elucidate aspects of Europe's present, rather than its past.

To develop these claims further, the next section delves into the process of sacralizing the state in order to explain how Indonesia transformed its secular postcolonial institutions.

SACRALIZING THE POSTCOLONIAL STATE

The sacralizing of Indonesian law is most apparent in four policy areas: education, recognition of religion, marriage law, and interfaith proselytizing. These areas have become radically transformed since independence. Each area has progressed differently and will be described separately in order to specify the determinants of the change. That said, oftentimes change happens for a convergence of reasons. For example, a law may be passed because an authoritarian leader wants more control over society, or because Islamic leaders want limits on Christian missionary activity, or because religious organizations want to protect their boundaries. Sometimes these logics overlap.

EDUCATION

Formal education in the Netherlands East Indies was initially reserved for a shallow elite of the traditional aristocracy groomed to be administrators under Dutch rule. The famous Dutch Orientalist Christiaan Snouck Hurgronje believed that education was an ideal vehicle for co-opting the native elites. This approach, known as the "Association Theory," educated the aristocracy in Dutch and incorporated them into European culture while marginalizing religious and ethnic leaders in order to forestall their political influence.[37] Religious education was not included in the elite Dutch-language schools (*hoogere burgerschool*). In the period after 1900, pressure from Amsterdam to institute more ethical policies led to the creation of a mass-education system of village schools covering basic literacy, numeracy, and practical skills. By 1930, there were 16,605 schools, and over 40 percent of Indonesian children attended them, albeit only sporadically. The effects were made clear by the 1930 census, which registered only 7.4 percent literacy.[38] And again, religious education was expressly excluded. Religious education did occur, however, in large numbers through private education by Christian missionaries and Islamic organizations. Java and Madura had recorded 10,830 Islamic schools in 1893, and by 1938, Muhammadiyah had 1,774 schools of their own.[39]

After independence, the Ministry of Education set up a commission to design an education system for the new country. The outcome was Law 4/1950 on Basic Education and Teaching in Schools and Law 12/1954, which incorporated optional religious education into all government schools. A letter from the minister of religion and minister of education instructed public schools to provide Islamic education, and a joint regulation by the minister of education and minister of religion in 1951 clarified that religious education was only necessary if there were at least ten students of that religion. The final act of the decade was in 1960, when the provisional parliament (Majelis Permusyarwatan Rakyat, MPRS), under the firm control of Sukarno, issued a law that reaffirmed that parents can choose for their child to opt out of religious-education classes.[40]

Six years later, religious education became mandatory when the MPRS, now under the control of Soeharto, exchanged the provision about optional religious education with "religious education is a compulsory subject in all schools, from primary through to university."[41] This forced parents to identify their children as belonging to one of the six recognized religions: Islam, Catholicism, Protestantism, Hinduism, Buddhism, and Confucianism. This policy, like the blasphemy law discussed below, helped Soeharto co-opt religious organizations while decreasing support for his communist opponents.

This policy has become formalized and institutionalized in the subsequent decades but remains essentially the same as when it was put into place in 1966. In 1975, Soeharto reaffirmed in a speech to mark the birthday of the Prophet Muhammad that religious education was not only necessary in public schools at all levels but also in private schools. In 1985, the minister for education reinforced that students must be educated in their respective religion and, further, that schools must provide at least two hours of religious education per week if there were more than ten students of that religion.[42] The only exception was for private religious schools, which were not required to provide religious institutions for students of other faiths, for example, Muslims in Christian schools. The legislature cemented this policy through Law 2/1989 on the National Education System, which required religious education alongside education in the Pancasila and citizenship.[43]

In the democratic period, the major legislation on schooling affirmed that religious education is a core concern of the Indonesian state and religious identity an important part of being a full citizen. Article 31 of the 1945 constitution was amended to include the clause committing the government to a "system of education that increases religious faith, devoutness, and character."[44] Article 31(3) of Law no. 20 of 2003 on the National Education System obliges the state to maintain and develop an education system that "increases faith, awareness of God and moral conduct" according to the religion students follow, and it must be taught by a teacher of the same religion. Article 12(1) is understood to require all schools, public and private, to provide religious education to all students, thereby overturning the exception for Christian schools. The subsequent Government Regulation no. 55 of 2007 on Religious Education for the Recognized Religions implemented the law and required that educational institutions comply by 2009 or be subject to sanctions, including closure.[45]

Although Christians and secular human rights organizations have opposed these changes, Islamic organizations see them as a necessary component of building the institutions of a strong society. While the Islamist party PKS declared the passage of Article 12 to be one of its chief political successes, these laws should not be interpreted as creeping Islamization or intolerance to religious minorities.[46] Muhammadiyah schools in Flores, West Kalimantan, and North Sumatra, where the students are majority Christian or Buddhist, have followed this template since the 1970s. There, teachers of any faith provide instruction in math, history, English, and other secular subjects to students of any religion. Doctrine is taught according to religious identity.[47] Muhammadiyah supports religious-self governance, with each faith tending after their flock. The often-referenced line from the Quran, "to you your religion, and to me mine" (*lakum dinukum waliyadin*), appears in many Muhammadiyah publications about appropriate relations with non-Muslims. In survey data, both NU and Muhammadiyah support having Christians, Hindus, and even Ahmadi Muslims teach in private Islamic schools as long as the content is secular. They are clear, however, that non-Muslims should not teach Islam in public or private schools. Likewise, Muslims should not teach the tenets of other faiths.[48]

Mandatory religious education is one way that Islamic organizations, political parties, the bureaucracy, and the executive have sacralized the policies of the secular postcolonial state. In comparative perspective, Indonesia is not unusual in making religious education mandatory; fourteen other democracies do the same. This policy is tolerant to Indonesia's recognized minority religions but discriminates against atheist students as well as those whose faiths fall outside those recognized by the state. One policy that could remedy this discrimination is for students of unrecognized religions to be accommodated in a class on comparative religions or ethics; Indonesia is unusual among democracies in not providing such an option. Greece has compulsory religious education in primary and secondary schools, but students may be exempted upon request. In Austria, attendance in religious instruction is mandatory for all students unless they formally withdraw at the beginning of the school year. Senegal provides formal education in multiple religions with an option to withdraw. In sum, democracies can mandate religious education in schools as long as students have a choice in which religion they are incorporated, including an option to study comparative religions or ethics. Such accommodations are important parts of making democracy work in places where the state and society see religious belief as an important component of national identity.

RECOGNITION OF RELIGION

As the Netherlands East Indies advisor on Arabian and native affairs, Hurgronje put into place another policy that would gradually be overturned after Dutch rule ended. In order to quell the influence of Islamic leaders in Aceh, West Java, and Central Java, Hurgronje counseled in favor of dividing Islam into two parts, one religious and one political. "Toward the former, Snouck counseled in favor of toleration: a policy of neutrality toward religious life."[49] Toleration entailed lowering obstacles for the pilgrimage to Mecca and even supporting a few Islamic schools, albeit with funds far below those given to Christian schools.

Toward the end of Dutch rule this policy began to crumble. The first major Islamic political coalition, the High Islamic Council of Indonesia (MIAI), was formed in 1937 in order to oppose the laws on marriage and Christian missionary activity (discussed below) as well as to organize Muslims for independence. While MIAI lasted only from 1937 to 1943, it profoundly influenced the institutions of the protostate. From 1942 to 1943, the occupying Japanese transformed MIAI from an Islamic federation into the political party Masyumi and embedded it in the institutional structures of the protostate through the Office of Religious Affairs, which became today's Ministry of Religious Affairs (MORA).[50] When the

Japanese occupation ended the following year, the Islamic organizations that had formed MIAI became the governing religious authorities in the new state. Since the MORA's creation, those organizations' control over the MORA and its penetration into every level of government have allowed it to shape the meaning of religion in Indonesia and the boundaries of recognition.

Article 28e, paragraph 1 of the 1945 constitution provides that "Every person shall be free to adhere to a religion and to worship in accordance with his/her religion." Paragraph 2 states, "Every person shall have the right to the freedom to hold a belief, to express his/her thoughts and attitude in accordance with his/her conscience." The constitution also reads, however, that this freedom is not absolute. Article 28j, paragraph 2 says, "In exercising his/her rights and freedom, every person must be subject to the restrictions stipulated in laws and regulations with the sole purpose to guarantee the recognition of and the respect for rights and freedom of other persons and to fulfill fair demand in accordance with the considerations of moral and religious values, security, and public order in a democratic society." Furthermore, the definition of religion has been a source of contestation.

The MORA's mission included: (1) to make belief in the One and Only God an operative principle in public life; (2) to be watchful that every inhabitant is free to adhere to his own religion and to worship according to his own religion; and (3) to assist, support, protect, and promote all sound religious movements.[51] The first task is a reference to the national ideology of Pancasila, with belief in God as the first principle. The second professes freedom of religion, but the meaning of the Indonesian word for religion, *agama*, is narrower than its English equivalent. *Agama* was defined in 1952 by the MORA as a monotheistic religion with belief in the existence of One Supreme God, a holy book, a prophet, and a way of life for its adherents.[52] This definition closely resembled Muhammadiyah's definition of religion. Islam, Roman Catholicism, and Christianity (Protestantism) were recognized as religions in 1951; Hinduism and Buddhism were included in 1958 under pressure from Sukarno; and Confucianism was added in 2000. Recasting Hinduism, Buddhism, and Confucianism to meet this monotheist and Abrahamic definition of religion entailed some bureaucratic creativity, but that did not deter the MORA, which simply identified a godhead, a messiah figure, and a single holy book for each religion. The third task suggests the limits of official tolerance—"unsound" movements were designated deviant streams (*aliran sesat*) or faiths (*kepercayaan*) rather than religions.

Since the 1950s, adherents to deviant streams and faiths have been pressured to join the recognized religions. In 1954, the MORA set up a special Section for the Supervision of Faith Movements in Society that monitored heterodox, heretical, and apostate faiths.[53] The policing of heterodoxy got a boost in authority in 1965 when President Sukarno affirmed that there were only six recognized religions and declared that any group that threatened these religions should be prohibited. On January 27, 1965, he signed Presidential Order no. 1: "Every person shall be prohibited from deliberately before the public telling, encouraging, or soliciting public support for making an interpretation of a religion adhered to in Indonesia or performing religious activities resembling the activities of such religion when the interpretation and activities are deviant from the principal teachings of such religion."[54] Sukarno's "blasphemy law" formalized the orthodox definition of religion that the Islamic organizations had long sought. The law was announced flanked by a joint statement of support by NU, Muhammadiyah, Partai Sarekat Islam Indonesia, the traditionalist Islamic group Jamiatul Washliyah, and the Indonesian Joint Trade Union.[55] Mystical sects were only marginally tolerated; they were recognized as a category of faith rather than as religions and were not entitled to resources from or protection by the state.[56]

Like education, since 1965, the laws regulating recognition have become stronger. Laws concerning personal identity are based on membership in one of the six recognized religions inscribed on each individual's identification card. The state privileges recognized religions, and any educational institution under the auspices of the MORA receives funding while being subject to oversight. Lindsey notes that for a brief period in the mid-1970s the parliament upgraded the official status of beliefs.[57] Yet this was short-lived. By 1978, the regime backed down, and the minister of religion "formally reiterated that 'beliefs' were not religions."[58]

The result is that in contemporary, democratic Indonesia, faith organizations are not able to access funding from the government that is allocated to religions, and individuals have to identify as adherents of one of the six religions on their identity card and in order to register their marriage.[59] According to Crouch, since 2006 a person may leave the "religion/ belief" section of their identity card blank, although they are still required to register their religious affiliation with the government.[60] This allowance is highly contested; a 2014 announcement that Joko Widodo's new minister of home affairs planned to allow individuals to leave that section blank was met by outrage from religious leaders, and the proposal quietly disappeared. As a result, there are some regions home to large numbers of *kepercayaan* (belief associations) followers where the bureaucracy will allow individuals to leave their religion section blank, but most regions will not.[61]

An influential Constitutional Court decision of 2010 reaffirmed that the 1965 blasphemy law is valid and constitutional and does not contravene the constitutional right to freedom of religion. While the National Protestant Council and National Catholic Council called for the law either to be revoked or revised, most of Islamic civil society and representatives of the country's minority groups supported the law. Eight of the nine justices and the overwhelming majority of witnesses supported the continued exclusion of heterodox faiths from state recognition. In survey data, both NU and Muhammadiyah are supportive of Christians and Hindus receiving the rights and benefits of citizenship but do not accord the same rights to individuals with heterodox beliefs, liminal groups, or communists.[62] In practice, this means that the government has preserved its authority to ban deviant religious groups, distinguish between religions and mystical beliefs, and promote individual and collective adherence to universal religions.

Recognition of religions is another way that Islamic organizations have sacralized the policies of the postcolonial state. While jarring to proponents of secular or liberal government, Indonesia's multitiered system for religious recognition is not unique among democracies. In Romania, the state recognizes eighteen denominations that enjoy the right to build houses of worship and perform rites of baptism, marriage, or burial; a guarantee to state noninterference; and protection against public stereotypes and negative media campaigns. The second, lower tier is composed of religious associations that also get tax breaks but do not otherwise enjoy the advantages of recognition. A similar example is Austria, which has three tiers of registration.

That said, while democratic states that demand registration may promote religious values through recognized privileges, they must also allow heterodox groups to register and receive protection from persecution. In Indonesia, *kepercayaan* groups are currently denied access to funding for their schools, cannot list their religion on their ID cards, are prohibited from entering the military, and have refused to send their children to school because their children would be educated in one of the recognized religions. This stigmatization in society is inconsistent with basic democratic liberties. Remedying this discrimination means allowing all registered groups to list their religious identification on their identification card or to leave the column blank. That would be consistent with the protection of individual rights, the promotion of communal values, and the transparency that befits Indonesia's consolidated democracy.

MARRIAGE

Depending on the "law group" of the person, different laws governed marriages in the Netherlands East Indies. "Europeans" included Dutch and other nationals; their marriages were governed by secular civil law. "Foreign Orientals" included Chinese, Arabs, and South Asians, who were also covered by the Civil Code. "Indigenous" Indonesians were governed by customary law (*adat*), which was specifically privileged by the famous Dutch Orientalist Snouck Hurgronje over Islamic law for Christians and non-Muslims. Muslims were married according to the Shafi'i mazhab. Hurgronje argued that only when one could ascertain that Islamic law had been received into customary law would the courts enforce it. Hurgronje's "reception policy" meant civil courts, using customary law (*adat*), not religion, frequently governed matters of inheritance.[63] The existence of different marriage laws for different groups created a need for a mechanism to decide on regulations governing marriages between persons from different groups. To resolve this, the Regulation on Mixed Marriage of 1898 stated that interfaith marriage was explicitly allowed because "difference of religion, nationality or origin is not a hindrance to marriage."[64] The regulation further stated that marriage between persons of different law groups was to be performed according to the law applicable to the husband. Thus civil marriage, without respect to the religious identity of the participants, was a predominant feature of the East Indies law through to independence, when with independence in 1945 it was declared that existing laws would continue in force until replaced by new legislation.

On March 5, 1944, the Japanese colonial government announced the creation of regional offices for religious affairs. Each residency as well as Jakarta and the sultanates were to create a Religious Affairs section within their education bureau.[65] Importantly, these offices were given control of Islamic affairs, including marriage. Control over marriage laws, a longstanding priority for Muslims who had chafed at the dominance of civil and Dutch regulations, finally became a reality. The MIAI had included among its top concerns opposition to the legal structure of the Dutch government, specifically the policies regarding marriage, inheritance, and restrictions on religious propagation (discussed below). After independence, the government added Statute no. 22/1946, requiring registration of Muslim marriage by the newly created Office of Religious Affairs (Kantor Urusan Agama, KUA) under the MORA.

As we have seen, the Islamic organizations driving policy in the MORA have had significant autonomy in interpreting government statutes. In the 1950s the MORA refused to register a marriage between a Muslim woman and a non-Muslim man on the grounds that such marriages are not permitted under Islamic law. Thus the MORA privileged their interpretation of Islamic law over the 1898 statute. The Indonesian Supreme Court heard the case and affirmed the validity of the Mixed Marriage Regulation. That was not, however, the end of the debate: the Supreme Court decision was met by a mass demonstration in September 1952 opposing the Mixed Marriage Regulation, petitioning for a new law, and urging the new government to declare the marriage invalid.[66]

While replacing Dutch marriage legislation with national law was a priority for the new state, none of the proposals debated in the 1950s and 1960s were enacted. Cammack notes that the principal point of contention was whether to enact a single set of civil rules or to provide different marriage laws for different communities. The Soeharto government favored the former and presented a largely secular marriage law in 1973, tracking the language of the Dutch regulation permitting interfaith marriage.[67] An overwhelming majority of the legislature supported the bill, including the governing Golkar party, the PDI, and the armed forces.

Islamic civil society, however, felt differently. Ulama condemned the bill during Friday prayers and held mass demonstrations in Jakarta. Two prominent NU leaders, K. H. Bisri Sansuri and K. H. Masyukur, met with Soeharto to voice their opposition.[68] Muhammadiyah ran a series of articles arguing that the bill was a covert form of "Christianization" (Kristenisasi) intended to convert the Muslim community to Christianity. In later years Muhammadiyah even came out against all forms of interfaith marriage despite a general consensus within Islamic law that Muslim men are permitted to marry Jewish and Christian women.[69]

The intensity of opposition to the bill surprised Soeharto, who instructed the parties to work out a compromise. The result is that Article 2 and Article 11 of the 1975 Marriage Act say that marriage must be consistent with the religious law of the parties. The elucidation further states that "there is no marriage outside of the religious law of the parties," suggesting that civil marriage would no longer be recognized.[70] The clause that permitted interreligious marriage was dropped, but the law did not specifically state that interreligious marriage is prohibited.

Proponents of interreligious marriage point to the lack of a repeal of the Regulation on Mixed Marriage of 1898 to argue that it is legal under contemporary Indonesian law. Yet, as Cammack notes: "It is generally regarded as common knowledge in Indonesia that marriage between persons of different religions is not allowed." In December 1988, the Jakarta Civil Registry adopted the policy that it would not perform civil marriages. In January 1989, they adopted the policy that civil marriages would not be recognized. The 2006 Law on Civil Registration certified that there are separate marriage registries for Indonesian Muslims and non-Muslims, and the MORA maintains that interreligious marriage is not allowed.[71] And a 2015 Supreme Court decision reaffirmed that the 1974 prohibition on interfaith unions will endure under the democratic government.[72]

In prohibiting mixed marriage, the MORA policy reflects the opinion of the major Islamic organizations. Nahdlatul Ulama came out against interreligious marriages at a Muktamar in 1962, another in 1968, and in a fatwa in 1989.[73] The Indonesian Council of Ulamas (Majelis Ulama Indonesia, MUI) issued a fatwa prohibiting mixed marriage in 1980.[74] Muhammadiyah likewise declared interreligious marriage prohibited in 1989.[75] All three organizations have adopted this restricted policy out of fears that Christians might use intermarriage in order to convert Muslims.[76]

Indonesia's restriction on interfaith marriage and requirement that marriages be done according to religious law is another way that the state has become sacralized since the colonial period. Such a policy is not unusual in comparative perspective; as of 2008, thirty-four countries around the world have personal status defined by religion or clergy, and twenty-seven restrict interfaith marriages. But Indonesia is among a small number of democratic countries, including India and Israel, that prohibit intermarriage. In practice, however, as many of 50 percent of marriages in Indonesia are unregistered, and Cammack notes that the civil registry will sometimes record interfaith marriages.[77]

PROSELYTIZING

Limitations on missionary activity including proselytizing were included in the Constitution of the Netherlands Indies of 1854. According to Article 177, all Christian teachers, priests, and ministers were required to obtain permission from the governor-general to undertake mission work in a particular area.[78] Until 1928 this regulation was used to forbid missionary work in certain areas such as Aceh, West Java, and Bali because the government felt these were areas with strong faiths that would react negatively to missionary activity. In 1928, however, Article 177 was abrogated and all of the East Indies opened to missionary activity. By the end of the colonial period there were no restrictions on interfaith proselytizing.

Secular and Islamic leaders alike protested the removal of Article 177. Sukarno wrote an article against the abrogation of 177 and the admission of missionaries to Bali: "In that way we might in the future come to witness a Roman Catholic Bali, which would form a wedge between Java and the islands to the East. There is already such a Christian wedge between Aceh and Minangkabau, christened Batakland."[79] At its congress in May 1939, the MIAI presented a motion to reinstate Article 177.[80] In 1932, Hadji Fachruddin, a Muhammadiyah leader, issued a pamphlet protesting the Christian missionaries.[81] Elsewhere Muhammadiyah accused Christians of undertaking an effort at mass conversion: "According to God's commandment, the Christians and the Jews, in each of their tactics will always go against Islam and try to convert Muslims into their religions, out of Islam. Therefore we must be careful and always be ready to stand against them, through strengthening and spreading Islam all over Indonesia."[82] NU also protested the repeal of Article 177, criticizing the Christians for being insensitive to Muslim concerns and lamenting the political weakness of Muslims. At the same conference, NU criticized the unequal subsidies given to Christians and Muslims, which had earlier caused a furor in Muhammadiyah.[83]

Since the end of the colonial period, Indonesian Islamic organizations have sought to restrict Christian missionary work. In 1963, Muhammadiyah warned its members of a conference in East Java planning to convert the entire country within fifty years through interfaith marriage: "Word has spread in the community regarding the result of the Christian Conference in East Java to Christianize the country, with a 20-year plan for Java and 50-year plan for the whole country. Such [a] decision truly is a challenge to Islam, which is now embraced by the majority of Indonesians."[84]

Opposition to proselytizing peaked in the 1960s, when, by Alwi Shihab's estimate, the church helped two million syncretic (*abangan*) Muslims escape the mass killings by converting to Christianity. "For the Muslims, the church's protection of the former communists who turned Christian was an act of taking advantage of the political situation—fishing in troubled waters." Conversion strategies allegedly included building churches in historically *abangan* villages, financial aid, educational scholarships, and protection for accused communists. A "foster parent" system was introduced to ease the conversion to Christianity. In response, a 1964 pamphlet by Bisjron A. Wardy, *To Be Aware of Christian Activities* (*Memahami Kegiatan Nasrani*), repeated the allegation that Roman Catholic and Protestant churches had held a conference in 1962 in order to develop a plan to convert all of Java within fifty years. Lukman Harun of Muhammadiyah pointed to the Meulaboh incident of 1967 in West Aceh, where a church was erected in a community where no Christian lived. This was also alleged to have occurred in Ujung Padang, Jakarta, Bukit Tinggi, and elsewhere.[85] In response, Harun, a member of the House of Representatives, proposed a parliamentary interpellation on July 10, 1967, urging the government to regulate the building of places of worship, methods of religious propagation, and channeling of foreign aid. In 1967, a major conference of religious leaders from the large social and political organizations gathered in Jakarta with the intention of establishing an interreligious council and to establish boundaries on missionary activities. No agreement was reached, and the blame was directed at Christians for not agreeing to proselytize only to people without religion (that is, those not belonging to one of the recognized religions).[86]

Even without an agreement, the MORA issued a Joint Ministerial Decision of 1969 that gave local governments power to restrict missionary work and the building of new houses of worship.[87] Article 1 said that religious groups could spread and practice their faith but were not permitted to disturb public order. The decree further required local governments to grant permission for the establishment of houses of worship and to "ensure that efforts to promulgate a religion by its followers do not cause inter-religious disharmony."[88] Article 4 stated that to obtain a permit to build a place of worship, a religious community was required to obtain permission from the mayor/regent, and in making their decision, the mayor/regent would consider the recommendation of the MORA and local religious leaders.[89] The decree was the first stage in reintroducing the restrictions on missionary activity that had been repealed in 1928.

Muhammadiyah's opposition to Christian missionary work and pressure on the Ministry of Religion led to Government Decree 70 and 78 in August 1978.[90] Shihab notes: "As it is evident, the whole purpose of the interpellation was specifically aimed at curbing the activities of the Christian mission in Indonesia."[91] Number 70, Article 2 states that religious proselytizing is prohibited when it (a) is directed at a person who already has a religion; (b) employs the use of bribery (such as gifts, money, clothes, food and drink, medicine, etc.) in order to persuade a person to change his or her religion; (c) involves the distribution of pamphlets, bulletins, magazines, books, or other publications to people who already have a religion; or (d) involves approaching the private residences of people who already have a religion. Additionally, the provision relied on the 1969 Joint Ministerial Decree to affirm that the government can take legal action to ensure compliance with these rules if the propagation "destabilizes religious groups" or "social harmony."[92] By then these regulations were having their intended effect; Crouch notes that religious minorities began to use houses as places of worship because they were unable to get building permits. In response, in 1975 the Department of Home Affairs issued an instruction to the provinces clarifying that private houses could not be used as churches.[93]

Since the 1970s the limitations on proselytizing have become more restrictive. Article 86 of the 2002 Child Protection Law states that any person who uses deceit, lies, or entices children to choose another religion against their will is liable to a maximum jail sentence of five years and/or a fine of one hundred million rupiah.[94] A 2006 Joint Ministerial Decision from the minister for religion and the minister for home affairs introduced additional requirements for the establishment of places of worship.

Article 14 demands ninety signatures from members of a congregation and signatures of support from at least sixty local community members in order for the local government to grant permission to establish a place of worship. Lindsey notes that the sixty community members are usually interpreted as having to be from a religion different from the congregation's.[95] Article 13 requires that the establishment of a place of worship be based on the "real needs and composition of the number of residents for the service of the religious community in the region/village."[96] Articles 8, 9, and 10 require provinces and districts to establish Religious Community Communication Forums (FKUB, Forum Komunikasi Umat Beragama) in every regency and city. The makeup is to include one member from each religion in the region and is instructed to provide a forum for dialogue between religious communities. Critics of the FKUB allege that they provide legitimation for the religious majority to deny minorities the right to build houses of worship.

A comprehensive bill on "interreligious harmony" has been under development for many decades but has yet to pass the legislature. The MORA proposed a bill including limitations on proselytizing in 1982 and again in 1989, 1997, and 2003, and the most recent minister of religion claimed that a new bill would be released in 2015.[97] Should such a bill pass the DPR, it would likely not be of a secular character; the inclusion of moderate Islamic organizations in the bureaucracy and legislature has meant increasing limitations on Christian missionary activity.

Of the four policy areas under review, the limitations on proselytizing is the area where the laws are most clearly promoted by the majority to restrict the activities of one particular religious minority. Hindus, Confucians, and Buddhists in Indonesia do not proselytize. The Islamic practice of propagation (*da'wa*) has almost exclusively targeted secular or nonobservant Muslims. It is only the missionary practices of Evangelical and Pentecostal Christians that have been seen as an affront to religious harmony and led mainstream Muslims to feel that the threat of "Christianization" is real. These doctrinal differences exacerbate the sense that Christians are not "playing by the rules." It was not a conservative Islamist but rather Indonesia's most prominent spokesperson for liberal Islam, Ulil Abshar Abdalla, who expressed this sentiment most succinctly: "When I was in D.C., I met with a group of Christians, and they had a very sophisticated operation to promote freedom of religion. But I think this is not the same freedom that I am talking about. That is Christianization."[98] Abshar Abdalla highlights an important distinction between the right of Indonesians to explore their country's diverse belief systems and the right of rich foreign churches to build houses of worship in poor Muslim villages. He supports the first but not the second.

Indonesia's restrictions on proselytizing are the final way that the state has become sacralized in the postcolonial period. In comparative perspective, Indonesia's restrictions on both domestic and foreign missionaries are not unusual; forty-six countries put restrictions on domestic missionaries and religious workers, including twenty-four democracies. India limits proselytizing to specific locations, such as places of worship. Greece prohibits proselytism in Article 13 of the 2001 constitution, defined as attempts to intrude on the religious beliefs of a person of a different religious persuasion, with the aim of undermining those beliefs, or by fraudulent means or by taking advantage of their inexperience, trust, need, low intellect, or naivety. A total of thirty-four democracies put restrictions on proselytizing by foreign clergy or missionaries, including Switzerland, Belgium, the United Kingdom, Denmark, Austria, Bolivia, and Costa Rica—all of which frequently deny visas to foreigners who wish to proselytize. Switzerland allows proselytizing only if missionaries can demonstrate knowledge of Swiss customs and culture, are conversant in at least one of the main national languages, and hold a degree in theology.

Yet, in the Indonesian case, the fact that the 1969 and 2006 decrees have been used to prevent indigenous Christian congregations from building houses of worship contravenes the constitution's commitment to freedom of religion and is a problem for democratic practice. More generally, however, there is nothing in democratic theory that demands unrestricted religious freedom. Instead, as Alfred Stepan notes in the introduction to this volume, the goal of democratic theorists should be to find arrangements of mutual accommodation and toleration within the context of an ongoing political and legal order.

* * *

This chapter has presented a diachronic overview of four policy areas that have been sacralized in order to accommodate the preferences of Indonesian Islamic organizations. Other policy areas could have been included. For example, constitutional guarantees of free speech have been modified by the 1965 law prohibiting blasphemy and the 2008 law on pornography. Restrictions on heterodoxy and liminal faiths have become significantly more muscular. As a result, heterodox religious sects have been prosecuted for dishonoring Islam and, in some cases, Christianity.[99] And *zakat* collection, once a private practice, is now tax deductible and collected by the state.[100]

Some scholars see these developments as evidence of an incipient theocracy, "stealth Islamization," low-quality democracy, or illiberal democracy. I suggest an alternative reading by excavating the implications of the inclusion of Islamic organizations in the democratic process. Instead of being a secular democracy, Indonesia is similar to India, Romania, Bulgaria, Greece, Switzerland, and Austria in that it promotes religious values while synthesizing liberal individual rights and group-differentiated rights within a system of legal pluralism. More theoretically, this chapter suggests that strengthening democracy in the Muslim world demands looking beyond the American and European models of liberal secularism toward the policies of democracies in Africa, Asia, Latin America, and Eastern Europe.

NOTES

I am grateful to Rusanda Soltan and Madelyn Powell for their research assistance and to Laryssa Chomiak, Melissa Crouch, Donald Horowitz, Ani Sarkissian, and Alfred Stepan for their thoughtful feedback.

1. Mirjam Künkler and Alfred Stepan, eds., *Democracy and Islam in Indonesia* (New York: Columbia University Press, 2013). "Polity Score: 8 (2013)," http://www.systemicpeace .org/polity/ins2.htm. The Polity score is a single regime score that ranges from +10 (full democracy) to -10 (full autocracy) and aggregates information about whether there are institutions and procedures through which citizens can express effective preferences about alternative policies and leaders as well as institutionalized constraints on the exercise of power by the executive.

2. Samuel Huntington, *The Third Wave: Democratization in the Late Twentieth Century* (Norman: University of Oklahoma Press, 1991), 169.

3. Stathis Kalyvas, "The 'Turkish Model' in the Matrix of Political Catholicism," in *Democracy, Islam, and Secularism in Turkey*, ed. Ahmet Kuru and Alfred Stepan (New York: Columbia University Press, 2012), 192–196.

4. Stathis Kalyvas, "Commitment Problems in Emerging Democracies: The Case of Religious Parties," *Comparative Politics* 32, no. 4 (2000): 390.

5. Charles Kurzman and Ijlal Naqvi, "Do Muslims Vote Islamic?" *Journal of Democracy* 21, no. 2 (2010): 50–63.

6. Jason Brownlee, "Unrequited Moderation: Credible Commitments and State Repression in Egypt," *Studies in Comparative International Development* 45, no. 4 (2010): 468–489.

7. Kurzman and Naqvi, "Do Muslims Vote Islamic?" 57–59.

8. Jillian Schwedler, "Can Islamists Become Moderate? Rethinking the Inclusion- Moderation Hypothesis," *World Politics* 63, no. 2 (2011): 347–376.

9. Nancy Bermeo, "The Myths of Moderation: The Role of Radical Forces in the Transition to Democracy," *Comparative Politics* 29, no. 3 (1997): 311, 314.

10. Gunes Murat Tezcur, *Muslim Reformers in Iran and Turkey: The Paradox of Moderation* (Austin: University of Texas Press, 2010). Schwedler, "Can Islamists Become Moderate?"

11. Saiful Mujani and R. William Liddle, "Politics, Islam, and Public Opinion," *Journal of Democracy* 15, no. 1 (2004): 120.

12. NU is associated with the political parties Masyumi, Partai Nahdlatul Ulama (PNU), Partai Kebangkitan Nasional Ulama (PKNU), Partai Kebangkitan Bangsa (PKB), and Partai Persatuan Pembangunan (PPP). Muhammadiyah is associated with the political parties Masyumi, PPP, and Partai Amanat Nasional (PAN). Persis is associated with Partai Persatuan Pembangunan (PPP), Partai Bulan Bintang (PBB), Partai Keadilan (PK), and Partai Keadilan Sejahtera (PKS).

13. Pancasila is the basis of Indonesian national ideology; its five principles are belief in God, humanitarianism, national unity, democracy as expressed through representatives of the people, and social justice.

14. That said, the successor organization to Darul Islam, the Free Aceh Movement (GAM), moderated its demands as a result of inclusion in the political process. See Edward Aspinall, "From Islamism to Nationalism in Aceh, Indonesia," *Nations and Nationalism* 13, no. 2 (2007).

15. Jeremy Menchik, *Islam and Democracy in Indonesia: Tolerance Without Liberalism* (New York: Cambridge University Press, 2016).

16. Jeremy Menchik, "The Coevolution of Sacred and Secular: Islamic Law and Family Planning in Indonesia," *South East Asia Research* 22, no. 3 (2014): 359–378.

17. This is Schwedler's typology of moderation (2011).

18. Kalyvas, "Commitment Problems in Emerging Democracies"; Thomas B. Pepinsky, R. William Liddle, and Saiful Mujani, "Testing Islam's Political Advantage: Evidence from Indonesia," *American Journal of Political Science* 56, no. 3 (2012); Mona El-Ghobashy, "The Metamorphosis of the Egyptian Muslim Brothers," *International Journal of Middle East Studies* 37, no. 3 (2005).

19. Michaelle L. Browers, *Political Ideology in the Arab World: Accommodation and Transformation* (New York: Cambridge University Press, 2009); Janine Astrid Clark, "The Conditions of Islamist Moderation: Unpacking Cross-Ideological Cooperation in Jordan," *International Journal of Middle East Studies* 38, no. 4 (2006); Jillian Schwedler, *Faith in Moderation: Islamist Parties in Jordan and Yemen* (Cambridge: Cambridge University Press, 2007); Carrie Rosefsky Wickham, "The Path to Moderation: Strategy and Learning in the Formation of Egypt's Wasat Party," *Comparative Politics* 36, no. 2 (2004).

20. Bermeo, "The Myths of Moderation"; Huntington, *The Third Wave*; Wickham, "The Path to Moderation."

21. Charles Tilly, *Coercion, Capital, and European States, AD 990–1990* (Cambridge, Mass.: Blackwell, 1990).

22. Merle Ricklefs, *A History of Modern Indonesia Since c. 1200*, 4th ed. (Stanford, Calif.: Stanford University Press, 2008), 241, 253.

23. Harry J. Benda, "Christiaan Snouck Hurgronje and the Foundations of Dutch Islamic Policy in Indonesia," *Journal of Modern History* 30, no. 4 (1958): 176.

24. Sarah Elizabeth Parkinson, "Organizing Rebellion: Rethinking High-Risk Mobilization and Social Networks in War," *American Political Science Review* 107, no. 3 (2013).

25. R. Q. Mecham, "From the Ashes of Virtue, and Promise of Light: The Transformation of Political Islam in Turkey," *Third World Quarterly* 25, no. 2 (2004): 345–347, 354, 359.

26. Aspinall, "From Islamism to Nationalism," 248, 253–254.

27. See, for example, the special issue "Religious Parties: Revisiting the Inclusion-Moderation Hypothesis," ed. Manfred Brocker and Mirjam Kunkler, *Party Politics* 19, no. 2 (2013).

28. Peter Berger, *The Desecularization of the World* (Washington, D.C.: Eerdmans/Ethics and Public Policy Center, 1999); Sadia Saeed, "Desecularization as an Instituted Process: National Identity and Religious Difference in Pakistan," *Economic and Political Weekly* 48, no. 50 (2003): 62–70.

29. Robert Hefner, "Islamising Java? Religion and Politics in Rural East Java," *Journal of Asian Studies* 46, no. 3 (1987): 533–554.

30. Donald Horowitz, *Constitutional Change and Democracy in Indonesia* (New York: Cambridge University Press, 2013), 247.

31. Anies Baswedan, "Political Islam in Indonesia: Present and Future Trajectory," *Asian Survey* 44, no. 5 (2004): 669–690.

32. Ibid., 675.

33. Excluded are the parties Hanura and Gerindra, which are vehicles for former military leaders and have no clear ideology.

34. See Menchik, *Islam and Democracy in Indonesia*, chap. 7.

35. Alfred Stepan, "Democracy, the World's Religion, and the Problems of the 'Twin Tolerations,'" *Journal of Democracy* 11, no. 4 (2000): 37–57.

36. François Foret, *Religion and Politics in the European Union: The Secular Canopy* (Cambridge: Cambridge University Press, 2015).

37. The policy was a spectacular failure; the new elites became the leaders of the emergent nationalist movement.

38. M. C. Ricklefs, ed., *A New History of Southeast Asia* (London: Palgrave Macmillan, 2010), 279–280; M. C. Ricklefs, *Polarising Javanese Society: Islamic and Other Visions (c. 1830–1930)* (Singapore: NUS, 2007), 215.

39. Ricklefs, *Polarising Javanese Society*, 154, 70, 216.

40. Melissa Crouch, "Proselytisation, Religious Diversity, and the State in Indonesia: The Offence of Deceiving a Child to Change Religion," in *Proselytising and the Limits of Religious Pluralism in Contemporary Asia*, ed. Michael Feener and Juliana Finucane (Singapore: ARI Springer Asia Series, 2013), 20–22; Law 4/1950 on Basic Education and Teaching in Schools; Law 12/1954; Joint Regulations of the Minister of Education and the Minister of Religion no. 17678/1951 on Religious Education; Decision by the MPR No. II/MPRS/1960, article 2(3).

41. MPRS No. XXVII/MPRS/1966 on Religion, Education and Culture.

42. Crouch, "Proselytisation, Religious Diversity, and the State in Indonesia," 21; Joint Decision of the Minister of Education and the Minister of Religion 35/1985 on the Implementation of Religion Education in Schools.

43. Crouch, "Proselytisation, Religious Diversity, and the State in Indonesia," 21; Government Regulation 10/1990 on Higher Education; Government Regulation 27/1990 on Pre-School Education; Government Regulation 28/1990 on Primary Education; Government Regulation 29/1990 on Secondary School Education.

44. Horowitz, *Constitutional Change and Democracy in Indonesia*; Fourth Amendment to the 1945 constitution, August 10, 2002, art. 2(1).

45. Timothy Lindsey, *Islam, Law, and the State in Southeast Asia*, vol. 1: *Indonesia* (London: I. B. Tauris, 2012), 235–236.

46. Ibid., 237; Najwa Shihab and Nugroho Januar, "The Ties That Bind: Law, Islamisation, and Indonesia's Prosperous Justice Party," *Australian Journal of Asian Law* 10, no. 2 (2008): 248.

47. Dr. Abdul Mu'ti of the Central Board of Muhammadiyah, interview with the author, Jakarta, October 1, 2009.

48. Menchik, *Islam and Democracy in Indonesia*.

49. Benda, "Christiaan Snouck Hurgronje," 342.

50. Harry Benda, *The Crescent and the Rising Sun: Indonesian Islam Under the Japanese Occupation, 1942–1945* (The Hague: W. van Hoeve, 1958), 166.

51. B. J. Boland, *The Struggle of Islam in Modern Indonesia* (The Hague: Martinus Nijhoff, 1982), 108.

52. Andrew Abalahin, "A Sixth Religion? Confucianism and the Negotiation of Indonesian-Chinese Identity Under the Pancasila State," in *Spirited Politics: Religion and Public Life in Contemporary Southeast Asia*, ed. A. C. Willford and K. M. George (Ithaca, N.Y.: Cornell Southeast Asia Program Publication, 2005), 121.

53. Alalahin, "A Sixth Religion?" 134.

54. "Penetapan Presiden No. 1/1965 tentang Pentjegahan Penjalahgun Dan/Atau Penodaan Agama," *Suara Merdeka*, March 9, 1965.

55. "Pernjataan Bersama Partai-2 Dan Ormas Islam," Arsip Nasional (AN)/NU 106. See also "Pernjataan Bersama Partai-2 dan Ormas Islam," *Berita Antara*, March 18, 1965. NU's youth wing issued a similar statement on March 23: "Putjuk Pimpinan Gerakan Pemuda Anshor," AN/NU 106, no. PP/616/B/III/1965.

56. Julia Howell, "Muslims, the New Age, and Marginal Religions in Indonesia: Changing Meanings of Religious Pluralism," *Social Compass* 52, no. 4 (2005): 473; Ricklefs, *Polarising Javanese Society*, 340.

57. Lindsey, *Islam, Law, and the State*, 1:60; MPR Decision no. IV 1973, no. IV 1978.

58. Lindsey, *Islam, Law, and the State*, 1:60.

59. Melissa Crouch, "Law and Religion in Indonesia: The Constitutional Court and the Blasphemy Law," *Asian Journal of Comparative Law* 7, no. 1 (2012): 26–27.

60. Ibid., 4.

61. Author interview with Robert Hefner, Boston, November 14, 2014.

62. Jeremy Menchik, "Productive Intolerance: Godly Nationalism in Indonesia," *Comparative Studies in Society and History* 56, no. 3: 591–621.

63. John Bowen, *Islam, Law, and Equality in Indonesia: An Anthropology of Public Reasoning* (Cambridge: Cambridge University Press, 2003), 48–50; Mark Cammack, "Legal Aspects of Muslim–Non-Muslim Marriage in Indonesia," in *Muslim–Non-Muslim Marriage: Political and Cultural Contestations in Southeast Asia*, ed. G. Jones, C. Leng, and M. Mohamad (Singapore: Institute for Southeast Asian Studies, 2009), 104.

64. Cammack, "Legal Aspects of Muslim–Non-Muslim Marriage,"105, in reference to *Regeling op de Gemengde Huwelijken* 1898, no. 158.

65. Benda, *The Crescent and the Rising Sun*, 162, 269n54.

66. Cammack, "Legal Aspects of Muslim–Non-Muslim Marriage," 107–108.

67. Ibid., 110.

68. Ibid., 134.

69. H. M. Rasyidi, "RUU Perkawinan," *Suara Muhammadiyah* 17 (September 1, 1973): 6. "The food of those who have received the Scripture is lawful for you, and your food is lawful for them. And so are the virtuous women of the believers and the virtuous women of those who received a divine revelation" (Qu'ran Sura 5:4).

70. Cammack, "Legal Aspects of Muslim–Non-Muslim Marriage," 113.

71. Ibid., 129, 119, 127.

72. Eriwn Sihombing, "Interfaith Marriage Still Unsanctioned as Court Rejects Judicial Review," *Jakarta Globe*, June 18, 2015, http://thejakartaglobe.beritasatu.com/news/inter faith-marriages-still-unsanctioned-court-rejects-judicial-review/.

73. Nahdlatul Ulama, *Ahkam al-Fuqaha' fi Muqarrarat Mu'tamarat Nahdlati al-'Ulama: Solusi Problematika Aktual Hukum Islam Keputusan Muktamar (1926–1999)* (Surabaya: Lajnah Ta'lif Wan Nasyer Jawa Timur and "Khalista" Surabaya, 2007), 433–437.

74. Majelis Ulama Indonesia, *Himpunan fatwa Majelis Ulama Indonesia* (Jakarta: Majelis Ulama Indonesia, 1997), 120–122.

75. Abdurrahman, Asyumuni, and Moelyadi, eds., *Tanya-Jawab Agama II* [Question and answer about religion] (Yogyakarta: Yayasan Penerbit Pers Suara Muhammadiyah, 1992), 173–174.

76. Interestingly, the more doctrinally strict Persis says that Muslim men may marry Jewish and Christian women but that Muslim women may not marry non-Muslim men. Ma'sum Hassan and H. Mahmud Aziz, *Soal-Jawab Tentang Berbagai Masalah Agama* (Bandung: CV Penerbit Diponegoro, 2007), 263–264.

77. Cammack, "Legal Aspects of Muslim–Non-Muslim Marriage," 125–126.

78. Crouch, "Law and Religion in Indonesia," 14.

79. M. P. M. Muskens, *Partner in National Building: The Catholic Church in Indonesia* (Aachen: Missio Aktuell Verlag, 1979), 165.

80. J. S. Furnival, *Netherlands India: A Study of Plural Economy* (New York: Cambridge University Press, 1944), 279.

81. Mizan Sya'roni, "The Majlisul Islamil a'la Indonesia (MIAI): Its Socio-Religious and Political Activities (1937–1943)," MA thesis, McGill University (1998), 76n13.

82. Muhammadiyah, *Suara Muhammadiyah* 1 (April 1939): 11.

83. Nahdlatul Ulama, "Majlis ke II: Tentang Hal yang Bersangkutan dengan Pemerintah," *Verslag-Congres Nahdlatul Ulama Yang ke 14 di Kota Magelang* (July 3, 1939), 48–49, 55.

84. Muhammadiyah, "Mempertajam Kewaspadaan Islam Tentang Berita Hasil Konferensi Katolik / Protestan Jawa Timur akan Mengkristenkan Seluruh Indonesia," *Suara Muhammadiyah* 25 (1963): 5.

85. Alwi Shihab, "The Muhammadiyah Movements and Its Controversy with Christian Missions in Indonesia," PhD thesis, Temple University (1995), 306, 309, 312n67; citing Lukman Harun, conference paper, "Endeavors to Create Religious Harmony Among Believers of Different Religions in Indonesia," Monash University, February 2–5, 1991.

86. Crouch, "Proselytization, Religious Diversity and the State in Indonesia," 25.

87. Joint Ministerial Decree no. 01/BER/mdn-mag/1969 on the Implementation of the Tasks of Government Law Enforcers in Guaranteeing the Order and Fluidity of the Development and Practice of Religion by Its Followers.

88. Lindsey, *Islam, Law, and the State in Southeast Asia*, 1:54–55.

89. Melissa Crouch, "Implementing the Regulation on Places of Worship in Indonesia," *Asian Studies Review* 34, no. 4 (2010), 2.

90. Keputusan Meteri Agama no. 70 dan 77 tahun 1978.

91. Shihab, "The Muhammadiyah Movements," 314.

92. Crouch, "Law and Religion in Indonesia," 26–27.

93. Crouch, "Implementing the Regulation on Places of Worship in Indonesia," 3.

94. Law 23/2003 on Child Protection.

95. Lindsey, *Islam, Law, and the State in Southeast Asia*, 55.

96. Joint Ministerial Decree of the Minister of Religion no. 8 of 2006 and the Minister of Home Affairs no. 9 of 2006 on Guideline for Heads and Deputy Heads of Regional Government in the Implementation of Their Duties of Protecting Religious Community Harmony, Empowering of the Religious Community Communication Forum, and Establishing Places of Worship.

97. Crouch, "Implementing the Regulation on Places of Worship in Indonesia," 43–44; Lindsey, *Islam, Law, and the State in Southeast Asia*, 58.

98. Ulil Abshar Abdalla, interview by the author, Jakarta, June 12, 2009.

99. Lindsey, *Islam, Law, and the State in Southeast Asia*, 406.

100. Horowitz, *Constitutional Change and Democracy in Indonesia*, 247; Law 38/1999.

9

INDIAN DEMOCRACY AND THE WORLD'S LARGEST MUSLIM MINORITY

HILAL AHMED AND SUDIPTA KAVIRAJ

G ANDHI, WITH HIS GIFT for expressing profound thoughts in lapidary form, said that whether a society is civilized is shown by how it treats its minorities. Note that Gandhi's claim is fundamental: if minorities are not treated well, he implies, it is a travesty of civilization, not just of democracy. Analyzing the place of Muslims in Indian democracy offers a crucial test of the functioning of democratic institutions in a society marked by intense religious beliefs and immense social diversity.

PLURAL PATHWAYS OF MODERNITY

"Minority" is a very thin and in some ways underdetermined characterization of a group. Being in a minority is not always or under all circumstances viewed as a handicap or a danger. People who earn much more than an average citizen are a minority, as were the members of premodern aristocracies, but neither group seemed particularly apologetic or troubled by their minority status. As we shall see, nor were the aristocratic ancestors of India's Muslims in medieval India—where they sometimes regarded their community as a rulers' race. Being in a minority is considered a beleaguered fate in circumstances typical of modern politics, particularly under a model of the nation-state evolved through European modernity. On this view, when people look at the history of Western Europe in the early modern era, what they view is not merely a regional, provincial story of the past in a part of the world but the story of their own obligatory future. But there is a large literature now that casts doubt on what was regarded as the obligatory narrative of a normative modernity that originated in Europe in the eighteenth and nineteenth centuries and spread identical institutional structures throughout the rest of the world. It would be reasonable to surmise that if the trajectories of modernity itself become increasingly complex and plural, discrete processes like secularity will also follow the same logic of a complex path of pluralized extension: that is, secularity as a process of transformation of the place of religion in societies subject to the logic of modernity and of secularism as an innovative form of political institutions that would assume plural forms.[1] After all, if we examine Western "secularism" closely, that too reveals plural paths of institutional modulation rather than an inexorable replication of a single institutional model. It does not require much argument today to establish that the way France, the United States, and the United Kingdom and the Scandinavian countries evolved their historical institutional designs were significantly different.[2] Western secularism does not refer to an invariant structure but something like a "structure" in the sense in which structuralist linguists use that word— to refer to a set of elements that are selected and combined in contextually innovative ways similar to the manner in which people create words out of the limited structure of an alphabet. The alphabet of secularity has been developed through the historical experiences of plural or pluralizing societies of different parts of the world, and each group of political elites seeks to fashion institutions that respond to the peculiar predicaments their history throws at them. Since the story of secularity is a constitutive part of the narrative of the unfolding of modernity, it is reasonable to expect that, like multiple modernity, we shall encounter multiple forms of the secular. If a constitution is not exactly like the French, that does not indicate that it is not secular, only that it does not replicate the French conception of secularity.[3]

THE PREHISTORY OF CONSTITUTIONAL SECULARISM

Institutional structures of Indian democracy emerged from a historical context of continuous intellectual debate spanning nearly a century—from the mid–nineteenth century, when concerns about minorities and secularist principles were first inchoately sensed, to the establishment of the postcolonial constitution in 1951. Like historically sensitive observers across the world, from the mid–nineteenth century, Indian Muslim intellectuals sensed an impending historic change in the nature of political power. Syed Ahmed Khan (1817–1898), a pioneer in modern Indian political thought, felt troubled by what he saw as a historical shift from one mode of power to another.[4] His works engaged in an insistent effort at a double persuasion. Khan sought to persuade Muslim elites—particularly in northern India—alienated by British hostility after the 1857 rebellion to cooperate with British rule and offer a qualified embrace to colonial modernity. Simultaneously, he tried to persuade the British to rely on premodern elites[5] instead of creating an entirely modern substitute in English-educated modern Bengalis.[6] A traditional elite skilled in military knowledge and statecraft who possessed historical knowledge of the exercise of power had already existed in northern India for centuries: the British should employ this group as their collaborators rather than shift power under the colonial dispensation to the upstart Bengali elite. Somewhat paradoxically, while deriding the idea that these pen-wielding babus (petty clerks) could replace the sword-wielding aristocrats, he advised the former wielders of the sword to acquire greater facility with the pen, and with modern education, if they did not want to be consigned to the dustbin of history. An emerging unease, still vague and half-articulated, is a significant part of his political reflections, a sense that, historically, Muslims were in the process of turning from one kind of minority into another. They were always an aristocratic minority[7]—aristocracies, after all, were minorities by definition—but in the great transformation to modern politics—based on numbers and logics of representation—they would become a statistical minority against the Hindus. This line of thought became a founding trope of Islamic political thought after the mid–nineteenth century. At least one strand of Islamic thought insistently focused on this impending misfortune and worked out institutional responses to this political reduction. There were contending strands of political argument as well, but political circumstances gave greater salience to this line of argument. The political future of Indian Muslims was under the shadow of two dangers: first, educational backwardness compared to some segments of the Hindus, for example, the Bengali bhadralok groups who eagerly embraced modern education and consequently monopolized modern professions and the colonial bureaucracy; and, second and increasingly significantly, becoming a "minority" in a postcolonial form of representative government after British rule, in which democracy would fail to provide them an adequate role in public political life.

British political strategies certainly contributed to the exacerbation of these anxieties. Indian nationalists referred to these policies as techniques of "divide and rule"—which British authorities followed explicitly from the Partition of Bengal in 1905.[8] Political stratagems of colonial authorities alone did not explain such unease: Orientalist ideologies—accepted uncritically by Indian elites—made a decisive contribution on one particularly crucial point. Through the colonial contact with British political life, Indian intellectuals became intimately familiar with discussions about democracy in Europe. But Orientalism always asserted as an incontrovertible fact that the societies in Britain and in India were fundamentally differently constituted, particularly when it came to the habitual self-identification of people and, consequently, to the grounds of political action. European societies had gone through a process of irreversible individuation, and therefore the division of majority and minority—crucial to the process of democratic governance—was in terms of how interests divided on a particular decision. Earlier traditions of Western political thought—British, French, and German—had prepared the ground for thinking about individual, sectional, and "universal" interests of modern societies.[9] In European discussions on democracy, a majority was standardly a decisional majority.[10] In India, by contrast, social actors recognized only one preeminent ground for their identities and therefore of all possible social action—their religious communities. The concept of the majority—and corresponding minority—therefore meant a decisional majority in European contexts but, through an Orientalist reversion, an identity majority in the Indian. Interestingly, late-colonial British governments—irrespective of party affiliation—relentlessly followed this Orientalist logic and applied it to their colonial or semicolonial possessions in India, Palestine, and Ireland.[11] If this profound translation of democracy was accepted, this determined and gave a fixed character to the whole political debate in India. A dominant section of Muslim political leaders stubbornly stuck to this conception because they were deeply concerned about its implications.[12] Oddly, leaders of the Indian Congress party did not attack this conception with sufficient clarity or tenacity[13]—though in the works of Gandhi and Nehru references to this confusion occur intermittently. Rather, instead of focusing on this critical and fundamental substitution on the basis of an entirely colonial ideology, they focused their efforts on offering constitutional and political safeguards and reassurances to the Muslim League leadership. We do not mean to suggest that the presence of identity minorities is not a serious problem in democratic politics, but it is essential to point out that this is a significant issue only in certain classes of questions, not in everything.[14]

THE LAST STAGE OF COLONIAL RULE

When independence became visible on the horizon—in the 1930s—some major Islamic political thinkers made another crucial move with far-reaching consequences. Starting with Muhammad Iqbal's famous Allahabad speech in 1930, where he made the first serious suggestion for something like a separate "sovereign" state for Indian Muslims,[15] leaders of the Muslim League began to draw attention to the inappropriateness of some constitutional solutions to the Indian communal problem. If we read them closely, we can detect two separate ideas unclearly intertwined in that discussion. Iqbal, for instance, thought that an application of the institutional model of the European nation-state would negatively affect the status of Indian Muslims. Minorities in a state based on an explicit or implied sense of a homogeneous national people would face a situation like that of European Jews.[16] Debates before independence on constitutional matters are strewn with constant and emotively charged references to Europe's Jewish minorities.[17] But when thinkers like Iqbal debated the contrast between Europe and the Indian subcontinent, they usually make a crucial substitution. Although their objection and concerns are regarding the state form of the nation-state, they turn their criticisms against the constitutional form of electoral democracy.[18] After clarification through the work of scholars like Lijphart,[19] we can see that what they were "seeking" was a constitutional design that was consociational rather than simply majoritarian, but they consistently misexpressed this reservation as a general rejection of democratic constitutionalism.[20]

INSTITUTIONAL DESIGN IN INDEPENDENT INDIA

At the time of constitution making, India's political elite did not have to face down these arguments, because the Muslim leaders who were with the Congress had already decisively rejected them. But these concerns could be relevant for other types of minorities as well, not just religious ones. The Indian Constituent Assembly continually debated these institutional questions.

Unlike Pakistan, which followed European state models more directly to establish a monolingual state form, at least formally, India adopted a more pluralist constitutional design with numerous significantly consociational features.[21] Besides that, as Lijphart partly noted in his analysis,[22] India practiced for several decades a two-layered consociationalism—it supplemented the formal provisions of the constitutional document with the pragmatic, unlegal, practically supple, contextually agile consociationalism through the functioning of the Congress Party. This meant that if the legal consociational rules failed to function, the informal rules of party operation could cover for its lapses.[23] Nehru, in particular, forcefully advocated special provisions in the constitution for the reassurance of religious minorities. His thinking regarding the treatment of the Muslim minority in India, on closer inspection, shows two interlinked arguments. Nehru supported two types of legal provisions to produce reassurance among the Muslim community—a vast twelve million or more—who remained in India despite Partition. Nehru felt that the assurance of Muslims, though they constituted a minority, was of the greatest importance for India's institutional claim to be a genuine secular state, so that claim critically depended on how India's Muslims viewed the postindependence settlement. First, some provisions were postulated because they were considered right in principle, that is, philosophically critical for a democratic and pluralist state, but, second, he supported some measures not because these were similarly right in principle but right under the circumstances.[24] After the trauma of Partition, the minorities could be offered measures that would simply generate their trust in the new institutions of power, though their philosophical justification was not unquestioned. The constitution offered protection to minorities for cultural and educational rights—like a special provision to establish schools for the protection of cultural forms. India's rich heritage of religious accommodation and mutual respect was formalized in terms of public holidays on the religious festival days of minority groups. Informal reassurance was provided, for instance, by support for special religious activities, such as Muslims' annual hajj pilgrimage. In Nehru's political thinking, these measures simply acknowledged and cemented a long tradition of religious accommodation and transaction. Some other measures were less directly in line with Nehru's secular-democratic beliefs. Separate and unequal treatment in the minorities' favor was carried a step further, in retrospect possibly unwisely, by the exemption of Muslim personal laws from comprehensive reforms. After assuming office, Nehru's government adopted far-reaching legislative reform of Hindu family laws regarding family and inheritance.[25] Although reform of Muslim family law could have been supported by similar arguments, Nehru did not press for parallel reform. Nehru defended these decisions by a theory of contingently right decisions in specific historical circumstances:

treating all religious communities equally was philosophically right, but under the historical circumstances after Partition, it was historically right to try to reassure the Muslim minority that their cultural practices would not be invaded by a majoritarian Hindu-inclined state. By implication, this emphasized a subtle but profoundly important judgment about the historical life of democracy: majority rule and majoritarianism are different things—the first is essential to democracy, the second fatal to its existence.[26] On another subject highly significant to the Muslim minority Nehru was less vigilant. Urdu was the common literary language of Indian Muslims and thus a very important constituent of their cultural heritage. Nehru sought to secure recognition for Urdu as a second language of the state of Uttar Pradesh—a traditional center of Muslim high culture. But, to his frustration, after the shock of Partition, even moderate Congress leaders were reluctant to accept that advice; Urdu was denied status as a second language of that state. This remained a point of resentment among Muslim communities. Some commentators believe that it might have been better had Nehru made the opposite political moves—if he had allowed Muslim personal laws to be reformed in line with the refashioning of Hindu legal codes but insisted on the status of Urdu as a state language of Uttar Pradesh.[27]

Nehru has drawn mild criticism for a second reason: some have suggested that he might have tried to consult the Islamic community more directly—representing one moment of Stepan's "twin tolerations"—to get the community's commitment to its acceptance of the rules proposed by the state.[28] But two counterarguments could be advanced from Nehru's side: first, selection of ecclesiastical leaders to represent the community would have conferred a gratuitous eminence on religious leaders, who were likely to be the most conservative representatives of the community's collective opinion; this would have infringed on the secular character of political life. There is an additional difficulty of finding the voice of the community in case of religious cultures that are not institutionally centralized like Christian churches. Both Hindu and Muslim communities in South Asia are utterly decentralized; choosing representatives as interlocutors thus confers an indirect power on the state. Second, Nehru would have argued that the best means of eliciting the opinion of a community—without going through the conventional traditional channels—is through electoral devices, not seeking out unelected, self-appointed religious leaders.

GEOGRAPHIC DISPERSAL AFTER PARTITION

Political experience in democracies is determined, or at least modulated, through the specific sociological features of social groups. What is significant in shaping political action is not the absolute number of a group but its topological distribution—how these numbers are distributed across space. Partition resulted in a fundamental transformation of the spatial and demographic structure of the Muslim community. With a single stroke, it reduced one of the leading social groups in India's political life to one of the most vulnerable; it became vulnerable in two ways. First, the community was significantly reduced in terms of absolute and proportional numbers. From more than 30 percent it was reduced to about 12.5 percent of the total population. Also, a more fundamental numerical shift took place—although 30 percent of the total population, Muslims constituted a majority in major parts of pre-Partition India; they were regional majorities. Spatial concentration of this numerical majority in Punjab and Bengal was highly significant in the political balance of power and in constitutional negotiations. After independence, Indian Muslims lost this local dominance. Though a considerable minority in several important states, they did not constitute a majority except in the peculiar instance of Jammu and Kashmir. Numerical power could no longer be used as an effective counterweight. Not surprisingly, these altered demographics of the Muslim community had an effect on their modes of political functioning. Except in a few states, the influence of the Muslim League as an identity-based political party faded. As the main contentions of political life were primarily ideological during the years of Nehru's leadership, Muslim groups supported mainstream political parties based on ideological affiliations. Recent memory of Partition also reinforced this choice by creating a revulsion against communal polarization. The Hindu nationalist political party, Jana Sangh, floated in 1951 to ride the revanchist anger among Hindus in the first general elections, did not gather substantial support, securing only three seats and 3.06% of votes—not enough to trouble the secularity of state institutions and the ideological dominance of Nehru's pluralist nationalism. Occasional communal clashes continued to flare up locally—mainly in North Indian cities with a history of communal conflict, but these did not threaten to spread uncontrollably across entire regions. Muslims were generally content to accept the ordinary everyday functioning of democratic politics and did not complain of peculiar marginalization.

ELECTIONS AND THE SEARCH FOR RELIGIOUS VOTES

Indian democracy went through quite a different phase during the times of Indira Gandhi. By then, the Congress Party did not enjoy the default support—bequeathed by the vivid memory of the nationalist movement—that Nehru had enjoyed. She had to work under quite different conditions of democratic party competition. During this period too there was no separate grievance of the Muslim community and no pressure to organize through separate party channels. Indira Gandhi's government continued to follow ritualistic pluralistic forms—for example, the appointment of Muslims as presidents of the republic or the inclusion of Muslim politicians in the central cabinet. But some political occurrences showed troubling trends for a democratic polity. The first change from Nehru's political practice was the abandonment of his strict avoidance of communal appeal in electoral mobilization. Nehru, unsurprisingly, was particularly sensitive to the memory of Partition and not merely avoided the use of religious appeals by his own Congress Party but also aggressively campaigned against "communal" politics in general. In an increasingly more frantic search for electoral majorities from the 1960s, Indira Gandhi's Congress began to revise that belligerent anticommunal stance. In electoral politics, Indira Gandhi's Congress made clear appeals to religious communities that were placed in a relatively vulnerable condition in mixed-population states to attract their votes by playing on their sense of vulnerability. This was a complex, paradoxical political practice with an insidious long-term effect. To take three separate instances, the states of Jammu and Kashmir, Punjab, and Uttar Pradesh all had religiously mixed populations: Uttar Pradesh was 79 percent Hindu and 20 percent Muslim, Punjab was 60 percent Sikh and 37 percent Hindu, and Jammu and Kashmir was 67 percent Muslim and 29 percent Hindu. However, in the Jammu region, Hindus constitute 65 percent and in the Kashmir Valley Muslims were 97 percent of the population—giving the two religious groups overwhelming region-specific majorities. Indira Gandhi's Congress began to appeal to the Hindus in Jammu to vote for the Congress as a "secular" party against the domination of Muslim parties, and it made an identical appeal to the Muslims in Uttar Pradesh to vote for the Congress against Hindu nationalists. Similarly, it appealed to the Hindus in Punjab against a government by the Akali Dal, a Sikh party. This demonstrated a strange form of "secularism" or pluralism in action. True, Congress was not appealing to any single religious community against others and certainly not to the majority of Hindus all over India. But it engaged in a strange kind of minority politics—seeking exclusive support from minorities in all religiously mixed states—and offering to protect them from vague threats coming from their rivals. In effect, it used religious appeals to all religious minorities, with two dangerous consequences. First, it projected the religious divide as the central political conflict in electoral contests. Second, it invited religious minorities to view themselves and vote as religious communities, overturning Nehru's principles of electoral mobilization. Communal mobilization of this type could easily shift to more openly religious parties—which is what happened in later years. So, Indira Gandhi, without being a communal politician, fostered a general move toward communal self-identification of religious groups in electoral politics.

EMERGENCY AND MUSLIM ALIENATION

A specific event during her tenure increased Muslim sensitivity about discrimination and perception of isolation. During the period of the Emergency—which suspended democratic rule for nearly two years in 1975–1977—local Congress leaders supported an entirely gratuitous "beautification drive" in the old city of Delhi, a predominantly Muslim residential area—displacing its inhabitants. This was further exacerbated by a coercive campaign for sterilization as part of a family-planning drive. Both of these local moves were seen as specifically targeting the Muslim inhabitants of Delhi's old city, producing huge resentment and occasional skirmishes with law enforcement. Rumor enlarged these incidents, and they circulated as stories of defiance against a violently repressive state. These incidents also led the Shahi imam of Delhi's Jama Masjid (mosque) to come out as a major figure of popular criticism and resistance against Indira Gandhi's regime.[29] Although these campaigns were relatively short-lived and predominantly unsuccessful, they left a long memory of bitterness against the Congress, which had once been seen as the "natural" party of support for minorities.

Indira Gandhi's divisive and desperate electoral politics left behind another undemocratic, polarizing legacy. Although she did not mobilize a Hindu-majority nationalism directly targeting Muslims, her policies had effects deeply injurious to democratic pluralism. By appealing to religious minorities, playing on their fears, and inviting them to vote on the basis of their religious identity, she inevitably hardened, by rebound, a similar consolidation of the Hindu majority. In some cases, the Hindu communities she mobilized as minorities in their states, as in Jammu and Kashmir, would eventually align with the Hindu majority party, BJP, which offered them support and alignment with the vast majority of Hindus in India. Without being a communal politician, Indira Gandhi contributed significantly to the currency of religious identity as an electoral tool.

The politics of the 1980s were marked by a strange but not explicable logic of electoral competition. The surprising rise of the BJP's electoral fortunes after it separated itself from the grand coalition against Indira Gandhi's Emergency and a significant reworking of its ideological arguments set in motion a process in which the Congress sought to retain its conventional support among Muslims by making concessions to more reactionary opinions inside the community. An example of that policy of conservative accommodation was the treatment of the Shah Bano case by Rajiv Gandhi's government. By refusing to provide Muslim widows the cover of more secular legislation, he succeeded in alienating both ordinary Hindu electors and the progressive Muslim intelligentsia. Instead of stemming the rise of Hindu nationalists, it gave them a foothold in portraying Muslims as "backward looking," dominated by conservative leaders, who, contrary to its stated social principles, were favored by Congress governments. It also helped them turn the question of a uniform civil code for all citizens into an issue for particularly divisive campaigns.

MUSLIMS AND THE SPECTER OF MAJORITARIANISM

In the last decades, the significant problem for the Muslims has been a negative, defensive one: how to respond, through electoral politics, to the rise and increasing stridency of Hindu nationalism. After a disastrously bad performance in the elections of 1984—which the Congress under Rajiv Gandhi won with an unprecedented majority—Hindu nationalist forces gradually worked an ideological redesignation of their politics, eventually appropriating for their purposes a bizarre form of "historical wrong." Just as lower-caste groups have mounted a persistent campaign around the "historical injustice" of caste oppression in Hindu society, the BJP claimed a parallel "historical wrong" enacted by Muslim conquerors in destroying Hindu temples during medieval times. Supporters of the BJP drew up a list of temples desecrated and destroyed in medieval India and demanded "restitution" of those temples, including the already inflamed instance of a temple in the North Indian city of Ayodhya.[30] During the conflict around the Ayodhya mosque, Syed Shahabuddin, a Muslim parliamentarian, sought to dissuade the more conservative Muslim ulemas from issuing a fatwa.[31] The BJP campaign targeted the Muslim community in a particularly perverse form. Existing Muslim communities could not be represented as a threat to the Hindu community in contemporary India in any conceivable sense—neither because of their numbers, nor spatial concentration, nor control over economic wealth or the levers of bureaucratic power. After the departure of a large segment of Muslim elites to Pakistan after Partition, Indian Muslims had been reduced to a "disadvantaged" community—in terms of wealth, education, and political representation, as attested by the government's own commissions of enquiry.[32] Since Congress leaders were irreconcilably opposed to religious reservation, unlike other caste-based backward groups, Muslims could not avail themselves of the opportunities of affirmative action to come out of their collective state of disadvantage. Even the minor avenues of improvement offered to the former untouchable castes were denied in their case.[33] The BJP's campaign ingeniously focused on events that had occurred centuries earlier, claiming these were parallel cases of "historical injustice." If caste injustice could be repaired in the present, why not religious injustice?

A curious aspect of the political conflict ignited by the BJP's new demands around the Babri Masjid and its subsequent demolition by Hindu nationalist volunteers in 1992 was that this turned into a confrontation between Hindu nationalist and secular opinion, spanning the Congress, other secular parties, militantly secular leftist parties, and highly assertive secular intellectuals; it was not acted out as a confrontation between Hindu and Muslim groups. In fact, what Muslim political representatives thought about the issue was largely eclipsed by this visible and bitter political contestation. Recent research reveals that although there was considerable overlap between Muslims and secularists, the issues of concern for Muslim leaders like Syed Shahabuddin were quite specific and distinct—which secularist intellectuals often neglected.[34] The Babri Masjid controversy thus showed a paradoxical aspect of Indian democracy: in defending the minorities volubly, secularists often unwittingly disregarded their real opinions and diminished their own collective agency.

This renewed campaign of the BJP on the basis of a doubtful "event" of the sixteenth century[35] gave the party significant electoral success. Other circumstances likely helped produce this result. A steep decline in the credibility of the Congress Party, mired in accusations of corruption, evident governmental inefficiency, and tied to a blatantly undemocratic dynastic leadership, created a space for a new definition of Indian nationalism, and the BJP sought to replace the pluralist conception of nationalism historically pursued by the Congress by its own exclusive conception of a Hindu nation.[36] After 1996 the BJP twice emerged as the single largest party in Parliament and formed coalition governments, but two factors joined to keep its antipluralist agenda in abeyance. Governmental power was controlled by a faction inside the party less enthusiastic about its antipluralist platform,[37] and its government depended on the support of other coalition partners who did not endorse its Hindu nationalist program—restraining its designs and actual government policy. But the BJP's internal structure was uneven, and in some states, its leadership was more aggressive in its antiminority attitudes. In 2002, the BJP government in Gujarat did not intervene in time to stop large-scale violence and massacres in which more than a thousand Muslims were killed. Though the central government under the BJP at the time showed uneasiness about the occurrence, the government of Gujarat, under its chief minister, Narendra Modi, showed no signs of contrition. Eventually, some functionaries of the government, including a junior minister, were found guilty and convicted by the judiciary.[38] But the Gujarat government under Modi failed to acknowledge its failure of public responsibility in providing equal security to Muslim citizens. In the general elections of 2014, Narendra Modi was elected to power as BJP's national leader. After Modi's installation in office, small-scale riots against Muslims have occurred in many parts of the country.[39] The victory of the BJP, under a more divisive agenda, has set off different resulting trends. Attacks on Christian institutions have increased, and some alarming incidents of murderous attacks on Muslims have been condoned or ignored by BJP officials. When a party with a divisive ideology occupies governmental office, this tends to enable its more extreme supporters to take populist action on their own initiative. Party functionaries are constrained to rationalize or cover up these incidents, for fear of losing their following. This can set off a constantly radicalizing logic of polarization, pushing minority groups into more perilous situations. A countervailing trend has also appeared in some contexts. In a state election in Delhi about six months after the parliamentary elections, the Aam Aadmi Party (Common Man's Party) swept the polls, handing the triumphant BJP a humiliating defeat. In a remarkable development, during these elections, the influential imam of Delhi's Jama Masjid declared support for the AAP and advised Muslims to vote for it. Interestingly, the leader of the AAP publicly refused the endorsement from a religious leader, asking Delhi's electorate, including its Muslim constituents, to vote on secular rather than religious grounds. In late 2015, barely a year after BJP's victory in national elections, it fought another election for the legislative assembly of the important northern state of Bihar. Once again, the BJP was decisively defeated by a coalition of secular parties focusing on issues of development and religious pluralism. Electorally, these two recent results make it hard to read the historic trend. The election of the BJP led by Modi in 2014 seemed to signal a victory, at least transiently, of BJP's antipluralistic revision of Indian nationalism. But the AAP's landslide victory six months later in Delhi, and its repeat in Bihar by another secular coalition, seems to indicate a swift disillusionment with the BJP's version of nationalism and voter support in the opposite direction—for parties that demonstratively repudiate that version of Indian identity. Apart from elections, there have been cases of selectively provocative legislation—like the recent extension of restrictions on the sale of beef in the state of Maharashtra under a Hindu nationalist state government. If these trends toward a selective politics of provocation against Muslims continue, Muslim groups might be led by negative incentives to organize into defensive political organizations. That might lead to a fundamental revision backward of the major positive effect of postcolonial democratic politics, that of rejecting the idea of parties based on religious identity that claim to offer a comprehensive representation of these communities.

But there are some peculiarities of Muslim politics in India that have to be recorded in any careful analysis. As the community has not been organized, after independence, through identity-based unifying political parties, the "politics" of Indian Muslims represents a considerably decentralized field of both systematic, consistent, and episodic action.[40] The remainder of the pre-Partition Muslim League in India fragmented into essentially local political groups, responding to regional and subregional circumstances, pursuing the politics of minute local-scale coalitions. Civil society groups like NGOs, wakf (charitable trust) boards, or leading cultural institutions like the historically eminent madrasa at Deoband often advance articulate, independent responses to large political questions. The instance of the Deoband school is particularly interesting. Not merely has the school revised its syllabus to keep with changing cognitive demands— with emphasis on science, mathematics, and computer education—but it has reacted to large political concerns with formal statements.[41] With the rise of terrorist militancy in South Asia and in the world, representatives of the Deoband school have followed individual incidents of terror and violence with an irenic commentary. The remarkable example of the persistent pluralism of Indian Muslims is generally lost in the general international reckonings of Muslim politics. Although this is not the place to present that historical narrative, Indian Islam has been marked historically—from the twelfth century on—by practices and explicit arguments in favor of pluralism. It is remarkable that the pluralist and accommodative arguments have emerged not only from the Sufi traditions of theology but also from major figures who exercised political power.[42] The interpretative interventions of Indian Islam are accorded little significance in global understandings of the continuing Islamic interpretation of living history. This is a pity: India has one of the largest Islamic communities in the world, one with a long self-conscious tradition that emphasizes its exceptional trajectory. In India, durable structures of Islamic political power coexisted with communities of subjects who practiced a fundamentally different faith— which imposed an interpretative requirement of drawing out the predominantly irenic principles from Islamic faith. A long line of South Asian Muslim thinkers recognized this as a distinctive feature of the traditions of Indian Islam.[43] Recent pronouncements of Islamic religious figures reveal that that historic tradition of interpretation is still intensely active. Despite the rise of Islamic militancy in neighboring Pakistan and to a lesser extent in Bangladesh, Indian Muslim politicians and community leaders have defended an assertively pluralist reading of their faith.

It is not surprising that in opinion-poll surveys India's Muslim citizens have consistently expressed unambiguously strong support for democracy. A full 62 percent of Muslim respondents prefer democracy to any other form of government.[44] Their level of support is at par with electors of other religious communities—rendering false the idea that the Islamic faith inclines its adherents intrinsically against democratic principles. Since they do not have a regional concentration of numbers, except in the frontier region of Kashmir, organizing exclusively on the basis of a religious identity does not appear attractive to them. In that respect, Muslim interests in Indian democracy are articulated in ways that are similar to how they are expressed in the United States, where Muslim interests are not organized through an exclusive political organization but through both major parties. Recent intensification of the United States' conflict with Islamic extremism has threatened to create a more tense atmosphere—with widespread fear of terrorist violence and a reciprocal fear among Muslims of more frequent discrimination. The politics of Hindu nationalism creates a similar vulnerability among Indian Muslims by specifically targeting and cornering them, which might push them toward a politics of despair. They do not identify themselves in politics either as theologically unified or sociologically uniform, making the lure of identity politics rather weak. Instead of being suspect supporters of democratic government, Indian Muslims seem to find the only promise for security in the assurances of dignity afforded by a framework of constitutional democracy.

A historical overview of the behavior of Muslims in Indian democracy shows three significant tendencies. The first is reflected in the altered character of the Muslim League. With the establishment of democratic rule, a party based on the claim that it comprehensively represented an entire religious community and therefore could act on their behalf effectively moved away from that idea and started engaging in ordinary coalition politics with other parties not based on religious affiliation. Second, in cases where a highly visible and contentious problem surfaced involving Muslim religious interests, like the Babri Masjid, the community decided to seek a solution through general constitutional principles. Its defense of its religious interests, therefore, instead of undermining democratic procedures, called for a stricter adherence to constitutionalism. Finally, increasingly sections of the community have veered toward an articulation of their interests in ways that strengthen their coalitional relation with non-Muslim communities affected by similar circumstances. Pasmanda Muslim leaders have accordingly sought reservation based on caste—which rejects religious exclusivity and aligns members of the community with the more general cause of social justice. Thus, overall, in the context of Indian democracy, Muslims take a lively part in politics not on grounds of communal exclusivity but by sharing demands with other groups—for constitutional propriety and the extension of social justice.

SOME GENERAL IMPLICATIONS

Thinking about Indian democracy through Alfred Stepan's thesis of the "twin tolerations" reveals a sociological underdetermination. The state side of this exchange of toleration is straightforward—by its very nature the state is unified, and at least it acts as a relatively coherent political agent,[45] but what toleration from the side of religious communities would mean depends to a large extent on those communities' internal sociological structure, which could show a great deal of variation. Christianity has a relatively structured and unified institutional form[46] that makes a decision regarding an acceptance of the state's offer of accommodation relatively straightforward. Both major religions in India—Hinduism and Islam—have, sociologically, a highly decentralized decisional structure. If collectively "Hindus" have to extend tolerance toward the state's policies, it is not clear whom this move should come from—making it hard to attain a collective decision binding on the community as a whole. Small groups centered around local organizations or interests can breach a decision made by larger, formal institutions of the community. A second potential problem is regarding institutional channels of representation. We saw in our discussion about Nehru that some observers feel that the opinion of the community should be elicited more directly. This could be done, as some European governments have tried to do, while pursuing a specific conception of "multiculturalism," by seeking opinions of religious leaders—like imams of mosques, alims of madrasas, or priests in the case of Sikhs or Hindus. But this assumes that religious communities are solidly united behind their ecclesiastical leaders. Alternatively, it is equally possible to see the community as being represented by their elected representatives: indeed, in a democratic system, electoral representatives are more appropriate carriers of the opinion of social groups into the deliberative process. Existence of political parties that exclusively represent religious communities—like the presence of the Muslim League in preindependence India—makes this process possible, but at a great cost. Presence of a political party of that kind stokes the illusion that religious identity is equivalent to a solid, comprehensive interest, which implies, falsely, that on every single issue of significant democratic debate, a religious community must have a distinctive and uniform opinion or preference. This is clearly incorrect. Religious groups may have distinctive positions on *religious* issues—for example, conversion, preservation of cultural aspects of their life, languages that are deeply linked to their spiritual expression, and freedom of religious practice. On other questions, a religious community of vast numbers and immense diversity—like Muslims in India—should not be expected to have a distinct and internally uniform opinion or interest.[47] It is more usual for members of the community to express their perceptions of interest—as peasants, workers, the poor, or groups belonging to specific regions—through parties that represent these interests. It is not surprising that Indian Muslims, despite the existence of religious political parties, have not worked through these as primary vehicles of their opinions or collective interests. Usually, they have voted in favor of secular parties like the Congress or leftist parties who profess a more consistent and vigilant secularism and are more sharply opposed to Hindu nationalism. In some cases, some political parties, like the Samajwadi Party, mainly concentrated in the state of Uttar Pradesh, the largest in the federation, have sought to attract Muslim support by playing on fears of the BJP and the insecure secularism of the Congress. Electoral analyses show a steady support of Muslim voters for the Samajwadi Party in Uttar Pradesh, but that often comes at a cost of a different kind. By becoming identified with Muslim votes, the Samajwadi Party stokes direct confrontations with Hindu nationalists. Just before the parliamentary elections of 2014, provocative campaigning by the BJP in the state of Uttar Pradesh sparked local conflicts and rioting—which tended to assist both parties by polarizing communal votes at the cost of a general deterioration of the communal situation in that state.

In analyzing the politics of large Muslim communities in democratic states, it is important to note a specificity of the Indian situation. It is true that India has one of the largest Muslim populations in the world, living under a democratic constitution, but it is still a minority. Its relation to the democratic constitution is quite different from that of large Islamic communities in states like Indonesia or Tunisia, which are largely Muslim countries with relatively small non-Islamic minorities. They are not threatened by a potentially majoritarian religious domination, as they could be in India. Even if the political system turns undemocratic, that will not threaten them with *religious* domination by other religious denominations. Under these circumstances, it is not hard to understand the support Indian Muslims evince for democratic institutions. The danger they face is a subtler transformation of democracy into a majoritarian form of government under the electoral government of Hindu nationalism. And the history of democratic constitutionalism shows that democratic government can be undermined more surreptitiously by a translation to majoritarianism than by the direct hostility of explicitly authoritarian politics. Authoritarian forces have to deny fundamental democratic principles, but majoritarian populism can pretend to extend and intensify them, using democratic principles against themselves.

NOTES

1. For an expanded argument for why modernity must be viewed as plural, see Sudipta Kaviraj, "Outline of a Revisionist Theory of Modernity," *European Journal of Sociology* 46, no. 3 (2005): 497–526.

2. For a recent discussion of these issues, see Charles Taylor, *A Secular Age* (Cambridge, Mass.: Harvard University Press, 2008); Alfred Stepan and Charles Taylor, eds., *Boundaries of Toleration* (New York: Columbia University Press, 2014); Akeel Bilgrami, ed., *Beyond the Secular West* (New York: Columbia University Press, 2016).

3. See Alfred Stepan's chapter in this volume. For a general discussion of secularity that "provincializes" the canonical secularity of the West, see Taylor, *A Secular Age*; for a wide-ranging discussion about how Taylor's argument could be viewed in other cultural and civilizational contexts, see Stepan and Taylor, eds., *Boundaries of Toleration*; Akeel Bilgrami, ed., *Can Secularism Travel?* (New York: Columbia University Press, forthcoming).

4. In Syed Ahmed Khan's works, these two modes of power are not given any definite or standardized conceptual titles, but it is quite clear that he saw that British colonialism was slowly giving rise to a new "modern" regime of social power. For Sir Syed and his historic influence, see David Lelyveld, *Aligarh's First Generation* (Delhi: Oxford University Press, 1996).

5. Though Sir Syed's arguments are read rather narrowly in terms of the interests of the Muslim elite, he generally included parallel Hindu political elites whose preeminence was equally imperiled by the rise of modern Bengalis whose skills fitted them to triumph in examinations rather than battles. Syed Ahmed Khan, *The Present State of Indian Politics* (Lahore: Sang-e-Meel, 1982).

6. Syed Ahmed Khan, *Causes of the Indian Mutiny* (1858), http://www.columbia.edu/itc/mealac/pritchett/oourdu/asbab/.

7. There was an obvious difficulty with this argument: large numbers of Muslims were actually converts from Hinduism and did not belong to the aristocracy, but Sir Syed was concerned primarily about the prospects of decline of the Muslim elites.

8. See Sumit Sarkar, *The Swadeshi Movement in Bengal* (Kolkata: Orient Blackswan, 2011), for a forceful statement of this line of argument.

9. Analyses of societies and the bases of political action in a long line of thinkers in all three traditions examined individual and collective agency; the process of formation of sectional interests of ethnic groups, economic classes, and other such potential forms of common aggregative interests; and their relation to "universal" interests of the state as a whole. These are reflected in the works of a number of major Western thinkers: Bentham and Mill, Saint-Simon and Fourier, Hegel and Marx. Some of these disparate reflections were drawn together into a tight and stylized contrast in Ferdinand Toennies, *Community and Civil Society* (Cambridge: Cambridge University Press, 2001), which initiated the conceptual binary of *gemeinschaft* and *gesellschaft*.

10. Concerns were often expressed about the outcomes of simple majorities, and this gave rise to the debates about proportional representation, but the underlying idea was that the "majorities" were always decisional majorities.

11. For a discussion that compares Pakistan to Israel, see Faisal Devji, *Muslim Zion* (Cambridge, Mass.: Harvard University Press, 2013), chap. 2.

12. Unfortunately, the works of dissenting intellectuals within the Muslim community, like Maulana Abul Kalam Azad, who mobilized evidence of a long pluralist tradition in medieval Islamic doctrine and appealed to the long tradition of pluralism of South Asian Islam, have been comparatively neglected. See, for a forceful and interesting analysis of his thought, Aijaz Ahmed, *Lineages of the Present* (London: Verso, 2000).

13. Congress leaders did not forcefully attack this conceptual substitution from decisional to identity majorities: they sought to reassure the Muslim leadership that constitutional devices could take care of their concerns. In a confused way, the Congress's claim to represent all Indians made this claim, but in a form that only provoked the Muslim leadership even more.

14. Minorities certainly have a solid common interest in those cases where policies will affect their position as a group—as in the case of their religious activities or demands, but it is fallacious to believe that on every significant issue the "interests" of a religious minority would be different from those of others.

15. Muhammad Iqbal, "Speech to Annual Session of the Muslim League," Allahabad, December 1930. Iqbal's suggestion was startling but remarkably vague. His negative arguments are clearer than the positive ones. Clearly, Iqbal believed that modern states must necessarily resemble European nation-states as a mandatory political form, and he was evidently concerned about the state of religious minorities—like the Jews. He also believed that for Muslims it was essential to have an environment where their communal social life could flourish. It is not clear if he wanted to propose the formation of a sovereign state or a large unit inside a loose confederation. According to some commentators, such ambiguities characterized even the very late and frantic negotiations about the creation of Pakistan. For this particular reading of the evidence, see Ayesha Jalal, *The Sole Spokesman* (Cambridge: Cambridge University Press, 1994).

16. For a revealing discussion of the political status of European Jews and its slow change toward legal equality, see Ira Katznelson in *Religion and the Political Imagination*, ed. Ira Katznelson and Gareth Steadman Jones (Cambridge: Cambridge University Press, 2012).

17. In a parallel case, in the debates in the Bengal legislative assembly, immediately before partition, some Hindu representatives used the Jewish example to make their point. Neither side entertained the alternative idea that precedents of European history might not be binding on postcolonial states and that there could be other ways to construct state institutions to suit other cultures.

18. See Iqbal's strictures against Westminster institutions—which British opinion regarded as the ideal form of government—in his "Speech to Annual Session of the Muslim League." These critics were not actively seeking a consociational model; their political imagination was crucially limited to existing European designs, but a consociational or nonmajoritarian design may have answered some of their concerns.

19. Arend Lijphart, *Patterns of Majoritarian and Consensus Government in Twenty-One Countries* (New Haven, Conn.: Yale University Press, 1984); Arend Lijphart, "The

Puzzle of Indian Democracy: A Consociational Interpretation," *American Political Science Review* 90, no. 2 (1996): 258–268.

20. See Iqbal, "Speech to Annual Session of the Muslim League"; and, more significantly, the presidential address by Muhammad Ali Jinnah to the Lahore Session of the Muslim League, March 22, 1940.

21. Like aspects of federalism, adoption of multiple languages rather than a single national language, provisions for minority schools, etc.

22. Lijphart, 'The Puzzle of Indian Democracy."

23. Rajni Kothari famously presented such an argument without using the familiar technical terms. Rajni Kothari, "The 'Congress System' in India," *Asian Survey* 4, no. 12 (December 1964): 1161–1173.

24. It can be argued in Nehru's favor that political justification always follows this double principle of "what is right"—using philosophical or historical justifiability. The trouble with the second type of measures is that, if not rectified and reconsidered under altered circumstances, these can produce unintended negative consequences.

25. For a detailed analysis, see Narendra Subramaniam, *Nation and Family: Personal Law, Cultural Pluralism, and Gendered Citizenship in India* (Redwood City, Calif.: Stanford University Press, 2013).

26. It should be noted that fascist critics of liberal democracy, often puzzlingly admired by radicals, seek to undermine liberal democracy precisely by a deliberate conflation of these two conditions.

27. Although it can be persuasively argued that this was a serious defect in Nehru's handling of post-Partition politics, his formal options appear, in retrospect, to have been limited. Under the formal division of constitutional powers, education was a "state" subject and not under the central legislature that Nehru could influence. In some of his letters of the time he expresses acute disappointment with leaders of his own party. For a detailed analytical account of Uttar Pradesh politics, see Guyanesh Kudaisya, *Region, Nation,"Heartland": Uttar Pradesh in India's Body Politic* (Washington, D.C.: Sage, 2006).

28. For instance, Akeel Bilgrami, "Secularism, Nationalism, and Modernity," in *Secularism and Its Critics*, ed. Rajeev Bhargava (Delhi: Oxford University Press, 1998), 380–417.

29. Hilal Ahmed, *Muslim Political Discourse in Postcolonial India* (New York: Routledge, 2014), chap. 4.

30. In Ayodhya, a mosque established by the first Mughal emperor, Babar, has been targeted by Hindu activists, as they believed it was constructed over a destroyed temple at the birthplace of the Hindu deity Rama. The mosque was destroyed by a Hindu mob in December 1992.

31. Shahabuddin described Muslims as a political community, noting that "Muslim Indians are . . . a pan-Indian community which sometimes reacts uniformly to a given stimulus but it is by no means a monolithic or homogeneous community, linguistically, ethnically or culturally." He further noted, "No doubt Muslim Indians see themselves, above all as a religious community, but they have to realise that they can protect their religious

status or religious rights flowing from the constitution only through political action. Once they are conscious of this imperative, they become a political community." In this conceptualization, Shahabuddin highlights two important sociological aspects of the Indian Muslim community. First, he argues for a plural Indian Muslim community, stressing that there are different social and linguistic communities in India that follow Islam as a religion. There are several Muslim sects and subsects in India, and the understanding of Islam of these communities is also not homogeneous. Second, Shahabuddin at the same time argues forcefully for the common concerns of this plural Muslim community. It does not mean that these Muslim communities do not recognize their Islamic identity. He notes, however, the "common concerns and priorities are more often overshadowed by local preoccupations and problems." The questions of being a political community and of becoming a political community are contingent upon the ways by which Indian Muslims communities react to "external pushes" and internal self-perceptions. Thus, for Shahabuddin, "being a religious community and becoming a political community, in larger and in national sense, are indeed, only two faces of the same coin–inseparable from each other." Syed Shahabuddin, "Muslim Indians as a Political Community," *Muslim India* 64 (April 1988): 1–3.

32. The Report of the Sachar Commission showed that Muslims as a whole trailed behind other groups in terms of income, education, and social power.

33. Interestingly, recently movements by Pasmanda Muslims, the most disadvantaged among the Muslims in caste terms, have mounted a strong program demanding caste reform with a recognition that the "caste question" persists within the Muslim community as well.

34. See Ahmed, *Muslim Political Discourse in Postcolonial India*.

35. There is evidence of the demolition of temples and desecration of images in medieval history, but the idea that a specific Hindu temple to Lord Rama was destroyed and a mosque built in its place is contested by liberal and secular historians. See S. Gopal, ed., *Anatomy of a Confrontation* (New York: Viking, 1991). However, it is important to point out that the destruction of a mosque was a wrongful act, irrespective of the historical question, and goes against constitutional guarantees to minorities.

36. The BJP's ideological position is often fraught with flagrant contradictions. It claims to respect the historic Hindu "tradition of tolerance" while advocating that such principles ought to be abandoned. Actively supporting the demolition of mosques on the pretext that these were built on ravaged temples is not the practice of a policy of religious tolerance.

37. After the election victories of the BJP, its prime minister, Atal Bihari Vajpayee, steered the government's policies away from agendas of mosque demolitions and even adopted peace initiatives with Pakistan.

38. Maya Kodnani, a minister at the time, was convicted by the courts in August 2012.

39. As Amrita Basu's study *Violent Conjunctures in Democratic India* (Cambridge: Cambridge University Press, 2015) points out, these events are not riots in a conventional sense but one-sided violence against Muslims.

40. For a concise analysis of these trends, see Hilal Ahmed, "Muslims as a Political Community," *Seminar* 602 (Delhi, October 2009), http://www.india-seminar.com/2009/602/602_hilal_ahmed.htm.

41. Darul Uloom Deoband issued a press release on September 8, 2014, characterizing Al-Qaida Chief Ayman al-Zawahiri's videotape announcing the outfit's India wing as "anti-Muslim and a mischievous act." Vice Chancellor Mufti Abul Qasim Nomani reasserted that "Indian Muslims are nonviolent, and they love their country. They will never be persuaded by a terrorist group." Reacting to the video message from Al-Qaeda announcing the creation of its branch in the Indian subcontinent, Mufti Nomani said, "Islam is a nonviolent religion which talks about propagating peace across the world. Followers of this peaceful religion would never buy arguments of the terrorist groups." He emphasized that Indian Muslims have a firm belief in the Indian secular constitution and the judiciary; therefore such provocations may not attract the attention of Indian Muslims. But he expressed concern that Ayman al-Zawahiri's new videotape could adversely affect the Indian Muslims because the communal forces in the country could seize this opportunity to spit venom against Muslims. The vice chancellor feared that the move might cause the arrest of innocent Muslims in false terror cases, just as numerous Muslim youths had previously been subjected to torture and imprisonment on the account of being members of so-called SIMI, or Indian Mujahidin. Mufti Nomani also cited the antiterrorism fatwa issued by Darul Uloom and the All-India Anti-Terrorism Conference held in February 2008, which was applauded in the national and international media. The vice chancellor urged the government, intelligence agencies, and the media to investigate the truth behind the videotape fairly. According to him, it might be part of the conspiracies hatched against Indian Muslims in order to incriminate them. See http://www.darululoom-deoband.com/english/.

42. Kaviraj, "Modernity, State, and Toleration in Indian History," in Stepan and Taylor, eds., *Boundaries of Toleration*, 243–254.

43. Even historical accounts of Islamic thought in India tend to disregard this strand, represented by important figures like Maulama Azad, and focus exclusively on figures who advanced the "two-nation" theory.

44. *Democracy in India: A Perspective* (Delhi: Lokniti Programme for Comparative Democracy, Centre for the Study of Developing Societies, 2015), 15–19. The full report is available at http://www.lokniti.org/democracy-india-citizens-perspective.php.

45. The state is of course influenced by different kinds of political forces, but the instrument of the state is identifiable.

46. This is a massive overstatement: in different cultural settings, Christianity, like Islam, interacted with local cultures in its vast spread across the world and adapted to conditions of religious belief.

47. Muslim intellectuals including Asghar Ali Engineer have passionately argued this position.

SELECTED BIBLIOGRAPHY

Abalahin, Andrew. "A Sixth Religion? Confucianism and the Negotiation of Indonesian-Chinese Identity Under the Pancasila State." In *Spirited Politics: Religion and Public Life in Contemporary Southeast Asia*, ed. Andrew Clinton Willford and Ken M. George, 119–142. Ithaca, N.Y.: Cornell Southeast Asia Program Publication, 2005.

'Abd al-Ghani al-Gamsi, Muhammad. *Mudhakkirat al-Gamsi: Harb Uktubr 1973* [Gamasi's memoirs: The 1973 October War]. San Francisco: Dar Buhuth al-Sharq al-Awsat al-Amayrikiyya, 1977.

Abdel-Malek, Anwar. *Egypt: Military Society—The Army Regime, the Left, and Social Change Under Nasser.* New York: Random House, 1968.

Ahmad, Irfan. *Islamism and Democracy in India: The Transformation of Jamaat-e-Islami.* Princeton, N.J.: Princeton University Press, 2009.

Ahmed, Aijaz. *Lineages of the Present.* London: Verso, 2000.

Ahmed, Hilal. *Muslim Political Discourse in Postcolonial India.* New York: Routledge, 2014.

——. "Muslims as a Political Community." *Seminar* 602 (October 2009). http://www.india-seminar.com/2009/602/602_hilal_ahmed.htm.

Aspinall, Edward. "From Islamism to Nationalism in Aceh, Indonesia." *Nations and Nationalism* 13, no. 2 (2007).

Baghdadi, Abd al-Latif al-. *Mudhakkirat* [Memoirs]. Cairo: al-Maktab al-Misri al-Hadith, 1977.

Basu, Amrita. *Violent Conjunctures in Democratic India.* Cambridge: Cambridge University Press, 2015.

Baswedan, Anies. "Political Islam in Indonesia: Present and Future Trajectory." *Asian Survey* 44, no. 5 (2004): 669–690.

Baz, Mohammad al-. *al-Aqrab al-Sam. Omar Suleiman, General al-Moukhabarat al-Ghamid.* Cairo: Konouz, 2013.

——. *al-Mouchir wa al-Fariq, al-Malaffat al-Siyassia li Tantawi wa Annan.* Cairo: Konouz, 2013.

Be'eri, Eliezer. *Army Officers in Arab Politics and Society.* New York: Praeger, 1970.

Beisinger, Mark R., Amaney A. Jamal, and Kevin Mazur. "Explaining Divergent Revolutionary Coalitions: Regime Strategies and the Structuring of Participation in the Tunisian and Egyptian Revolutions." *Comparative Politics* 28 (October 2016).

Benda, Harry J. "Christiaan Snouck Hurgronje and the Foundations of Dutch Islamic Policy in Indonesia." *Journal of Modern History* 30, no. 4 (1958).

——. *The Crescent and the Rising Sun: Indonesian Islam Under the Japanese Occupation, 1942–1945.* The Hague and Bandung: W. van Hoeve, 1958.

Benkraiem, Boubaker. *Naissance d'une armed nationale, la promotion Bourguiba.* Tunis: Maision d'edition de Tunis, 2009.

Berger, Peter. *The Desecularization of the World.* Washington, D.C.: Eerdmans/Ethic and Public Policy Center, 1999.

Bermeo, Nancy. "The Myths of Moderation: The Role of Radical Forces in the Transition to Democracy." *Comparative Politics* 29, no. 3 (1997).

Besheer, Margaret. "G8 Commits $80 Billion to Arab Spring Democracy." *Voice of America.* September 19, 2011. http://www.voanews.com/content/g8-commits-80-billion-to-arab-spring-democracy-130242553/158882.html.

Bessis, Sophie. "Khadija Cherif, la femme qui fait peur au pouvoir tunisien." *Le Monde.* February 9, 2015.

Bhargava, Rajeev. *Democracy in India: A Perspective.* Lokniti Programme for Comparative Democracy, Centre for the Study of Developing Societies. Delhi, 2015.

Bilgrami, Akeel, ed. *Beyond the Secular West.* New York: Columbia University Press, 2016.

——, ed. *Can Secularism Travel?* New York: Columbia University Press, forthcoming.

——. "Secularism, Nationalism, and Modernity." In *Secularism and Its Critics,* ed. Rajeev Bhargava, 380–417. Delhi: Oxford University Press, 1998.

Bitar, Sergio, and Abraham Lowenthal, eds. *Democratic Transitions: Conversations with World Leaders.* Baltimore, Md.: Johns Hopkins University Press, 2015.

Boland, B. J. *The Struggle of Islam in Modern Indonesia.* The Hague: Martinus Nijhoff, 1982.

Boukhars, Anouar. *The Reckoning: Tunisia's Perilous Path to Democratic Stability.* Carnegie Endowment. April 2015.

Bou Nassif, Hicham. "Coups and Nascent Democracies: The Military and Egypt's Failed Consolidation." *Democratization* 23, no. 5 (2016).

——. "A Military Besieged: The Armed Forces, the Police, and the Party in Ben Ali's Tunisia, 1987–2011." *International Journal of Middle East Studies* 47 (2015): 65–87.

Bowen, John. *Islam, Law, and Equality in Indonesia: An Anthropology of Public Reasoning.* Cambridge: Cambridge University Press, 2003.

Brecher, Michael. *Nehru: A Political Biography.* London: Oxford University Press, 1959.

British Broadcasting Corporation (BBC). "Tunisia After the Revolution." November 17, 2014.

Brocker, Manfred, and Mirjam Kunkler. "Religious Parties: Revisiting the Inclusion-Moderation Hypothesis." *Party Politics* 19, no. 2 (2013).

Browers, Michaelle L. *Political Ideology in the Arab World: Accommodation and Transformation.* Cambridge: Cambridge University Press, 2009.

Brown, Nathan. "Egypt's Constitutional Cul-de-Sac." Chr. Michelsen Institute Insight, March 2014.

——. "Regimes Reinventing Themselves: Constitutional Development in the Arab World." *International Sociology* 18, no. 1 (March 2003): 33–52.

Brown, Nathan J., Amr Hamzawy, and Marina Ottaway. "Islamist Movements and the Democratic Process in the Arab World: Exploring the Gray Zones." Carnegie Endowment for International Peace, 2006.

Brownlee, Jason. "Unrequited Moderation: Credible Commitments and State Repression in Egypt." *Studies in Comparative International Development* 45, no. 4 (2010): 468–489.

Burgat, Francois, and William Dowell. *The Islamic Movement in North Africa.* Austin: University of Texas Press, 1997.

Cammack, Mark. "Legal Aspects of Muslim–Non-Muslim Marriage in Indonesia." In *Muslim–Non-Muslim Marriage: Political and Cultural Contestations in Southeast Asia*, ed. G. Jones, C. Leng, and M. Mohamad. Singapore: Institute for Southeast Asian Studies, 2009.

Carey, John M. "Why Tunisia Remains the Arab Spring's Best Bet." Conference presentation for Dartmouth and IISS. September 9–11, 2013.

Carter Center. "The Carter Center Congratulates Tunisia's National Constituent Assembly on Final Draft of Constitution and Urges Safeguards for Human Rights." June 12, 2013.

Cavatorta, Francesco, and Fabio Merone. "Moderation Through Exclusion? The Journey of the Tunisian Ennadha from Fundamentalist to Conservative Party." *Democratization* 20, no. 5 (2013): 857–875.

Charrad, M. M. *States and Women's Rights in the Making of Postcolonial Tunisia, Algeria, and Morocco.* Berkeley: University of California Press, 2001.

Chebbi, Ahmed Najib. "A propos d'une derive." February 2006.

——. "Amorce d'un débat." March 2006.

Clark, Janine Astrid. "The Conditions of Islamist Moderation: Unpacking Cross-Ideological Cooperation in Jordan." *International Journal of Middle East Studies* 38, no. 4 (2006).

Collectif du 18 Octobre pour les Droits et les Libertés. "Communiqué de Presse." December 4, 2005.

Crisis Group. "Marching in Circles." Cairo, May 25, 2013. http://www.crisisgroup.org/en /publication-type/media-releases/2013/mena/marching-in-circles-egypts-dangerous-second -transition.aspx.

Crouch, Melissa. "Law and Religion in Indonesia: The Constitutional Court and the Blasphemy Law." *Asian Journal of Comparative Law* 7, no. 1 (2012): 1–46.

——. "Proselytisation, Religious Diversity, and the State in Indonesia: The Offence of Deceiving a Child to Change Religion." In *Proselytising and the Limits of Religious Pluralism in Contemporary Asia*, ed. Michael Feener and Juliana Finucane. Singapore: ARI Springer Asia Series, 2013.

Dekmejian, Hrair. *Egypt Under Nasser: A Study in Political Dynamics.* Albany: SUNY Press, 1971.

Devji, Faisal. *Muslim Zion*. Cambridge, Mass.: Harvard University Press, 2013.

Diamond, Larry. "Tunisia Is Still a Success." *Atlantic*, March 23, 2015.

Diouf, Mamadou, ed. *Tolerance, Democracy, and Sufis in Senegal*. New York: Columbia University Press, 2013.

Dunne, Michele. "Egypt's Draft Constitution Rewards the Military and Judiciary." Carnegie Endowment for International Peace, December 2013.

Fadel, Monica. "The Hands of the Gulf in Tunisia." *Gulf House for Studies and Publishing*. http://gulfhsp.org/en/posts/1322/.

Feldman, Noah. "A Peace Prize for Tunisia's Exceptionalism." *Bloomberg*. October 9, 2015.

Filali-Ansary, Abdou. "Building Consensus in Post-Revolutionary Tunisia." *Open Democracy*, January 30, 2015.

Filiu, Jean-Pierre. *The Arab Revolution: Ten Lessons from the Democratic Uprising*. London: C. Hurst, 2011.

Foret, François. *Religion and Politics in the European Union: The Secular Canopy*. Cambridge: Cambridge University Press, 2015.

Freedom House. "The Recurrent Temptation to Abdicate to the Military in Egypt." *Freedom at Issue* 13 (January 2012).

Frei, Eugenio Ortega. *Historia de una Alianza Política*. Santiago: CED, CESOC, 1992.

Furnival, J. S. *Netherlands India: A Study of Plural Economy*. New York: Cambridge University Press, 1944.

Gad, Ibrahim. *Tamarrad . . . Wal Tarik ila 30 Youlyou*. Cairo: Markaz al-Mahroussa, 2014.

Geisser, Vincent, and Eric Gobe. "Un si long règne . . . Le régime de Ben Ali vingt ans après." In *L'année du Maghreb*. CNRS Éditions, 2008.

George, Alexander L., and Andrew Bennett. *Case Studies and Theory Development in the Social Sciences*. Cambridge, Mass.: MIT Press, 2005.

Ghannouchi, Rached. "Tunisia's Perilous Path to Freedom." *Wall Street Journal*, January 15, 2015.

Ghobashy, Mona El-. "The Metamorphosis of the Egyptian Muslim Brothers." *International Journal of Middle East Studies* 37, no. 3 (2005).

Gobe, Eric. "Les avocats tunisiens dans la Tunisie de Ben Ali: économie politique d'une profession juridique." *Droit et Société* 79 (2011).

Göle, Nilüfer. *Islam and Secularity: The Future of Europe's Public Sphere*. Durham, N.C.: Duke University Press, 2015.

Gopal, S. *Anatomy of a Confrontation*. New York: Viking, 1991.

Grewal, Sharan. "Why Tunisia Didn't Follow Egypt's Path." *Washintgon Post*. February 4, 2015.

Guellali, Amna. "The Problem with Tunisia's New Constitution." Human Rights Watch, February 24, 2015.

Habermas, Jürgen. "Religion in the Public Sphere." *European Journal of Philosophy* 14, no. 1 (2006).

Haddad, George. *Revolution and Military Rule in the Middle East: The Arab States*. Vol. 2: *Egypt, the Sudan, Yemen, and Libya*. New York: Robert Speller and Sons, 1973.

Hamid, Shadi. *Temptations of Power: Islamists and Illiberal Democracy in a New Middle East*. Oxford: Oxford University Press, 2014.

Hammad, Abdel Azim. *Al-Thawra al-Taiha. Siraa al-Khouza wa al-Lihya wa al-Maydan. Rou'yat Chahid Ayan.* Cairo: Markaz al-Mahroussa, 2013.

Hammad, Gamal. *Asrar Thawrat 23 Yuliyu* [Secrets of the July 23 Revolution]. Cairo: Dar al-'Ulum, 2011.

Hassan, Ma'sum, and H. Mahmud Aziz. *Soal-Jawab Tentang Berbagai Masalah Agama.* Bandung: CV Penerbit Diponegoro, 2007.

Hefner, Robert. "Islamising Java? Religion and Politics in Rural East Java." *Journal of Asian Studies* 46, no. 3 (1987): 533–554.

Hibou, Beatrice. *The Force of Obedience: The Political Economy of Repression in Tunisia.* London: Polity, 2011.

Hidibi, Ibrahim al-. "An Motalabat 'Awdat al-Jeish." *Al-Shouroq.* March 8, 2013.

Horowitz, Donald L. *Constitutional Change and Democracy in Indonesia.* New York: Cambridge University Press, 2013.

Houfi, Nachwa al-. *Ya Nokhba Ma Tammit.* Cairo: Dar Dawwin, 2013.

Hourani, Albert. *Arabic Thought in the Liberal Age: 1798–1939.* New York: Cambridge University Press, 1983.

Howell, Julia. "Muslims, the New Age, and Marginal Religions in Indonesia: Changing Meanings of Religious Pluralism." *Social Compass* 52, no. 4 (2005).

Human Rights Watch. "Egypt: Rab'a Killings Likely Crimes Against Humanity: No Justice Later for Series of Deadly Mass Attacks on Protesters." August 12, 2014.

Huntington, Samuel. *The Third Wave: Democratization in the Late Twentieth Century.* Norman: University of Oklahoma Press, 1991.

Iqbal, Muhammad. "Speech to Annual Session of the Muslim League." Allahabad, December 1930.

Jinnah, Muhammad Ali. "Speech to the Lahore Session of the Muslim League." March 22, 1940.

Kalyvas, Stathis. "Commitment Problems in Emerging Democracies: The Case of Religious Parties." *Comparative Politics* 32, no. 4 (2000).

——. "The 'Turkish Model' in the Matrix of Political Catholicism." In *Democracy, Islam, and Secularism in Turkey,* ed. Ahmet Kuru and Alfred Stepan, 192–196. New York: Columbia University Press, 2012.

Kandil, Hazem. *Soldiers, Spies, and Statesmen: Egypt's Road to Revolt.* London: Verso, 2012.

Katznelson, Ira, and Gareth Steadman Jones, eds. *Religion and the Political Imagination.* Cambridge: Cambridge University Press, 2012.

Kaviraj, Sudipta. "Outline of a Revisionist Theory of Modernity." *European Journal of Sociology* 46, no. 3 (2005): 497–526.

Keath, Lee, and Maggie Michael. "Popular Wave Could Lift Egypt Army Chief to Office." *Associated Press.* January 30, 2014. http://news.yahoo.com/popular-wave-could-lift-egypt-army-chief-office-223857617.html.

Kepel, Gilles. *Jihad: The Trail of Political Islam.* Cambridge, Mass.: Harvard University Press, 2002.

Khan, Syed Ahmed. *Causes of the Indian Mutiny.* 1858. http://www.columbia.edu/itc/mealac/pritchett/00urdu/asbab/.

——. *The Present State of Indian Politics.* Lahore: Sang-e-Meel, 1982.

Kothari, Rajni. "The 'Congress System' in India." *Asian Survey* 4, no. 12 (December 1964): 1161–1173.

Kudaisya, Guyanesh. *Region, Nation, "Heartland": Uttar Pradesh in India's Body Politic.* Washington, D.C.: Sage, 2006.

Künkler, Mirjam. "How Pluralist Democracy Became the Consensual Discourse Among Secular and Nonsecular Muslims in Indonesia." In *Democracy and Islam in Indonesia*, ed. M. Künkler and A. Stepan, 53–72. New York: Columbia University Press, 2013.

Kuru. Ahmet T. "Passive and Assertive Secularism: Historical Conditions, Ideological Struggles, and State Policies Toward Religion." *World Politics* 59 (2007).

——. *Secularism and State Policies Toward Religion: The United States, France, and Turkey.* New York: Cambridge University Press, 2009.

Kurzman, Charles, and Ijlal Naqvi. "Do Muslims Vote Islamic?" *Journal of Democracy* 21, no. 2 (2010): 50–63.

Lelyveld, David. *Aligarh's First Generation.* Delhi: Oxford University Press, 1996.

Lijphart, Arend. *Patterns of Majoritarian and Consensus Government in Twenty-One Countries.* New Haven, Conn.: Yale University Press, 1984.

——. "The Puzzle of Indian Democracy: A Consociational Interpretation." *American Political Science Review* 90, no. 2 (1996): 258–268.

Lindsey, Timothy. *Islam, Law, and the State in Southeast Asia.* Vol. 1: *Indonesia.* London: I. B. Tauris, 2012.

Linz, Juan J. *Breakdown of Democratic Regimes: Crisis, Breakdown, and Reequilibration.* Baltimore, Md.: Johns Hopkins University Press, 1978.

Linz, Juan J., and Alfred Stepan. *Problems of Democratic Transition and Consolidation: Southern Europe, South America, and Post-Communist Europe.* Baltimore, Md.: Johns Hopkins University Press, 1996.

MacCulloch, Diarmaid. *The Reformation.* London: Viking, 2003.

Majelis Ulama Indonesia. *Himpunan fatwa Majelis Ulama Indonesia.* Jakarta: Majelis Ulama Indonesia, 1997.

Marks, Monica. "Complementary Status for Tunisian Women." *Foreign Policy*, August 20, 2012.

——. "Convince, Coerce, or Compromise? Ennahda's Approach to Tunisia's Constitution." Brookings Institution, February 10, 2014.

——. "How Egypt's Coup Really Affected Tunisia's Islamists." *Washington Post*, March 16, 2015.

——. "Islamism in Transition: Compromise and Contention Inside Tunisia's Ennahda After the Revolution." Unpublished doctoral dissertation, Oxford University.

——."Tunisia's Ennahda: Rethinking Islamism in the Context of ISIS and the Egyptian Coup." Brookings Institution. August 2015.

——. "Tunisia Opts for an Inclusive Coalition." *Washington Post*, February 3, 2015.

——. "Who Are Tunisia's Salafis?" *Foreign Policy*. September 28, 2012.

Marks, Monica, and Omar Belhaj Salah. "Uniting for Tunisia?" *Sada.* Carnegie Endowment. March 28, 2013.

Marx, Karl. *The Eighteenth Brumaire of Louis Bonaparte* [1864]. New York: International Publications, 1964.

Marzouki, Nadia. "Dancing by the Cliff: Constitution Writing in Post-Revolutionary Tunisia, 2011–2014." In *Constitution Writing, Religion, and Democracy*, ed. Asli Bali and Hanna Lerner. Cambridge: Cambridge University Press, 2016.

al-Masry al-Youm. "Profile of Hejazi." March 27, 2014. http://www.almasryalyoum.com/news/details/418190.

Materi, Moncef el-. *De Saint-Cyr au Peleton d'execution de Bourguiba.* Tunis: Arabesques, 2014.

McCarthy, Rory. "Protecting the Sacred: Tunisia's Islamist Movement Ennahda and the Challenge of Free Speech." *British Journal of Middle Eastern Studies* (2015).

Mecham, R. Q. "From the Ashes of Virtue, and Promise of Light: The Transformation of Political Islam in Turkey." *Third World Quarterly* 25, no. 2 (2004): 339–358.

Menchik, Jeremy. "The Coevolution of Sacred and Secular: Islamic Law and Family Planning in Indonesia." *South East Asia Research* 22, no. 3 (2014): 359–378.

——. *Islam and Democracy in Indonesia: Tolerance Without Liberalism.* New York: Cambridge University Press, 2016.

Merone, Fabio, and Francesco Cavatorta. "The Emergence of Salafism in Tunisia." *Jadaliyya.* August 17, 2012.

——. "Salafist Mouvance and Sheikh-ism in the Tunisian Democratic Transition." Working Papers in International Studies. Dublin City University, 2012.

Middle East Eye. "Row in Tunisia Over Claims That UAE Is Buying Political Influence." May 24, 2015. http://www.middleeasteye.net/news/row-tunisia-over-claims-uae-buying-politic al-influence-1185267817#sthash.KA6tfRik.dpuf.

——. "UAE Threatens to Destabilise Tunisia for Not Acting in Abu Dhabi's Interests." November 30, 2015. http://www.middleeasteye.net/news/uae-threaten-destabilise-tunisia -not-acting-abu-dhabis-interests-1261316730#sthash.jCvzKdsO.dpuf.

Middle East Online. "Tunisia Follows in Footsteps of Egypt: 'Tamarrod' to Challenge Ennahda's Constitution." July 3, 2013. http://www.middle-east-online.com/english/?id=59870.

Muhammadiyah. "Mempertajam Kewaspadaan Islam Tentang Berita Hasil Konferensi Katolik / Protestan Jawa Timur akan Mengkristenkan Seluruh Indonesia." *Suara Muhammadiyah* 25 (1963).

——. *Suara Muhammadiyah No 1* (April 1939): 11.

Mujani, Saiful, and R. William Liddle. "Politics, Islam, and Public Opinion." *Journal of Democracy* 15, no. 1 (2004).

Murphy, Emma. *Economic and Political Change in Tunisia: From Bourguiba to Ben Ali.* New York: Palgrave Macmillan, 1989.

Muskens, M. P. M. *Partner in National Building: The Catholic Church in Indonesia.* Aachen: Missio Aktuell Verlag, 1979.

Muslim Brothers, Ministry of Transport. *Akhbar al-Youm.* December 31, 2013.

Nahdlatul Ulama. *Ahkam al-Fuqaha' fi Muqarrarat Mu'tamarat Nahdlati al-'Ulama: Solusi Problematika Aktual Hukum Islam Keputusan Muktamar (1926–1999).* Surabaya: Lajnah Ta'lif Wan Nasyer Jawa Timur, 2007.

O'Donnell, Guillermo, Philippe C. Schmitter, and Laurence Whitehead. *Transitions from Authoritarian Rule*. Baltimore, Md.: Johns Hopkins University Press, 1986.

Parkinson, Sarah Elizabeth. "Organizing Rebellion: Rethinking High-Risk Mobilization and Social Networks in War." *American Political Science Review* 107, no. 3 (2013).

Patton, Calum. "Tunisia: Violence on the Streets of Kasserine as Youth Return to Protest Incomplete Revolution." *International Business Times*. January 21, 2016. http://www.ibtimes .co.uk/tunisia-violence-streets-kasserine-youth-return-protest-incomplete-revolution-1539357.

"Penetapan Presiden No 1/1965 tentang Pentjegahan Penjalahgun Dan/Atau Penodaan Agama." *Suara Merdeka*. March 9, 1965.

Pepinsky, Thomas B., R. William Liddle, and Saiful Mujani. "Testing Islam's Political Advantage: Evidence from Indonesia." *American Journal of Political Science* 56, no. 3 (2012).

Perlmutter, Amos. *Egypt: The Praetorian State*. New York: Transaction, 1974.

Pion-Berlin, David, ed. *Civil-Military Relations in Latin America: New Analytical Perspectives*. Chapel Hill: University of North Carolina Press, 2001.

Polity IV Project, Center on Systemic Peace. "Polity Score: 8 (2013)." http://www.systemic peace.org/polity/ins2.htm.

Rasyidi, H. M. "RUU Perkawinan." *Suara Muhammadiyah* 17 (September 1, 1973).

Read, Christopher. *Allegiance: Egypt Security Forces*. Thesis, Naval Postgraduate School, 2013. https://calhoun.nps.edu/bitstream/handle/10945/38998/13Dec_Read_Christopher.pdf.

Redissi, Hamadi. "Ennahdha entre au gouvernement. Les politiques ont trahi le peuple." *Leaders*, February 7, 2015.

Republic of Indonesia. Constitutional Court. "Constitutional Court verdict, 2010." Decision no. 140/puu-vii/2009, section 3.34.10.

Reuters. "Egypt Got $23 Billion in Aid from Gulf in 18 Months—Minister." March 2, 2015. http://uk.reuters.com/article/uk-egypt-investment-gulf-idUKKBN0LY0UT20150302.

Ricklefs, Merle. *A History of Modern Indonesia Since c. 1200*. 4th ed. Stanford, Calif.: Stanford University Press, 2008.

——, ed. *A New History of Southeast Asia*. London: Palgrave Macmillan, 2010.

——. *Polarising Javanese Society: Islamic and Other Visions (c. 1830–1930)*. Singapore: NUS, 2007.

Rogers, Joshua S. "There Is No Room for a Religious Party: Negotiating the Islamist Challenge to State Legitimacy in Tunisia, 1987–1991." Master's thesis, Oxford University. 2007.

Rosefsky Wickham, Carrie. *The Muslim Brotherhood: Evolution of an Islamist Organization*. Princeton, N.J.: Princeton University Press, 2013.

Saeed, Sadia. "Desecularization as an Instituted Process: National Identity and Religious Difference in Pakistan." *Economic and Political Weekly* 48, no. 50 (2003): 62–70.

Saleh, Heba. "Tunisia Forms Coalition in Advance from Autocracy." *Financial Times*. February 2, 2015.

Sami, Farah. "Eight Years Ago Today, When Leftists and Islamists Got Along." *Tunisia Live*, October 18, 2013. http://www.tunisia-live.net/2013/10/18.

Sarkar, Sumit. *The Swadeshi Movement in Bengal*. Kolkata: Orient Blackswan, 2011.

Schwedler, Jillian. "Can Islamists Become Moderates? Rethinking the Inclusion/Moderation Hypothesis." *World Politics* 63, no. 2 (2011): 347–370.

——. *Faith in Moderation: Islamist Parties in Jordan and Yemen*. Cambridge: Cambridge University Press, 2007.

Shahabuddin, Syed. "Muslim Indians as a Political Community." *Muslim India* 64 (April 1988).

Shahin, Emad El-Din. "The State, Liberals, and the Muslim Brotherhood in Egypt: From Competition to Eradication." Paper presented at an international conference on Tunisia's democratic transition in comparative perspective, March 25, 2015, Columbia University, and revised October 1, 2015.

Shihab, Alwi. "The Muhammadiyah Movements and Its Controversy with Christian Missions in Indonesia." PhD thesis, Temple University, 1995.

Shihab, Najwa, and Nugroho Januar. "The Ties That Bind: Law, Islamisation, and Indonesia's Prosperous Justice Party." *Australian Journal of Asian Law* 10, no. 2 (2008).

Sihombing, Erwin. "Interfaith Marriage Still Unsanctioned as Court Rejects Judicial Review." *Jakarta Globe*, June 18, 2015. http://thejakartaglobe.beritasatu.com/news/interfaith -marriages-still-unsanctioned-court-rejects-judicial-review/.

Sikimic, Simona. "Profile: Mohammed Dahlan, Gaza's Comeback Kid." *Middle East Eye*. April 7, 2014. http://www.middleeasteye.net/news/profile-mohammed-dahlan-gazas-come back-kid-1305037516.

Sinnawi, Abdullah. فصن القنا.. بال فصن ا.تقاق. *al-Shourouk*, August 20, 2012. http://www .shorouknews.com/columns/view.aspx?cdate=20082012&id=078ef184-b91f-4ee5-b902-6a2 857929a61.

Siyam, Chahata. *Al-'Askariyoun wa al-Thwara al'Mankousa*. Cairo: Rawafad lil Nachr wa al'Tawzi', 2013.

Steavenson, Wendell. *Circling the Square: Stories from the Egyptian Revolution*. New York: Harper Collins, 2015.

Stepan, Alfred. *Arguing Comparative Politics*. Oxford: Oxford University Press, 2001.

——. "Fernando Henrique Cardoso: The Structural-Historical Scholar-President of Brazil." In *Cardoso and Approaches to Inequality*, ed. Dietrich Rueschemeyer and Richard Snyder. Boulder, Colo.: Lynne Reiner, forthcoming.

——. *The Military in Politics: Changing Patterns in Brazil*. Princeton, N.J.: Princeton University Press, 1971.

——. "Religion, Democracy, and the 'Twin Tolerations.'" *Journal of Democracy* 11 (October 2000): 32–52.

——. "Rituals of Respect: Sufis and Secularists in Senegal in Comparative Perspective." *Comparative Politics* (July 2012): 379–401.

——. "Tunisia's Transition and the Twin Tolerations." *Journal of Democracy* 23 (2012): 89–103.

Stepan, Alfred, Juan J. Linz, and Yogendra Yadav. *Crafting State Nations: India and Other Multinational Democracies*. Baltimore, Md.: Johns Hopkins University Press, 2011.

Stepan, Alfred, and Charles Taylor, eds. *Boundaries of Toleration*. New York: Columbia University Press, 2014.

Subramaniam, Narendra. *Nation and Family: Personal Law, Cultural Pluralism, and Gendered Citizenship in India*. Redwood City, Calif.: Stanford University Press, 2013.

Sya'roni, Mizan. "The Majlisul Islamil a'la Indonesia (MIAI): Its Socio-Religious and Political Activities (1937–1943)." MA thesis, McGill University, 1998.

Taylor, Charles. *A Secular Age*. Cambridge, Mass.: Harvard University Press, 2008.

Tezcur, Gunes Murat. *Muslim Reformers in Iran and Turkey: The Paradox of Moderation*. Austin: University of Texas Press, 2010.

Thapar, Romila. "Is Secularism Alien to Indian Civilization?" In *The Future of Secularism*, ed. T. N. Srinivasan, 83–108. New York: Oxford University Press, 2007.

Tilly, Charles. *Coercion, Capital, and European States, AD 990–1990*. Cambridge, Mass.: Blackwell, 1990.

Toennies, Ferdinand. *Community and Civil Society*. Cambridge: Cambridge University Press, 2001.

Tunisie Numerique. "Tunisie: Crise Diplomatique entre la Tunisie et las Emirats Arabes Unis: Dessous et Enjeux." September 21, 2015. http://www.tunisienumerique.com/tunisie-crise-diplomatique-entre-la-tunisie-et-les-emirats-arabes-unis-dessous-et-enjeux/266972.

Ulama, Nahdlatul. "Majlis ke II: Tentang Hal yang Bersangkutan dengan Pemerintah." *Verslag-Congres Nahdlatul Ulama Yang ke 14 di Kota Magelang*, July 3, 1939.

Wickham, Carrie Rosefsky. "The Path to Moderation: Strategy and Learning in the Formation of Egypt's Wasat Party." *Comparative Politics* 36, no. 2 (2004).

Wolf, Anne. "Can Secular Parties Lead the New Tunisia?" Carnegie Endowment. April 2014.

Yahyaoui, Mokhtar. "Nida'a Tunis, Nida'a el-mustaqbal." Parts 1 and 2. May and July 2003.

Youness, Sharif. *Nida' al-Shaab. Tarikh Naqdi li al-ideologia al-Nasiriya* [The call of the people. A critical history of the Nasserite ideology]. Cairo: Dar al-Shourouq, 2013.

CONTRIBUTORS

Hilal Ahmed is associate professor at the Centre for Studies in Developing Societies in Delhi, India, and a Rajya Sabha Fellow. He works on political Islam, Muslim modernities/representation, and the politics of symbols in South Asia. His book *Muslim Political Discourse in Postcolonial India: Monuments, Memory, Contestation* (2014) looks at these thematic concerns to make sense of the nature of contemporary Muslim political discourse. As a Rajya Sabha Fellow (2015–2016) Ahmed worked on the politics of Muslim political representation in postcolonial India. Ahmed was a visiting fellow at Victoria University Wellington (2013–2014), visiting Asia fellow at the University of Dhaka (2011), and visiting professor at the University of Pune (2011). He has produced a documentary, *Encountering the Political Jama Masjid* (2006), and is working on his second film, *Images of Qutub Minar.*

Nathan Brown is professor of political science and international relations at George Washington University. He has written numerous books, including *Constitutions in a Nonconstitutional World* (2001); *The Rule of Law in the Arab World* (1997); and, with Amr Hamzawy, *Between Religion and Politics* (2010). He serves on the Advisory Committee for the Middle East and North Africa Divison of Human Rights Watch and is on the board of trustees of the American

University in Cairo. He served as an advisor for the committee drafting the Palestinian Constitution. From 2013–2015 he served as president of the Middle East Studies Association.

RACHED GHANNOUCHI is one of the most influential Islamic democratic thinkers and political activists in the world. He is the founder and president of the Ennahda (Renaissance) Party in Tunisia. For his oppositional activities Ghannouchi was imprisoned and sentenced to death by President Bourguiba and then exiled for twenty-one years by President Ben Ali. After the fall of Ben Ali in February 2011, Ghannouchi returned from exile and his party won a plurality in the free election for the National Constituent Assembly. Ennahda, along with two secular parties, led the 2011–2014 ruling coalition that helped write Tunisia's inclusive constitution. Ghannouchi is the author of hundreds of articles in Arabic, French, and English on the relationship between Islam and democracy and the role of a party with Islamic ideals in a modern democracy. His biography by Azzam S. Tamimi, *Rachid Ghannouchi: A Democrat Within Islamism*, was published in 2001.

SUDIPTA KAVIRAJ is professor of Indian politics and intellectual history at Columbia University. Previously he had taught at Jawaharlal Nehru University in Delhi and SOAS University of London. He is a member of the Subaltern Studies Collective. His books include *The Enchantment of Democracy and India* (2011); *The Imaginary Institution of India* (Columbia, 2010); *Civil Society: History and Possibilities*, coedited with Sunil Khilnani (2001); *Politics in India* (1999); and *The Unhappy Consciousness: Bankimchandra Chattopadhyay and the Formation of Nationalist Discourse in India* (1995). Kaviraj helped create the "multiple modernities" literature with his article "An Outline of a Revisionist Theory of Modernity," published in the *European Journal of Sociology* (2004).

MONICA MARKS is a Rhodes Scholar completing her PhD in political science on Tunisia's Ennahda Party at St Antony's College, Oxford University. She has carried out four years of research in Tunisia and has been a visiting professor at Bogaziçi University in Istanbul. She conducts research in Arabic, French, and Turkish. Her research and analysis pieces on Tunisia and Middle Eastern politics are published regularly by outlets including the *Guardian*, *Washington Post*, *New York Times*, and the Brookings Institution.

RADWAN MASMOUDI was born in Tunisia and received a PhD in Engineering from MIT but decided to devote his life to human rights and democracy in the Islamic world, especially Tunisia. He became the founder and president of the Center for the Study of Islam and Democracy (CSID), based in Tunis and Washington, D.C., which now has programs in approximately twenty countries. He has published articles in the *Journal of Democracy* and numerous op-eds throughout Europe, the Middle East, and the United States. Masmoudi appears frequently on CNN, Al-Jazeera, MBC, Fox News, and Algerian TV.

JEREMY MENCHIK is assistant professor of international relations and political science at Boston University. From 2007–2015 he carried out extensive field research in Indonesia, including the first-ever stratified sample of religious elites from Indonesia's three largest and oldest religious institutions. He is the author of *Tolerance without Liberalism: Islam and Democracy in Indonesia* (2015) and articles in the *South East Asia Review* and *Comparative Studies in Society and History*, as well as numerous op-eds in Indonesia and the United States. Menchik has been a Luce Fellow at the Center for Democracy, Toleration, and Religion at Columbia University.

HICHAM BOU NASSIF is assitant professor of political science at Carleton College. He holds a doctorate in international law from the Université Saint-Esprit de Kaslik, Lebanon and a PhD in political science from the University of Indiana. He was a field reporter for the Lebanese Broadcasting Corporation. He has conducted more than a hundred interviews with Egyptian and Tunisian military officers. Using these interviews and official documents in the public record, he compiled the first-ever data on military postretirement positions in the private and public economies of Egypt and Tunisia.

ALFRED STEPAN (1936–2017) was the Wallace C. Sayre Professor Emeritus of Government and director of the Center for the Study of

Democracy, Toleration, and Religion at Columbia University. He was previously the founding rector of the Central European University in Budapest, the Gladstone Professor of Government at Oxford University, and a fellow of All Souls College at Oxford University. His numerous books, which have been translated into over a dozen languages, include *Problems of Democratic Transition and Consolidation*, with Juan Linz (1996); *Crafting State Nations*, with Linz and Yogendra Yadav (2011); *Arguing Comparative Politics* (2001), which includes the widely translated article "The World's Religious Systems and Democracy: Crafting the 'Twin Tolerations'"; and *Rethinking Military Politics* (1988). He edited *The Boundaries of Toleration* (Columbia, 2014) with Charles Taylor. He received the International Political Science Association's Karl Deutsch Award in 2012. He was a member of the American Academy of Arts and Sciences and the British Academy. His articles appeared the *New York Review of Books, Economist, Guardian*, and frequently in Project Syndicate.

CARRIE ROSEFSKY WICKHAM is professor of political science at Emory University. She has been conducting extensive fieldwork and interviews in Egypt since 1990. She is a recipient of the American Political Science Association's Aaron Wildavsky Best Dissertation Award. She is the author of *Mobilizing Islam: Religion, Activism, and Political Change in Egypt* (Columbia, 2002) and most recently *The Muslim Brotherhood: Evolution of an Islamist Movement* (2015). Her articles have appeared in academic journals such as *Comparative Politics*, in public-affairs journals such as *Foreign Affairs*, and in leading newspapers throughout the world including the *New York Times, Guardian*, and *El Pais*.

INDEX

Unless otherwise noted, all groups and organizations are Tunisian. Figures and tables are indicated by "*f*" and "*t*" after the page number.

RELIGION, CULTURE, AND PUBLIC LIFE

Series Editor: Katherine Pratt Ewing